QUEEN ELIZABETH GRAMMAR SCHOOL
WAKEFIELD

709.24

William Morris & Kelmscott

The Design Council

William Morris & Kelmscott

First edition published in the United Kingdom
1981 by
The Design Council
28 Haymarket, London SW1Y 4SU
in association with
West Surrey College of Art and Design
Farnham, Surrey

Designed by Mic Claridge
Printed and bound in the United Kingdom by
Balding + Mansell, London and Wisbech

© Leonard Stoppani, A. R. Dufty, Asa Briggs,
Joseph Acheson, Martin Shuttleworth,
Gillian Naylor, Stuart Durant, Patricia L. Baker,
Helen Snowdon, Dorothy D. Bosomworth,
John Brandon-Jones, Larry Baker,
Ray Watkinson, Jacqueline Herald,
Deryn O'Connor and West Surrey College of
Art and Design, 1981

British Library CIP Data

William Morris and Kelmscott.
  1. Morris, William
  709'.2'4   PR5083

  ISBN 0-85072-121-0   978 0850 721218

Cover: Detail from 'Vine and Acanthus' (T3).
(In the picture captions, the initials P, T, C, F, TF
and B refer to the six catalogues.)

Contents

William Morris, Kelmscott and Farnham

Kelmscott Manor in Oxfordshire was William Morris's country home from 1871 until his death in 1896. Since 1962, the house has been in the care of the Society of Antiquaries, who have not only restored it but cherished the paintings, drawings, tapestries, furniture, ceramics and books by Morris and his friends that have been in the house since the death of Morris's daughter, May, in 1938. The collection is now far more extensive than ever it was in Morris's lifetime, for it includes not only most of what was at the house in his day but also much brought from London after his death by his widow, Janey, and his daughter May, and much collected since.

For many years now, small groups of our students have been going to study there but, despite its grand title, the 'Manor' is relatively small. Indeed – as Morris himself confessed through the mouth of Ellen in *News from Nowhere* – the old house is far too small to hold 'a tithe of the folk' to whom he has made it belong in imagination; not very many of us at one time can crowd into Rossetti's Kelmscott studio or the separate bedrooms of Janey and William Morris. The great loft can hold a fair number of visitors but there is no other corridor or room in the Manor where a dozen is not a crowd; and besides – although individual scholars and parties of students can on occasion visit the house by appointment – the tenant has not the staff to open the house to the general public except on a limited number of days in the year.

It was this inevitable, if relative, inaccessibility of the treasures of Kelmscott that gave a member of our staff, Joseph Acheson, Senior Lecturer in Art History, the idea of persuading the Society of Antiquaries to allow us to put on an exhibition. He approached our Academic Board and Richard Dufty, who is the Honorary Curator of Kelmscott. Dick Dufty is not only the man who, more than any other, is responsible for the restoration of the house, but he is also the past President of the Society of Antiquaries, a sometime Chairman of our Governors, and a long-standing friend of this College. Dick and his fellow Antiquaries were at first cautious, but once they made up their minds to back us they committed themselves swiftly and totally to this most ambitious enterprise. Like all the best projects, it grew in the making. Where we felt what is in the house did not fully illustrate a particular facet of Morris or his friends' talents, we did not hesitate to borrow from other collections. The College commissioned 14 essays from external and internal contributors so that this book will provide not only a record of what is currently known of each work of art in the house and of its making, but also a lively reminder that William Morris and his ideas are as vigorous as ever they were.

That the universities are open to all today and that there have grown up colleges such as this where the study of the visual arts to degree level is open to all, we owe, in great measure, to people who long ago believed that the future was worth working for. Morris was a practical visionary who cared profoundly for both the freedom and the fulfilment of his fellow human beings; a man who believed that 'nothing should be made by man's labour which is not worth making or be made by labour degrading to the makers'; a man who came to believe that the Golden Age is not in the past but in the future. 'If a chap can't compose an epic poem while he's weaving tapestry', he once said, 'he had better shut up, he'll never do any good at all.' Not all of us have his energy, nor his many talents, nor that inherited wealth that allowed him to set up as a kind of one-man Crafts Council; but not all of us, either, have to cope with a Janey, or a Dante Gabriel Rossetti. Morris's life was no bed of roses. Had he not struggled fearlessly, had he not

7

made himself an artist of stature, we would never have heard of him. Had his friends not been men of talent too, we would not be bothering.

It is no bad thing to ask oneself: 'What was the world like when these people were students? What did they add to it?' The answers are in this book and in the exhibition which it was designed to complement. It was both a major, and a unique project. For help in mounting the exhibition we have to thank not only the Society of Antiquaries but also the Crafts Council, the Marc Fitch Fund, Mrs Jean Garnade, the South Eastern Arts Association, and our main backers, Johnson Wax Ltd. This American company were Frank Lloyd Wright's early patrons at home in America; ever since they have been in the area they have given generous support to Farnham, building the Johnson Wax Kiln Gallery at the Maltings and supporting many local causes. They contributed almost two thirds of the cost of the exhibition and helped to make it and this book possible. Our thanks go, too, both to museums and to private lenders: to the Visitors of the Ashmolean, the City of Bath, the City of Birmingham Art Gallery, John Brandon-Jones, the British Library, the Trustees of the British Museum, Richard Dufty, the Syndics of the Fitzwilliam Museum, Dr de Haas, Hammersmith and Fulham Public Library, the William Morris Society, the Tate Gallery, the Victoria and Albert Museum, as well as to several private collectors who wish to remain anonymous.

To Richard Dufty our debt is incalculable: he helped at every stage. Next our thanks must go to the Assistant Curator of the Manor, Mrs Jean Wells, who was in every way helpful, efficient and kind to our art historians, studio staff, photographers and students. I must also thank the outside contributors to this book: Lord Briggs of Lewes, Gillian Naylor, Stuart Durant, John Brandon-Jones and Ray Watkinson; and the able team at our publishers, The Design Council, who have patiently and efficiently seen us to press.

On our own staff the moving forces have been Joseph Acheson, the Exhibition Director; John Morris, Vice Principal; Mic Claridge, the designer of this book; Mike Southgate, the designer of the exhibition; Martin Shuttleworth, editor of this book; and Christopher Brighton, Director of the Symposium on 'Morris and Kelmscott'. The interior and exterior photography at Kelmscott Manor is by Dennis Anthony. John Knight photographed all the furniture, glass, ceramics, textiles and paintings, except for the cover, the tapestry *If I Can* and the portrait of Jane Morris, *Blue Silk Dress*, which were taken by Peter Sanger. The photographers were assisted by the following students: Richard Bush, Jamie Cabot, Colin Horsman and Andrew Rowley. Major contributions were made by Lawrence Baker, Patricia L. Baker, Dorothy D. Bosomworth, Jacqueline Herald and Helen Snowdon of the College's History of Art and Complementary Studies Department; Deryn O'Connor, Department of Textiles; Veronica Acheson, Department of Three-Dimensional Design; and Michael Sleigh, Foundation Studies.

Leonard Stoppani
Principal
West Surrey College of Art and Design
Farnham, Surrey

8

Kelmscott

A. R. Dufty

In a totally flat landscape midway between Lechlade and Faringdon lies a small village consisting of a church, a village hall and 21 dwellings, including an inn, containing 32 families. It has neither post office nor shop, and is inaccessible by public transport. Here space is not at a premium, and the buildings are sited well apart, apparently at random, alongside a minor road which deteriorates into a farm track and ends in the tow-path by the River Thames. Yet the name of this quiet, remote, unspectacular place, Kelmscott, is known throughout the civilised world. The fame is due to one man, William Morris, who from 1871 until his death in 1896 rented the Manor, which stands at the farthest end of the village where farm track merges into tow-path.

Though only his holiday retreat, which he visited but intermittently, Morris loved the house, and after it he named his London home, Kelmscott House in Hammersmith, and his private printing press, the Kelmscott Press. Hence the fame which, though by chance bestowed, the Manor reciprocates and complements by virtue of its traditional homespun character reflecting his tenets, and its contents illustrating something of his genius.

Morris said of it: 'A house that I love with a reasonable love I think: for though my words may give you no idea of any special charm about it, yet I assure you that the charm is there; so much has the old house grown up out of the soil and the lives of those that lived on it: some thin thread of tradition, a half-anxious sense of the delight of meadows and acre and wood and river; a certain amount (not too much let us hope) of common sense, a liking for making material serve one's turn, and perhaps at bottom some little grain of sentiment: this I think was

◀ The White Drawing Room, Kelmscott Manor

what went to the making of the old house.' Affection for it is implicit too in his factual description: 'The house is built of well-laid rubble stone of the district . . . buttered over, so to say, with thin plaster which has now weathered to the same colour as the stone of the walls; the roofs are covered with the beautiful stone slates of the district, the most lovely covering which a roof can have, especially when, as here, and in all the traditional old houses of the countryside, they are "sized down", the smaller ones to the top and bigger towards the eaves, which gives one the same sort of pleasure in their orderly beauty as a fish's scales or a bird's feathers.'

Effectively the Manor is of two dates. The original late-sixteenth-century house built probably by Richard Turner (d1600) and finished by 1571 stands complete and little altered. Remarkably, though dating from a generation or more after the end of the Middle Ages, it follows the typical medieval arrangement with a hall, screens passage and solar and kitchen wings, forming a half-H plan. Philip Webb himself noted the fact; of it he wrote: 'For so late a time of genuine native building, and from the modesty of the house altogether, it is singular how the regular plan of the old English form, of all degrees of importance, is enclosed in the earlier part of it.' The conspicuous wing on the north-east is of the second date, being an addition of about 1670 which is simply butted up against the front of the original house.

The addition is of interest for two related reasons, for certain architectural details of an exotic kind and for the evidence it gives of both social and economic advancement of the owning family, still the Turners, at the time. The suffix 'Manor' to the name of the house is, so to say, a courtesy one: it was the great house in the village, but it was never the principal house of the manor; this was in Broadwell. Obviously the

Turners though not of the squirearchy were of some standing in the sixteenth century as the size and appearance of the original building indicate. The family then evidently grew to have pretensions, presumably backed by profits from the sale of wool from the surrounding sheep farm, and in 1665 it obtained a grant of arms. The rise in status demanded a rise in the standard of living and that this should be seen, but the original house with its low-ceilinged rooms and rustic joinery was no more than the home of a successful farmer. The contrast in the 1670 addition is extreme, the lofty rooms and large transomed and mullioned windows expressing an elegance and a gentlemanly way of life doubtless more appropriate and congenial to a more affluent Turner, Thomas (1620–82).

By the same token, though perhaps reading more than is really there into the architecture of the addition, the curious mixture of traditional features of Tudor origin with contemporary features, even if *de minimis*, in the revived classical style suggests a certain awareness of fashion in the owner builder, evidently a man of emerging taste still with mud on his boots. Less explicable are two other more remarkable features, first, the batter of the external wall faces whereby the plane of the parapet is consistently 1ft 3in back from the plane of the base; secondly, the convexity of the wall faces. The former may indeed stem from indigenous medieval practice, though the sensitive purpose would seem to have been to give a visual impression of height. The latter, namely classical entasis, is however a quite extraordinary sophistication in a house of this date in so remote a place.

Nothing is known of the later vicissitudes of the house apart from family descent until in 1871 William Morris rented it from the trustees of Elizabeth, widow of James Turner (d1870), as co-tenant until 1874 with Dante Gabriel Rossetti

and then for a time with F. S. Ellis, the publisher of his earliest writings. Thereafter Morris remained the sole leasee to the time of his death in 1896. His widow, Janey, continued as tenant until she bought the house in 1913. On her death in 1914 May Morris the younger daughter inherited, the elder daughter being incapacitated. May died in 1938, having bequeathed the property to the University of Oxford, but in 1962 the bequest was declared invalid and, as a result, the whole reverted to the residue legatee of May Morris's estate, namely the Society of Antiquaries. Two facts of interest emerge from this account: first that, apart from certain family arrangements, Kelmscott Manor has changed hands by purchase only once since 1571; and, second, that its fame derives from a particular tenancy held between 1871 and 1896.

After Morris's death in 1896 his widow sold their London home, Kelmscott House in Hammersmith, and evidently brought the contents to the Manor; photographs of the interior of the former show many objects now in the latter. Similarly, and on similar evidence, at a later date May Morris brought her possessions from 8 Hammersmith Terrace, her London home. The conclusion seems to be that in Morris's time the 'Morris' contents were few, though an oak table designed by Philip Webb was made by Morris & Co for the Manor (and it is still there), and, as a result of the *ménage à trois* – Janey, William and Rossetti – subsisting there from 1871 to 1874, a number of pieces of furniture and pictures belonging to Rossetti were brought in; these too remain in the Manor. The negative evidence is that Morris, regarding the house as a holiday home, did little to make it comfortable; Janey did little more, and in 1889 Wilfrid Scawen Blunt, her lover succeeding Rossetti, described it as 'extremely primitive'. Subsequently, May Morris seems to have kept the contents intact, though a visitor in 1925 could still write: 'The house is damp; the plain, old-fashioned piano has to be put on legs in case of floods', and the state of the Manor in 1962 showed that conditions had remained so until May's death in 1938 and afterwards.

May's bequest of the property to Oxford University included certain effects that were to go with the gift; these she listed. Everything else was left to her companion, Miss Lobb, a landgirl during the First World War whom, following instant dismissal for foul language by the local farmer, she befriended and housed and who is remembered with awe locally because of her formidable size and daily attire of Norfolk jacket and yellow plus-fours. Miss Lobb died shortly after May and there followed a disastrous sale of her inheritance at Kelmscott in 1939 in pouring rain on the first day of petrol rationing when, among other things, several portraits of Janey by Rossetti, her clothes and jewels and much 'Morrisiana' were sold for a few shillings.

Fortunately the possessions listed by May remained in the house although, considering their importance, surprisingly little was done for their care and maintenance until 1962. For instance, the embroidered blue serge hangings designed by Morris and worked by Janey for their bedroom at Red House, and the earliest known of their joint productions, once assumed lost, were then found lying tumbled in dirt and cobwebs in the corners of various rooms in the Manor. Again the 'Vine and Acanthus (cabbage)' tapestry, Morris's first venture into tapestry weaving, which he designed and wove himself in 1879, was trailed on the floor.

When the Society of Antiquaries inherited the property the Manor was thus falling into ruin. The only recorded work of structural maintenance by Morris was the replacement of rotten floorboards with stone paving and the laying in the White Room of a wood-block floor in 1895, all under the supervision of Philip Webb; the latter must be an early example of its kind.

May Morris on an Icelandic pony

Miss Lobb with her dog

Certainly little more had been done to maintain the structure for a great many years except apparently the renewal of some exterior stonework. In 1962 the Society had no money to pay for restoration and therefore it proposed to sell the Manor, its contents and the greater part of Kelmscott village which went with the property, the cottages in their lack of any amenities and poor condition being scarcely less primitive than the Manor. However, in 1963 a most generous gift to the Society of shares in the Sun Alliance and Sun Life Assurance Co by Miss Susan Minet, daughter of a one-time treasurer of the Society, transformed the financial situation, enabling the property to be retained, and the whole put into a proper state of repair. The work of conservation was the responsibility of the architects Donald Insall & Associates primarily under the direction of Peter Locke, a Lethaby Scholar of the Society for the Protection of Ancient Buildings founded by Morris in 1877. The task lasted from 1964 to 1966. Meantime the entire contents were removed to Oxford for repair, cleaning and storage. In 1966 they were returned and reinstalled at the Manor, where they have remained properly cherished. By the kindness of the Antiquaries many of them were lent to the West Surrey College of Art for an exhibition in November 1981 which was intended to show something not only of the great gifts of William Morris and his associates but also of the character and peaceful ambience of Kelmscott Manor itself.

The exhibition catalogue (pages 125–183) records the known history of the exhibits and explains the craft processes by which they were created; it is thus in itself an important contribution to knowledge. The provenance of many of them is revealed in May Morris's list already mentioned, the more important having been in the exhibition. However, a number of additions to the contents of the Manor have been made in recent years which extend the *oeuvres* of Morris and his contemporaries therein; some of these too were exhibited. The more notable accessions include a selection of objects and books from the 'Morrisiana' collected by N. L. McMinn, an American one-time professor in the English department of Northwestern University, Illinois, among them the 'lost' portrait of Morris on his death-bed by Charles Fairfax Murray. Mrs Surtees has given a lock of Morris's hair in a silver frame designed by Philip Webb or possibly R. Catterson-Smith who wrought it. On indefinite loan from the estate of Mrs Hinman come the Merton *millefleurs* tapestry and many samples and lengths of woven wool fabrics which she had bought at Morris & Co's George Street shop in London in the late 1920s; she died in 1979 aged 100. Again on indefinite loan are many shop samples of velvets, chintzes, silks and wallpapers which previously belonged to Albert Earl, an employee in the Morris firm from about 1918 until about 1930. The splendid Morris carpet made at Merton Abbey in the 1880s, one of the most conspicuous exhibits, was transferred on permanent loan to the Manor in 1976. Finally, in recent months Lady Fairfax-Lucy has given a notable dish designed by De Morgan which was a wedding present from him to her mother in 1905.

The intention of the Society of Antiquaries is that Kelmscott Manor should be a home, not a museum, and thus retain something of the atmosphere which so much pleased and revitalised Morris. It is therefore let to a private tenant with an interest in him, his family and his works. Peace and tranquillity characterise the house and, although Morris suffered unhappiness and frustration during the time he was a tenant, it emanates no sadness. Even Rossetti who was a townee, out of sympathy with rusticity, wrote: 'It and its surroundings are the loveliest "haunt of ancient peace" that can well be imagined', and again: 'It is a most lovely old place, a desert in solitude, an Eden in beauty.' So it still is, and long may it so continue.

By way of epilogue a quotation from Morris's *News from Nowhere or an epoch of rest* is appropriate, indeed essential, in any account of Kelmscott Manor, for he could think of no better setting than this for the conclusion of the journey which from a paradise of imagination he describes. Ellen is an idealised companion:

'. . . almost without my will my hand raised the latch of a door in the wall, and we stood presently on a stone path which led up to the old house. My companion gave a cry of pleased surprise and enjoyment: nor did I wonder, for the garden between the wall and the house was redolent of the June flowers, and the roses were rolling over one another with that delicious superabundance of small well tended gardens which at first sight takes away all thought from the beholder save that of beauty. The blackbirds were singing their loudest, the doves were cooing on the roof-ridge, the rooks in the high elm-trees beyond were garrulous among the young leaves, and the swifts wheeled whirring about the gables. And the house itself was a fit guardian for all the beauty of this heart of summer.

'Once again Ellen echoed my thoughts as she said ". . . Yes, friend, this is what I came out for to see; this many-gabled old house built by the simple country folk of the long-past times, regardless of all the turmoil that was going on in cities and courts, is lovely still amidst all the beauty which these latter days have created: and I do not wonder at our friends tending it carefully and making much of it. It seems to me as if it had waited for these happy days, and held in it the gathered crumbs of happiness of the confused and turbulent past . . ."

'We went in, and found no soul in any room as we wandered from room to room, from the rose-covered porch to the strange and quaint garrets amongst the great timbers of the roof, where of old time the tillers and herdsmen of the manor slept, but which a-nights seemed now by the small size of the beds, and the litter of useless and disregarded matters – bunches of dying flowers, caddis worms in mugs and the like – to be inhabited for the time by children.

'Everywhere there was but little furniture, and that only the most necessary, and of the simplest forms. The extravagant love of ornament which I had noted in this people and elsewhere seemed here to have given place to the feeling that the house itself and its associations was the ornament of the country life amidst which it had been left stranded from old times, and that to re-ornament it would take away its use as a piece of natural beauty.

'We sat down at last in a room . . . which was still hung with old tapestry, originally of no artistic value, but now faded into pleasant grey tones which harmonised thoroughly well with the quiet of the place, and which could have been ill supplanted by brighter and more striking decoration.

'I asked a few random questions of Ellen as we sat there, but scarcely listened to her answers, and presently became silent, and then scarce conscious of anything, but that I was there in that old room, the doves crooning from the roofs of the barn and dovecot beyond the window opposite to me.'

Nowhere in the Utopian story is the house named, but the woodcut frontispiece commissioned by Morris for the published book and with a decorative border designed by him is of the east front of his beloved Kelmscott Manor, and there in reality is the room 'still hung with old tapestry'.

The Appeal of William Morris

Asa Briggs

With the development of interest in the Victorians at every level – serious and trivial – it was inevitable that there should be a growth of interest in William Morris. Born in 1834, three years before Queen Victoria came to the throne, Morris died in 1896, five years before the Queen. His own experience, therefore, as boy and man was what we would now call Victorian. In the background was the Industrial Revolution, with an unprecedented growth in material wealth. Yet there were continuities with the pre-industrial past and movements of discontent and protest seeking to shape a very different future. It was not a settled time, and if Queen Victoria had not lived for so long we would not have been tempted to treat everything that happened between 1837 and 1901 as being of one piece.

The Victorians were their own best critics. They were particularly critical of what they regarded as their two major national weaknesses – cant and complacency. Morris was more sharply critical than most. He described the society of his own age as 'hateful' and its so-called 'civilisation' as 'ugly', 'silly' and 'wrong'. 'Apart from my desire to produce beautiful things,' he exclaimed, 'the leading passion of my life is hatred of modern civilisation.' When he visited the Crystal Palace in 1851, at a time when the word 'Victorian' was first beginning to be used, he called it 'wonderfully ugly'. Later in his life, when he became a Socialist, he wrote to a friend in 1885 that the only hope for the future lay in revolution, adding 'now at last when the corruption of society seems complete, there is arising a definite conception of a new order'.

Morris came from a comfortable background and most of the people who read his first poems and bought the first beautiful objects he and his partners produced, came from a comfortable background too. Yet, like many Victorians, Morris criticised the middle classes of his day for hypocrisy, cowardice and joylessness. When he turned to the submerged working classes, he looked for virtues that were missing in the ranks 'above'. He distinguished himself from many other Victorian critics, however, in participating directly – and fervently – in working-class movements from 1883 onwards, sharing in the toil as well as in the excitement. While he was not alone in urging that after a century of so-called progress men should 'forego some of the power over nature . . . in order to become more human and less mechanical', few other critics who shared his philosophy drew from it the same practical conclusions as Morris. Joining in the class struggle, which is how Morris perceived it, gave him new hope for the future. Without it he would, he claimed, have despaired:

'There I was in for a fine pessimistic end of life, if it had not somehow dawned on me that amidst all this filth of civilisation the seeds of a great change, what we call Social Revolution, were beginnning to germinate. The whole face of things was changed to me by that discovery, and all I had to do then in order to become a Socialist, was to hook myself onto the practical movement.'

That 'practical movement' had registered only a few successes when Morris died or, indeed, when Queen Victoria died five years later. Yet as far as Morris himself was concerned, socialism came as a personal fulfilment as well as a conversion. As G. M. Young, not a socialist, put it in 1936, 'his socialism was the final synthesis of all his purposes: and without it his character would have been unfinished, his life incomplete'.

G. M. Young had much to do with the development of scholarly interest in the Victorians, an interest which soon widened outside intellectual circles, and by 1936 he had already sketched a brilliant portrait of Victorian England compared with which Morris's sturdy indictment seems a rough caricature. In fact, however, Morris's relationship with the rediscovered nineteenth century is more complicated than he could possibly have been aware of himself.

His appeal in the middle years of the nineteenth century had nothing to do with socialism. When *The Earthly Paradise* was published in 1868, the *Saturday Review*, itself not given to cant, noted how popular it was among people who as a rule do not care to read any poetry, and it singled out not working men, but 'political economists and scientific men to whom Shelley is a mystery and Tennyson a vexation of the spirit'. When his eventually famous 'Firm' came into existence in 1861 – producing all the 'beautiful things' desirable for a house (and some for a church or palace), including as the years went by glass, wallpapers, textiles, fabrics and furniture – the people who bought the products were rich, not poor. Moreover, the Firm was a commercial success.

It was Morris's own restlessness of spirit that made him dissatisfied with worldly tokens of success or with escape, as in *The Earthly Paradise*, into a dream world far removed from the realities of the nineteenth century. There was an element of personal tension, including estrangement from his wife, which drove him from within. Before he became a socialist in 1883 he wrote a new kind of poem 'Sigurd the Volsung' (1876–7), in which he showed how much he preferred the Vikings (and their values) to the Victorians (and theirs). He also took charge of the Firm and moved into liberal politics. In 1883, the year when he joined the Democratic Federation, describing himself simply on his membership card as a designer, he gave a lecture on 'Art under Plutocracy' in Oxford, with John Ruskin in the chair, in which he recommended the members of his privileged audience to 'cast in their lot with the working

men . . . Do not hold aloof from us, because we have not attained that delicacy of manners . . . which the long oppression of competitive commerce has crushed out of us.'

Morris by then had crossed what he called 'the river of fire', and he wanted everyone to know it. Yet some of his most powerful statements of personal commitment came not in public lectures but in private letters. To the Austrian Marxist socialist Andreas Scheu, for example, he wrote that, 'in spite of all the success' he had enjoyed, he had concluded that:

The art I have been helping to produce would fall with the death of a few of us who really care about it, that a reform in art which is founded on individualism must perish with the individuals who have set it going. Both my historical studies and my practical conflict [note his use again of the adjective 'practical'] *have forced on me the conviction that art cannot have real life and growth under the present system of commercialism and profit-mongering.'*

Andreas Scheu has left a vivid pen portrait of Morris at this time, which should be contrasted with the pen portraits of Morris as a young Pre-Raphaelite 30 years before, by turns fidgety and boisterous. Already by then Morris had grown the great beard that he never lost, and had begun to wear the flappy, unfashionable clothes. On Scheu, 'the fine, highly intelligent face of the man, his earnestness, the half-searching, half-dreaming look of his eyes, his plain unfashionable dress, made a deep impression'. That was the personal magnetism, a part of Morris's contemporary appeal, associated closely with a quest. The young Leeds socialist, Alf Mattison, described a visit to Kelmscott House in Hammersmith in 1892, four years before Morris died, as follows:

'What a pleasant time we had; there was Morris at the head of the table; May Morris at my side, and

18

about six or eight more comrades. Morris was in hearty and jovial mood . . . Tales were told and songs were sung.'

Another place of great fellowship was Kelmscott Manor.

Morris was more at ease with the concrete than with the abstract, although the 'half-dreaming look' in his eyes could not be ignored. (He was to make the most of his dreams in his writings, not least in *News from Nowhere*, 1890.) To try to place him among his contemporaries, however, we must go beyond appearances and inclinations, and trace three crucial relationships, two of which are concerned with ideas, and one of which was concerned with context. The first two are the relationships between Morris and Ruskin and between Morris and Marx, and the third is the relationship between Morris and the visual environment of his time, a changing environment which still included a rich, if persistently threatened, historical heritage.

Morris's life might have followed roughly the same outline had there been no Ruskin. Yet it is impossible to understand the English nineteenth century as it actually was without understanding Ruskin, one of its greatest critics, although a man who clearly belonged to it and to no other century. Ruskin, born in 1819, the same year as Queen Victoria, died in 1900, only one year before she did. He was not alone in favourably comparing past with present, particularly the lost past of the Middle Ages, in extolling the Gothic and, above all, in relating the visual – buildings and objects – to the social. Yet no one so prominently, except Thomas Carlyle, stood out as prophet as well as sage. Ruskin encouraged people to look in order to understand, and Morris always acknowledged his debt to him. He had warmed to Ruskin's indictment of the human and social failings of the century long before he had heard of Marx or felt attracted by socialism. Indeed, key passages in Ruskin (some of them with echoes of Carlyle before him) relate directly to what Morris came to feel with passion:

'You must either make a tool of the creature or a man of him. You cannot make both. Men were not intended to work with the accuracy of tools, to be precise and perfect in all their actions . . . It is verily this degradation of the operative into a machine, which, more than any other evil of the times, is leading the mass of the nations everywhere into vain, destructive struggling for a freedom which they cannot explain the nature of to themselves . . . It is not that men are ill fed, but that they have no pleasure in the work by which they make their bread, and therefore look to wealth as the only means of pleasure.'

The critique of commercialism and industrialism preceded Morris, therefore, nor was it specifically Marxist: its roots lay deep in a romanticism which preceded the full development of industry, and it had as much to do with a sense of nature as with a sense of society. Morris knew this. When once a socialist criticised Ruskin in the pages of *Commonweal*, the journal of the Socialist League, Morris himself added the note that, however much damage might have been 'done to his influence by his strange bursts of fantastic perversity', his 'feeling against commercialism' had been 'absolutely genuine' and 'his expression of it most valuable'. He had been able to stir disciples too, and Morris went on to suggest that through his writings, which had stopped short of socialism, he had 'made many socialists'.

There were, however, important differences between the two men who were never themselves in the simple relation of master to disciple. There was an inquisitorial element in Ruskin that was missing in Morris. The novelist Henry James once described Ruskin's world of art as being like 'a sort of assize court in perpetual session'.

Morris's world of art was by contrast a true garden of delight. Before he became a socialist he dreamed of a palace of art, open to all. After he became a socialist, the image of the garden seemed more natural. Morris wanted people to live in an uninhibited way, enjoying themselves both at work and at play. With Morris, who like many Victorians could contemplate even with some satisfaction the onslaught of barbarism, there was always a return to keel. With Ruskin, there was a 'darkening glass', ending in madness. Young referred to his 'wiry outline', a phrase of William Blake, and compared Ruskin's and Morris's behaviour before a Royal Commission: *'Ruskin, having said his piece, is all at sea; Morris knows what he is about from the first question to the last.'*

The biggest difference of all, of course, was that while Ruskin drew and painted as well as he talked and wrote, Morris actually made *things* – with other people working by his side. *'What is irresistible in Morris'*, a German observer explained, *'is the tangible character of his productions. Here culture takes a visible form and becomes reality: one sound mind working for the comfort of other sound minds.'*

The relationship between Marx, who was neither artist nor craftsman, and Morris, who was neither economist nor historian, has recently received far more detailed attention than that between Morris and Ruskin, although Morris's first biographers left it unconsidered. Such attention goes back to the 1930s, when the first signs of the Victorian revival, with different causes, can be traced. It was two years before Young reviewed May Morris's *William Morris: Artist, Writer, Socialist* in 1936 that Robin Page Arnot produced his little book *William Morris: A Vindication* which re-asserted Morris's Marxism. Edward Thompson's *William Morris, Romantic to Revolutionary*, a massive book with

a similar thesis, did not appear until 1955, and even then it was relatively little noticed when it was first published. Since then, Paul Thompson has produced his admirably comprehensive study *The Work of William Morris* (1967) and Paul Meier, in a huge two-volume French study translated into English in 1978 as *William Morris, the Marxist Dreamer*, has set out to assess in meticulous detail Morris's debt to Marx and Engels. In what is now mainstream Morris criticism, *News from Nowhere* is usually treated as orthodox Marxist description of the Communist future, though there are differences of opinion about the extent of Morris's originality.

Morris was certainly excited when he read parts of Marx, was directly involved with Engels, who did not fully appreciate him, in the tangled London socialist politics of the late 1880s, and echoed (or paralleled) much Marxist language in his speeches and writings. There is much in common between the thoughts of the young Marx and the middle-aged Morris. Yet Morris followed his own line of development in many of his pre-socialist lectures and had got near to the critique of industrialism which was given Marxist underpinning after his conversion. When he became a revolutionary, he knew from the start what commitment meant. The 'happy days' that lay on the other side of the 'river of fire' would be secured only after organised (and, if need be, bloody) action. It was at this point that Morris separated himself unequivocally from most of the other Victorian critics of Victorianism, such as Matthew Arnold. 'No rose water will cure us: disaster (and if need be bloody) and misfortune of all kinds, I think, will be the only things that will breed a remedy.'

Meier is right to emphasise both the unity of Morris's thought and its essential creativity. He is right, too, to note how Morris had broken earlier with what he called 'the rights of property, the necessities of morality and the interests of religion', treating them thereafter as 'sacramental words of cowardice that silence us'. These were the necessary props of Victorianism, not all of which other British non-Marxist socialists even wished to pull down; yet there were many differences between Marx and Morris apart from the obvious fact that one was grounded in Hegel and the other in Ruskin, and that Marx studied, analysed and gave orders, while Morris made things.

Marx was an intellectual in a sense that Morris never was, although both men wished to relate ideas to action, transforming action. Marx was a highly original political economist too, able to move from insight to system, while Morris never found political economy easy, though he recognised its importance, and had serious reservations about 'system'. Nor did Morris advance a distinctively Marxist approach to history. Marx would never have idealised the Middle Ages, as he did, or dismissed so sweepingly the Renaissance and all that followed it. Indeed, he would willingly have conceded many of the triumphs of the Industrial Revolution, one of the major themes of the Communist manifesto. Not least important, Morris did not regard the future triumph of socialism as inevitable, scientifically demonstrable. It depended on will more than on logic. Hopeful though he was that socialism would win, with the working classes in the vanguard, he was too imaginative to take it for granted. 'The revolt against capitalism may be vanquished.' He once wrote:

'The result will be that the working class – the slaves of society – will become more and more degraded, that they will not strive against overwhelming force, but stimulated by that love of life which Nature . . . has implanted in us, will learn

to bear everything – starvation, overwork, dirt, ignorance, brutality.'

To combat apathy as well as ignorance, Morris insisted on socialist education and set out to provide it himself, addressing no fewer than 249 meetings between 1885 and 1890 in what must have been one of the busiest of all socialist calendars:

'So I began the business, and in street corners I spake,
To knots of men. Indeed, that made my very heart ache.
So hopeless it seems, for some stood by like men of wood,
And some, though fain to listen, but a few words understood,
And some hooted and jeered; but whiles across some I came
Who were keen and eager to hear; as in dry flax the flame
So the quick thought flickered among them; and that indeed was a feast.'

There must have been many occasions when by natural inclination Morris would have chosen to feast at Kelmscott rather than in the back streets of England's cities. His relation to his environment is the third relationship that needs to be understood. He hated the smoke and noise and dirt of the cities. He also despised the engineering triumphs of the nineteenth century, dreaming of a return to an England where everything was on a more intimate human scale. As Young pointed out more perceptively than some recent writers, before he became conscious of the significance of class antagonisms, he was aware of the sharp Victorian contrasts between town and countryside. 'He was educated nominally at Marlborough, and really in Savernake and on the Marlborough Downs'. He loved landscape before he learned to love buildings: this was part of the appeal of Iceland. Young notes how he wrote of the ridge of hills near Faringdon that 'the hills are low but well designed', which he rightly observes was 'a proper compliment from one artist to another'. There was certainly a link between *The Earthly Paradise* and *News from Nowhere*, and it should be remembered that when he was once writing of industrial action, he remarked sensitively that 'when the day comes that there is a serious strike of the workmen against the poisoning of the air with smoke or the workers with filth, I shall think that art is getting on indeed and that schools of art have had a notable success'.

Old buildings he preferred to new ones. Nor did he like what nineteenth-century architects were prepared to do with old buildings. That was why he played such an important role in the founding in 1877 of 'Anti-Scrape', the Society for the Protection of Ancient Buildings. 'These old buildings do not belong to us only; they have belonged to our forefathers', he wrote, 'and they will belong to our descendants unless we play them false. They are not in any sense our property, to do with as we like. We are only trustees for those that come after us.' Once again, however, his aesthetic and historical interests led him to a political answer.

'You cannot abolish the slums of our great cities: you cannot have happy villagers living in pretty houses among the trees, doing pretty looking work in their own houses, or in the pleasant village workshops between seedtime and harvest, unless you remove the causes that have made the brutal slum-dweller and the starveling field labourer.'

It is because of what Morris had to say on such themes, which link concern for human relationships and for natural and built environment, and because of his relationship with Ruskin and to Marx, that Morris has retained and in many ways strengthened his appeal in the late-twentieth century. During the last few decades, indeed, interest in his work has grown substantially, not least outside circles sympathetically drawn to the Victorians. Thus, the William Morris Society includes many members who are not members of the Victorian Society. Some are more interested in his politics than in his craftsmanship. Others are interested in both and in the relationship between them. For those reasons, the appeal of Morris straddles two contrasting centuries and two contrasting segments of the divided world of this century. As our own world changes, different aspects of his

William Morris, c1890

work are singled out. Yet increasingly there is a desire to find out about the whole man. An exhibition can reveal at least as much about him as a book . . . and Morris himself knew this, much as he loved beautiful books and became increasingly concerned in his last years with printing and acquiring them.

How can we place all this in perspective? There are many people, loved or revered by their own contemporaries, who are forgotten by posterity, and there are some people who influence posterity far more than they ever influenced their contemporaries, Marx outstanding among them.

When Morris died in 1896, Robert Blatchford, socialist pioneer, wrote a moving obituary notice which revealed how interested he was in the relationship between contemporary judgements and the likely judgements of posterity. 'He was our best man and he is dead', he began, but he added at once: 'it is true that much of his work still lives and will live.' And then he went on to amplify his judgement:

'Great as was his work, he himself was greater. Many a man of genius is dwarfed by his own creations . . . Morris was of a nobler kind. He was better than his best. Though his words fell like sword strokes, one always felt that the warrior was stronger than the sword. For Morris was not only a genius, he was a man. *Strike at him where you would, he rang true.'*

This was an incomplete judgement, if memorable, for by concentrating on the words it left out the objects, and these had and can still have their own appeal. It was a somewhat misleading judgement, too, in that one sentence at least would have irritated Morris, the sentence referring to 'genius'. Morris associated art not with genius but with fellowship, and wanted above all to belong to a society of equals, and he was willing to labour to secure the necessary social and cultural transformation. Where

Blatchford's words would have appealed to Morris most was when he was speaking of Morris ringing true, whether he was being stricken or, he might have added, which was more likely, when he was striking others himself. He wanted to ring true, and he did. The appeal persists.

The reason why the appeal persists in 'east' and 'west' is that in both segments of the world, the development of twentieth-century socialism has followed lines which would not have appealed to him. He hated bureaucracy, militarism and the stifling of the human spirit. And he did not confuse socialism and welfare measures. He was not taken in by slogans. He tested societies not by what they said about themselves, but by their quality of life. There are essential features of his critique of industrialism which are as pertinent in 'communist' countries as they are in 'capitalist' ones. And he would have insisted on their relevance to the life of the individual as well as of the society. 'Art cannot be the result of external compulsions', he claimed, 'the labour which goes to produce it is voluntary.'

The nineteenth century allowed more of an accepted place for that 'voluntary' drive than the twentieth century, and Young was wise to include in his essay on Morris the words of a Regius Professor of Divinity in Oxford, words he feels Morris would have accepted, even though they were printed in the Tory *Quarterly Review*: *'There is a tendency deeply implanted in our best impulses, by which men are moved to make others partners of whatever good they themselves possess, to abnegate all superiority and disclose the very secret spring of it.'*

We know how Morris abnegated all superiority. We are less sure, perhaps, whether we have yet tapped 'the very secret spring'.

'An Artist of Reputation': Dante Gabriel Rosetti and Kelmscott Manor

Joseph Acheson

William Morris discovered Kelmscott Manor in May 1871 after a search of five years for 'some little country place which they might make more or less permanently their own' and 'avoid the discomforts of a holiday in lodgings'. Dante Gabriel Rossetti travelled to Kelmscott with Morris and his wife, Jane, to view the house with the idea of sharing the tenancy with Morris and finding somewhere which might offer him peace and 'restore him to bodily health'.[1]

Rossetti, who was six years older than his friend, had known Morris since the latter's Oxford days and been a valued member of Morris's 'Firm' since its formation in 1861. Morris, as head and chief designer of this successful firm of interior decorators, had fully justified the modest title 'designer', which he had attached to himself at the beginning.

Rossetti was by 1871 widely recognised as a painter of outstanding talent. Already famed, if not notorious, as the principal surviving painter of the Pre-Raphaelite Brotherhood (formed in 1848, defunct early in the 1850s on the election of Millais to the Royal Academy in 1853 and the departure of Hunt to the Holy Land in the following year), he had for many years attracted much attention as a creator of romantic idealisations of classical and medieval history and myth. As the 1860s drew to a close these works were frequently the subject of controversy, because of their aura of mystery, their tendency to gloominess and, increasingly from 1870 on, their 'decadent' and 'fleshly' sensuousness, especially evident in the series of his portraits of beautiful women that date from this time. The output of these portraits of 'stunners', as he called the women who inspired them, continued until his death in 1882. Jane Morris was the

model for many, sometimes painted from life, sometimes fantasised from the painter's memory.

In addition to the products of his own studies, Rossetti carried out his commitments to the Firm, as an 'artist of reputation' who had undertaken much work in most of the 'minor arts', especially during the decade before his arrival at Kelmscott, designs for jewellery, stained glass, tiles and furniture as well as some 11 fine and unusual book-bindings and several elegant picture frames, the latter designed in conjunction with Madox Brown. The jewel casket painted for Jane Morris by Rossetti and his wife Elizabeth (Siddal) and the pomegranate and lily design for a cushion cover at Kelmscott testify to his abilities as a designer.

Besides extensive attainment in the visual arts, by 1871 both Morris and Rossetti were acclaimed also as poets of distinction, and respected each other's talents, a mutual respect to be much tested during the next decade.

Morris's wife Jane, or Janey as she was called, was just over 30 when they first saw Kelmscott and a woman of striking and unusual beauty: 'so strangely lovely and majestic', thought the literary critic Buxton Forman; 'the most lovely woman I have ever known', said Watts Dunton, Rossetti's friend and legal adviser, and neither man was given to hyperbole. Even dull and sober William Rossetti said of her effect on his brother, 'a face created to fire his imagination and to quicken his powers'. Swinburne,[2] more extravagant in his words, commented in 1858, when he heard of Janey's engagement to Morris, 'to think of Morris's having that wonderful and perfect stunner of his to look at or speak to. The idea of his marrying her is insane. To kiss her feet is the utmost one should dream of doing.' Gabriel's own words are even more expressive, in his sonnet 'The Portrait', written in 1868 when the magnificent painting of her in a blue dress –

◀ *William Bell Scott, John Ruskin, Dante Gabriel Rossetti, 1863*

25

which is the chief of all the works of fine art at the Manor – was finished:

'Lo it is done. Above the enthroning throat
The mouth's mould testifies of voice and kiss,
The shadowed eyes remember and foresee.
Her face is made her shrine. Let all men note
That in all years (O Love, thy gift is this!)
They that would look on her must come to me.'[3]

Gabriel, a widower for nine years in 1871, had probably been in love with Janey since their first meeting in 1857 but – according to several accounts – as he was then committed to Lizzie Siddal he had encouraged Morris's infatuation for Janey, encouragement which led to Morris's marrying her in 1859. Whatever the truth of this supposition, he wrote ecstatically of his 'regenerate rapture' only a few months later than this 1868 sonnet.

On this subject Janey herself is enigmatic and mostly silent, although Wilfrid Scawen Blunt, who became Janey's lover after Gabriel's death, claims she told him that she had never loved Morris.[4] It is certain, however, that Morris loved her then and still did when they first came to Kelmscott.

With both men in her thrall, the three years at Kelmscott during their joint tenancy of the Manor were to witness the unfolding drama of love in turns both joyful and lyrical, and tragic and desperate.

The First Coming to Kelmscott
In July 1871 Morris took down to the Manor Janey and their two children, Jenny, aged ten, and May, aged nine; Rossetti followed soon after. Morris stayed for a few days only, returning to London to prepare for his first visit to Iceland, the climax of some 15 years' fascination with its heroic literature and admiration for the simple and self-reliant pattern of living of its people – as different as could be

from the degraded and polluted living of the working masses in Britain's industrial cities. For Rossetti, that summer was to be the sweetest and most memorable of his life, an image of happy existence that haunted him long after his final departure in July 1874, so that he was driven on numerous occasions in his remaining years to futile attempts to recreate elsewhere the experience which, in recall, steadily increased its hallucinatory power over him.[5]

For Morris, the attraction of Kelmscott remained until the end of his days, although he was always conscious of its 'melancholy, born of beauty'. It remained a physical symbol for him of the 'earthly paradise' that he sought for so long through literature, and later through social and political reform.

Early Days of Friendship and Collaboration
The relationship of these two men had begun in joy and optimism when Morris had first met Rossetti in London early in 1856, through the initiative of the first and greatest friend of his undergraduate days in Oxford, Edward Burne-Jones. Morris and Burne-Jones in consequence soon abandoned their theological ambitions, Morris to take up architecture, becoming articled to G. E. Street, the great architect of the Gothic Revival, then in Oxford, and Burne-Jones to seek a painter's training.

Thus began the careers of Morris and Burne-Jones as artists. By the autumn of 1856, they were enthusiastically studying painting together in London under Rossetti's guidance.

Morris, who was already writing poems, was further encouraged by the words of the new 'God', who worshipped Dante's *Vita Nuova* and *Purgatorio* and once claimed that Malory's

Blue Silk Dress, *Rossetti's portrait of Janey* ▶
Morris aged 26 (P1)

Morte d'Arthur and the Bible were the 'two greatest books in the world'.

Morris's poem 'Praise of My Lady', in his first volume *The Defence of Guenevere and Other Poems* published in 1858, gives evidence both of his talent and of a new awareness of Italy that had come from Rossetti.

'If any man has any poetry in him he should paint . . . the next Keats ought to be a painter', Rossetti advised his young friends, and it was advice that they promptly followed.[6]

By June 1857 Morris was busy with his first picture *La Belle Iseult* (sometimes known as *Queen Guenevere*), the only known easel painting by him, now in the Tate Gallery.

'O Tempera O Morris'
In 1857 Rossetti gained a major commission in Oxford through Woodward, the architect, to decorate the new Debating Hall (now the Library) in the Union Building. With the assistance of six of his friends, including Morris and Burne-Jones, he undertook the decoration of ten wall-bays, with subjects to illustrate incidents taken from Malory's *Morte d'Arthur*. By the following year six of the subjects had been completed. Because of the lack of experience of the artists involved in this 'Jovial Campaign', the paintings were carried out in distemper on whitewashed newly laid brick walls, and within six months they had sadly deteriorated.[7]

In a study by Rossetti of Guenevere and Launcelot for his painting *Sir Launcelot's vision of the Sanc Grael*, the finest of the Union series, we see Burne-Jones as Launcelot and Jane Burden (later to become Mrs Morris) as Guenevere. Rossetti and Burne-Jones had just met Jane at the theatre and had persuaded her to act as a model. The subject is 'Sir Launcelot

◀ La Belle Iseult *by William Morris, 1858*

prevented by his sin from entering the chapel of the Sanc Grael'. It illustrates appropriately the contemporary obsession for medievalism, inspired by Malory and especially by Tennyson, and this early emphasis on feelings of guilt is prophetic of so much of his work in the 1860s and 1870s.

This is the first drawing Rossetti made of Janey, who from then on was to replace Lizzie as the model for this painting, a symbolic act on his part, one might think, in view of later events.[8]

Sources of Rossetti's Art
Although Rossetti had never completed his course at the Royal Academy and his apprenticeship was limited to brief spells in Sass's Academy and Ford Madox Brown's studio, his potential as a draughtsman is evident.

One can see directness and assurance similar to that in the Sanc Grael study in the drawing at Kelmscott of Janey, one of two he made of her in 1861 when she was 21, for the altar-piece he was then painting for Llandaff Cathedral. May Morris considered these drawings 'particularly valuable as portraiture in their freedom from type-exaggeration'.[9] A study of Morris as David, made in 1862 for the same altar-piece, is now at Birmingham.

One is tempted to speculate how far his undeniable talents in objective drawing might have developed within the tenets of 'truth to nature' insisted upon by his other two more naturally gifted colleagues in the Brotherhood, Millais and Hunt, in their early years. They had both received the full range of academic instruction at the Royal Academy.

To assess Rossetti's potential for moral and social realism in art,[10] we have only the painting *Found*, begun in 1853, apart from his two early religious works *The Girlhood of Mary Virgin* of 1849 and the *Ecce Ancillae Domini* (later called the *Annunciation*, to escape allegations of 'popery'). Rossetti left the painting unfinished, and it was completed after his death by his assistant, Dunn, and by Burne-Jones. It is now in the Bancroft Collection, Delaware, U.S.A. A sketch for its composition and a study of the head of Fanny Cornforth, who was the model for the street woman, are both in the Birmingham Museum. We should let his sister, Christina, have the last word in her sonnet 'The P.R.B. is in its decadence . . . D. G. Rossetti shuns the vulgar optic'.

Red House and the Firm
In 1859 Morris married Jane Burden and, aided by an annual income of some £900 inherited in 1854 when he came of age, he embarked with the help of Philip Webb, Clerk of Works in Street's office, upon plans for building and decorating a home for his bride and himself at Upton in Kent, as well as establishing a workshop there, to be shared with all his friends who would first undertake the decoration of the house. Creating this artistic community at Red House proved an enjoyable task and was to occupy him for the next five years. To some extent he had realised his dream of a monastic workshop, in imitation of that of the German painter, the 'Nazarener' Carl Overbeck, set up outside Rome in the first decade of the nineteenth century – a dream that Morris and Burne-Jones had shared since their under-graduate days. The 'Nazarene' influence in painting had already been a powerful one in shaping the character of Pre-Raphaelite paint-ing, and of Rossetti's first works.[11]

'The Shadow of Dante'
For Rossetti primary Italian sources were paramount. Many of his drawings and water-colour paintings illustrate the works by Dante, particularly the *Vita Nuova*, which he had

translated into English in 1848 and with whose author he largely identified himself. The P.R.B. favoured a deliberate archaism with its attendant formality, linear character and artificiality. Encouraged by Ruskin's writing, they drew inspiration not only from German drawings but also from the early Quattrocento painters in Italy, especially the frescoes by Fra Angelico in the Campo Santo at Pisa. These the P.R.B. knew only from engravings, as none of them had as yet visited Italy. Rossetti never did visit his family's homeland, although two paintings of scenes in a North Italian town, possibly Mantua, which he owned (and which are now at Kelmscott) remind us of his attachment to the country. The drawing *The Anniversary of the Death of Beatrice*, dated 1849, shows Rossetti's response to those influences. He made a watercolour version of the same subject in 1853, now in the Ashmolean. This watercolour inspired Ruskin's first letter to Rossetti, in which he described it as a 'thoroughly glorious work', and confirms Ruskin's awareness and approval of Rossetti's response.

New Location and Consolidation of the Firm
The design and craft venture at Red House proved so encouraging that it became necessary to place it on a proper business footing and, in 1861, as Morris, Marshall, Faulkner and Co, the Firm began to move – slowly at first, but steadily gaining momentum. With success came fresh problems, however. Although one railway had reached them, Red House was still too in-accessible and too cold. Morris caught a chill commuting and was laid low with rheumatic fever. He decided in 1865, therefore, to bring back his family – now including his two lively daughters, Jenny and May – and all his work, to a new base in an old house in Queen Square, Bloomsbury.

The change was a wise decision, for in its new

premises the Firm flourished as never before.

The year 1865/6 was to prove one of furious activity for Morris and for his closest friend, Burne-Jones, the third artist whose work is well represented at Kelmscott Manor, mostly by illustrations made for the Kelmscott Press. The commission to the Firm from the Board of Works for the decoration of the Green Dining Room at the South Kensington Museum involved Burne-Jones in the painting of figures in a series of stained-glass windows designed by Webb, and 12 panels of the *Zodiac*, painted on a gold ground. Eleven drawings of the *Signs of the Zodiac*, now at Kelmscott, are related to these panels. They demonstrate the decorative charm of Burne-Jones's work at this time and his recent re-awakening to Italian art of the later Quattrocento and early Cinquecento, especially to the work of Botticelli and Mantegna. Here indeed was one artist who understood the 'appetite for beauty' and the 'virile air' attributed to Botticelli by contemporary tradition.[12] Through Ruskin he was to learn also that the vision of Botticelli is centred in his outlines. This he would demonstrate even more clearly in the numerous drawings he was to make to illustrate Morris's *The Earthly Paradise*.

In addition to all their other work, Morris and Burne-Jones began working together again – with renewed enthusiasm – upon *The Earthly Paradise*, a cycle of tales of love and heroism drawn from many sources, and with which they both hoped to rival the great collections of the Middle Ages, such as the *Decameron*, the *Arabian Nights* and the *Canterbury Tales*, and at the same time to challenge the declining standards of contemporary book production in England. Morris, often working into the small hours, turned these tales into verse with extraordinary but lamentable speed. There were to be 500 illustrations in all, which Burne-Jones

would design and Morris would cut for reproduction on wood. The method proposed was beginning to give way to photographic means of reproduction in the commercial field, a process which was much quicker, but which sacrificed most of the quality of the image.

Retreat from Society

While all this activity flourished, Rossetti had for several years withdrawn from the company of most of his old friends to lead an introspective and isolated existence at 16 Cheyne Walk, Chelsea, in an old house overlooking the river, where his model from early days in Blackfriars, the blonde and ample Fanny Cornforth, presided as both housekeeper and patient companion. His pattern of living was now punctuated by violent swings of mood, from frenetic hyperactivity to long periods of inaction, which left him overwhelmed by depression and an acute sense of failure. To add to this torment were neurotic fears of blindness, and feelings of guilt over Lizzie's death, so extreme that they amounted to paranoia, for this unfortunate *artiste maudit* whom Baudelaire would have understood so well.

Lizzie had committed suicide in 1862, following the death of their only child, a daughter stillborn the previous year. There is some evidence that Rossetti (who had certainly often neglected Lizzie during the last years of her life) could have anticipated and perhaps taken more positive action to prevent her tragic end.

The culmination of this guilt and Rossetti's obsessive and powerful attempts to expunge it, as well as his overwhelming awareness of the loss of both physical life and love, is the force that inspires the famous portrait of Lizzie as Dante's Beatrice, *Beata Beatrix*, dated 1864, but not completed until 1870. He came to think of himself as Dante and wrote of this picture: 'I made the figures of Dante and Love passing through the street and gazing ominously on one another, conscious of the event; while the bird, a messenger of death, drops the poppy between the hands of Beatrice.' The painting[13] is now in the Tate Gallery.

Self-reconciliation appeared to be well advanced when in 1866 he completed the portrait of Janey called the *Blue Silk Dress*, the finest of all his works at Kelmscott Manor. In the returning confidence of his renewed love for Janey, he had the coffin of Lizzie exhumed in 1869 to recover the manuscripts of his early poetry, which he had caused to be buried with her body. However, this restored confidence was traumatically shattered in the consequences of so emotive an action, and Rossetti suffered a serious relapse. During his slow recovery he stayed at Penkill Castle, on a wild part of the Ayrshire coast, at the invitation of its owner and hereditary 'laird', Miss Alice Boyd, *inamorata* of his great friend, the poet and painter William Bell Scott. His recovery was hastened by long walks, alone or in Scott's company, which diffused the pain of self-condemnation and exhausted him. An even greater numbness was induced by whisky, in order that he might overcome the dreaded insomnia that nightly denied him relief, a pattern of living he was to repeat so often at Kelmscott.

Janey too had been ill before coming to Kelmscott, and to improve her health she had been taken by her husband in 1869 to the German spa town of Ems. This event is illustrated by a caricature drawing by Rossetti, in which she is shown reclining in the bath while her husband reads to her from volume two of *The Earthly Paradise*.

The appalling tragedy of Rossetti's life is often made more bearable and comprehensible to the onlooker by such flashes of mordant humour.

Burne-Jones displays a similar predilection for graphic satire even more frequently. The 1860s and early 1870s was a period of outstanding achievement by British artists in 'black and white' such as Charles Keene, who contributed to the rapidly increasing number of popular journals such as *Punch* and the *Illustrated London News*, and magazines such as *Once a Week*, *Good News* and *Cornhill* (edited by Thackeray). Rossetti had the talent to have become a great illustrator, as his drawing for St Cecilia (which he made as early as 1856/7) demonstrates, but he became discouraged as did Morris by the inability of the craftsmen who cut the woodblocks to capture the spirit and quality of the original drawings. In another drawing he both demonstrates his skill and hints at his inability to face the realities of life and love: the famous 'Bogie' drawing, *How they met themselves*, which he drew on his honeymoon in Paris in 1860.

Rossetti at Kelmscott

Rossetti truly loved Kelmscott and its surrounding landscape, though for rather different reasons than Morris. During all his time there he set off daily on long walks of five or six miles at a time (he speaks of two 'splendid riverside walks', and how he could avoid all of Kelmscott village's 117 inhabitants by keeping to field paths). Soon he was encouraging the fragile Janey to keep him company, in his own words: 'her having developed a most triumphant pedestrian faculty', which surpassed even that of his companion Scott at Penkill the year before.

Gabriel loved children, especially the two Morris girls, claiming that he would like to adopt his favourite, the nine-year-old May. He had the gift of talking to them as if they were grown up, and they rewarded him with their love and confidence. Of May he said: 'quite a beauty the more one knows her, and will be a lovely woman'. It would be difficult to disagree with this judgement, looking at his drawing. May Morris, in later years, vividly remembered the early days of pleasure and informal living in Rossetti's company at the Manor, of his romping with the children and the five dogs, or sharing mealtime with Mossy the barn owl, or – as other commentators were to note also – of Rossetti sitting down to late breakfasts of many eggs and bacon.[14]

His fondness for animals is well known but rarely represented in his pictures. His garden at Cheyne Walk housed a strange menagerie of armadillos, wombats, woodchucks, peacocks and a kangaroo!

In 1871 Rossetti painted another happy portrait of Janey at Kelmscott, in the background of which there is a glimpse of the house and church, a rare reference by him to factual landscape.[15] The original portrait remained with Rossetti during his lifetime, but in 1890 – some years after his death – the American collector Samuel Bancroft bought it for his collection and it is now housed at the Wilmington Society of Fine Arts, Delaware. In 1893 he shipped the painting back to England for Charles Fairfax Murray to restore; at this time the copy now at Kelmscott was made by Fairfax Murray. Something of the charm of the original painting is revealed in Rossetti's sanguine drawing for the portrait still at Kelmscott. In Rossetti's words: 'the figure is meant to be, as it were, speaking to you, and embodying in her expression the penetrating sweetness of the scene and season', an apt comment on those early halcyon days together at Kelmscott.

Again at Kelmscott there is a drawing of Janey reclining on her sofa as was her wont, which belongs to the same period. One can imagine the scene, set in the large drawing room which he used as a studio in 1871, or in the tapestry room which he used in 1872 and 1873. There Gabriel would make drawings of her or read to her and instruct her in the works of Scott, Pepys and Boswell, bought especially for her from the bookdealer Ellis. Many of these books still remain in the house.

A token of their time together is the miniature drawing he made of her, a tiny icon to adorn the fly-leaf of a volume of Burton's *Anatomy of Melancholy*, which he gave her as a Christmas present in 1873.

Rossetti's miniature of Janey (P26)

In September 1871, Morris returned from Iceland and quickly made haste to Kelmscott, to rejoin his family in 'my own little old house', as he put it, and to enjoy the delights of boating and fishing and riding his sturdy little pony, Mouse, brought back with him from Iceland.

Rossetti observed Morris's fishing with his usual sardonic humour in another caricature drawing: he shows a rotund Morris seated in a punt reading *The Earthly Paradise*, oblivious to the fish leaping about him, under which he has written,

'Enter Morris, moored in a punt
and Jacks and tenches exeunt'.

Rossetti's Decline
As winter approached Morris returned to London, taking Janey and family with him, and leaving behind a disconsolate Rossetti. For Rossetti this most idyllic phase of his life was over. He returned to London, and to the arena of literary criticism, to be the subject and first victim of a fierce attack upon the 'Fleshly School of Poetry' of which he and Swinburne were regarded as leaders.[16]

These additional troubles and separation once more from Janey led to an even deeper trough of despair, and eventually to his attempted suicide in London at Whitsuntide 1872. He took an overdose of chloral, just as Lizzie had done ten years before. However by September, after convalescence again in Scotland, he had recovered sufficiently to return to Kelmscott, and was determined to revive the ecstatic days of the previous summer.

Once again he writes of the 'perfect paradise' of life with Janey and the 'kids': 'here all is happiness again . . . such lovable children'. But Janey and family soon returned to London, this time to help her husband seek a new base in town between Hammersmith and Turnham Green.

The Morris and Burne-Jones families c1874

Rossetti alone at Kelmscott
Rossetti remained alone at Kelmscott through the cold and severe winter of 1872, when several great elms were laid low by violent storms. In spite of 'double glazing' installed by a Lechlade carpenter, he was driven by the cold from his studio in the tapestry room. Before the attention of the architects introduced by the Society of Antiquaries in 1962, there were few comforts in the house; Wilfrid Scawen Blunt, who eventually succeeded Rossetti as Janey's lover, was to confirm this with feeling in his journal many years later. Many other visitors before and after him and old photographs all confirm the house's spartan character.

Gabriel, frequently sleepless and frustrated, lamented:
'. . . how far away
The night shall be from the day that was'.
Possessive and jealous of the loss of anything that linked his life with Janey, he caused all his

drawings of her to be sent to Kelmscott. He hung many in the tapestry room where some still hang.

But there were to be only a few more joyful stays at Kelmscott for Rossetti. There were two brief periods in 1873: when Morris was in Italy with Burne-Jones, and later when Morris had gone off to Iceland for the second time. We read then of Jenny and May plucking flowers for the elderly Mrs Rossetti 'with her dear old face', who had come to stay, and of Gabriel commenting: 'I have done nothing but my daily painting all my time here', with a consequent improvement to his generally shaky financial status. He was able to write: 'I shall be much better stocked with tin than is my wont.'[17]

In 1873 he was working on two of his 'fleshly' masterpieces at Kelmscott, one was *Proserpine*, the other *La Ghirlandata*. Janey came down for a week at a time to pose as Proserpine – apt comment on the situation, for Proserpine the enchained and unhappy wife of Pluto was ever doomed to divide her life between the freedom and light of the upper world and slavery and misery in the underworld, chained to a husband she did not love.

Here we see in blatant display the 'inhuman icon of narcissistic obsessive sensuality', in the words of John Gere, written exactly a century later for his introduction to the catalogue of the last major exhibition of Rossetti's work in this country.[18]

For the second work Rossetti used his beloved little May as model for the two angel figures, but for the 'stunner' brought down the dressmaker Alexa Wilding, of 'beautiful face and sunburnt hair' and 'soft and mystical repose', whom in 1865 he had 'picked up' in the Strand. She was one of the few to attend his funeral, and laid a wreath on his grave.

In 1874 Janey came back again but in July departed to join Morris on a visit to Bruges, to stay in the very same room that they had occupied on their honeymoon 15 years before. This blow left Rossetti 'overstrained and fanciful', to use his brother's careful words, leading eventually to quarrels with both locals and the few friends who remained loyal to him. Suddenly Rossetti departed for London, never to return to Kelmscott, 'to Morris's relief for many reasons', says the tactful Mackail, 'and the estrangement between the powerful and self-centred personalities was final'.

The Last Act
Painting and poetry are linked more closely than ever during the last act of the drama. In 1881 a second edition of Rossetti's *Poems*, first published in 1870, appeared together with another book, *Ballads and Sonnets*, which contained a sonnet sequence – 'The House of Life'. In this sequence we have the full revelation of guilty love and brazen sensuality for which

Janey Morris photographed c1860

35

only death could provide expiation and relief. In verse, as in painting, there will be fierce clashes on the very Victorian battlefield of sexual mores, between the intellectual urgencies of spiritual decarnalisation and those of physical fulfilment and explicit sexuality, with champions of both sides engaged in bloody battle. Ruskin and Patmore pitted themselves against Rossetti and Swinburne, and weaker rebels such as Burne-Jones withdrew from the fight when the heat became too great. In painting, the sensuous restless forms of Rossetti and Burne-Jones, in rich, exotic and sometimes oppressively heavy colour, provided examples for imitation by numerous lesser artists of the *fin de siècle*. Their painting considerably influenced painters abroad, especially the Symbolist school in France during the 1880s and 1890s.[19]

The path to Art Nouveau is clear, and is especially evident in the paintings of Burne-Jones, from the *Perseus* and *Cupid and Psyche*

cycles in the Fulham Public Library.

The curtains closed finally on the tragedy of Rossetti's life and art with his death aged 54 on Easter Day 1882, in most miserable circumstances at Birchington-on-Sea, Kent. The Manor then returned to its role as a peaceful haven for all who were and are still to live there, although its beauty will always be shadowed.

Peace came to Morris too with his death in 1896 at the comparatively early age of 62, the final cause being given as tuberculosis.[20] Charles Fairfax Murray made an impressive death-bed portrait of him.

These two great men, Morris and Rossetti, had lived out heroic roles. As an epilogue one might add Rossetti's last lines to go below the final major work for which Janey was model, the *Astarte Syriaca* of 1877:

'That face, of Love's all penetrative spell
Amulet, talisman, and oracle –
Betwixt the sun and moon a mystery.'

William Morris as David, *1860 aged 26 (P8)*

Janey Morris *in 1861 aged 21 (P7)*

The principal sources consulted for general information on the lives and work of William Morris, Dante Gabriel Rossetti and Edward Burne-Jones are the earliest standard works:

The Life of William Morris by J. M. Mackail, London, 1899.

D. G. Rossetti as Designer and Writer by W. M. Rossetti, London, 1889.

Dante Gabriel Rossetti, Illustrated Memorial of his Art and Life by H. C. Marillier, London, 1899.

Memorials of Edward Burne-Jones, by G(eorgiana) B(urne)-J(ones), 2 vols, London, 1904.

More recent sources which have given valuable assistance are:

A Victorian Romantic, Dante Gabriel Rossetti by Oswald Doughty, 2nd edition, London, 1960.

Edward Burne-Jones, A Biography by Penelope Fitzgerald, London, 1975.

Detailed information of individual works has been taken from the following catalogues:

Dante Gabriel Rossetti, 1828–1882, The Paintings and Drawings, a Catalogue Raisonné by Virginia Surtees, Oxford, 1971.

Dante Gabriel Rossetti, Painter and Poet, The Royal Academy of Arts, London and City Museum and Art Gallery, Birmingham, London, 1973.

Burne-Jones, the paintings, graphic and decorative work of Sir Edward Burne-Jones, The Arts Council of Great Britain, London, 1975.

These source books and catalogues will be referred to by the following abbreviations:

The Life of William Morris	Life WM
D.G.R. Designer and Writer	Rossetti
D.G.R. Illustrated Memorial	Marillier
Memorials of E. Burne-Jones	Memorials
Victorian Romantic, D.G.R.	Doughty
E.B.J. A Biography	Fitzgerald
D.G.R. Catalogue Raisonné	S. (eg: S.370)
D.G.R. RA 1973	DGR Cat. RA
B.J. Arts Council 1975	EBJ Cat. AC

I have been greatly assisted by the succinct, lively and often witty notes written in both catalogues by Mrs Virginia Surtees.

I am also indebted to A. R. Dufty, past President of the Society of Antiquaries and Honorary Curator of Kelmscott Manor, for his unstinting information and advice, especially concerning Rossetti's and Burne-Jones's works at Kelmscott Manor.

(References to Fine Art entries relate to the Catalogue of Paintings, Prints and Drawings, pages 125–138.)

1 Life WM, chap VII, 'Morris and Kelmscott', pp213–39.

2 Algernon Swinburne, undergraduate at Balliol College, Oxford found the Rossetti circle in Oxford c1857. He was acquainted with the verse of Rossetti and his friends in the *Oxford and Cambridge Magazine* and was attracted to the Pre-Raphaelite group 'by its seriousness, imagery, symbolism, mystery, by a quality often cruel, and melancholy in its pictures, poems and tales'. 'Now we were four in company and not three', said Burne-Jones later. See Doughty, p232. Increasing estrangement between Rossetti and Swinburne took place during the 1870s in spite of the latter's efforts to heal the breach.

3 'The portrait', *Willow-wood* (four willow-wood sonnets) all written in December 1868. See Doughty pp377, 476 and 687.

4 Wilfrid Scawen Blunt, diplomat, poet, traveller and 'man-about-town', who succeeded Rossetti as Janey's lover soon after his death in 1882. He writes very frankly in *My*

Diaries, 1916, about the relationship between Morris and his wife, as well as life in the *ménage à trois* at Kelmscott Manor, pp28–9. He states that in his view 'One thing only, I think, he did not know, much as he had written about it, the love of women, and that he never could bear to discuss.' *Ibid*, pp30–1. Blunt bequeathed his letters from Janey, and his diaries and notebooks, to the Fitzwilliam Museum, Cambridge, on his death in 1922. Peter Faulkner of the University of Exeter is currently preparing a new edition of these diaries, with hitherto undisclosed information. Elizabeth Longford has also written a detailed and interesting biography, *A Pilgrimage of Passion*, London, 1979.

5 The views of Rossetti and Morris were understandably opposed concerning the former's life at Kelmscott. Doughty (p542) states that Rossetti had refound the peace he sought, and quotes from a letter to William, 'Here all is happiness again, and I feel completely myself . . . such charming and lovable children.' For him Kelmscott was a 'perfect paradise'. Yet Mackail (Life WM, p308) reports Morris comments on Rossetti's time at Kelmscott as follows: 'he has all sorts of ways so unsympathetic with the simple old place that I feel his presence there is a kind of slur on it'.

6 See Life WM, chap IV, pp109–17, 129 and Doughty pp209–10 for details of life at Red Lion Square. According to Mackail, Morris's mother blamed 'Ned' Jones for her son's second and unexpected change of career to one as a painter (p111) and states that he became moody and unstable in consequence, 'I want to imitate Gabriel as much as I can' he replied to all criticism of this slavish devotion to a new master.

7 The hilarious story of the painting of the Union murals is first told by Mackail (pp118–22) and again later by Doughty (pp117–26). They all thought it a 'great lark, throwing buckets of dirty water over each other, and disturbing the undergraduates studying in the adjacent library with their songs, jokes, laughter and scuffles. Reputedly hidden among the ceiling paintings were painted images of a rotund "Topsy" (Morris) legs straddling like Henry VIII.' 'Unnaturally and unnecessarily curly, but growing fat', quipped 'Ned' Jones. Mackail tells again of Morris 'embedded in iron (armour specially made to his design in a local forge) the visor of the basinet (helmet) immovable, dancing with rage and jammed inside'. This schoolboy humour in Oxford was typical of their Bohemian life-style in London and at Red House, Upton also during these early years.

In spite of the failure Mackail can record the original colourful appeal of the completed paintings which they were so soon to lose, quoting Coventry Patmore, in the *Saturday Review* for Boxing Day 1857, speaking of the colour 'as sweet, bright, and pure as a cloud in the sunrise . . . so brilliant as to make the walls look like the margin of an illuminated manuscript'. Morris could have asked for no higher praise, and one notes his influence on Rossetti whose use of colour became brighter and more decorative.

8 The story of W. Deverell's discovery of Elizabeth Siddal in a bonnet shop in Leicester Square is well known: John Gere suggests, somewhat unkindly (*Pre-Raphaelite Painters*, 1948, p32), that it was perhaps his most important contribution to the Pre-Raphaelite movement, see also pp27–8. His action followed a pattern of 'picking up' models, often in the street, a practice of all three principal members of the P.R.B., but one in

which Rossetti excelled, and continued for longer than the others.

9 Richard Dufty quotes May Morris's remarks in his *Illustrated Guide*, published by the Society of Antiquaries, London, in 1977. Although very brief and condensed, the *Guide* contains a summary of most important information on the present collection at Kelmscott Manor, including the works of fine art.

10 The oil painting *Found* is Rossetti's painting of a 'modern life' subject with intended moral significance. Begun in 1854 when he was living at Blackfriars, it was left unfinished on his death, probably because of his inability to face realities in both life and art. The stirrings of conscience regarding the plight of the poor and the appalling conditions that existed for workers in the new industries, factories, mines, etc, producing the wealth of Victorian Britain (and of Morris too) were becoming evident in the writings of those who 'seeming to be idle, work, and are the cause of well-ordained work in others' – Madox Brown's explanation of the presence of Carlyle and the Rev. F. D. Maurice, leader of the Christian Socialist Movement, in his painting *Work* (1852–65).

Holman Hunt responded early to such pressures: his painting *The Awakening Conscience* of a kept woman, exhibited at the Royal Academy in 1854, is the most complete example. Rossetti's subject is a moral one also, representing a 'street prostitute crouching against a brick wall, who is being discovered in the early morning by a country farmer, as he brings his cart to market over Blackfriars Bridge, and recognised as the woman he once loved' (DGR Cat. RA, p31). He painted the prostitute from Fanny Cornforth kneeling against 'a wall of a churchyard', where 'the wicked cease from troubling and the weary are at rest'. The painting of the calf, painted at Brown's house at Finchley, 'trammelled in the net, and helpless, carried in the cart to its death, points to the past and present life of the girl', continued to give him trouble.

11 For a brief reference to the influence of the German 'Nazarene' community and their painting on the Pre-Raphaelite style, see Life WM, pp62–3, Doughty, pp70–1, and *Pre-Raphaelite Painters*, 1948, pp9–10.

12 Lionello Venturi in his work on *Sandro Botticelli*, Vienna, 1937, gives a succinct and perceptive analysis of the nineteenth-century English reaction by critics such as Ruskin and Pater, to Botticelli's painting and the links between his work and that of both Fra Angelico and Michaelangelo (pp7–13).

13 Although dated 1864, the painting was begun 'many years before' his wife's death in 1862, cf Rossetti's letter of 22 December 1863 to Ellen Heaton, and the Dunn Papers (S168, p93). It would seem however that he regarded it as a memorial to her and it was always painfully associated in his mind with her death.

He explained its subject as follows: 'The picture illustrates the *Vita Nuova*, embodying symbolically the death of Beatrice as treated in that work. The picture is not intended at all to represent death, but to render it under the semblance of a trance, in which Beatrice seated at a balcony overlooking the city is suddenly rapt from Earth to Heaven.'

Following his words quoted in this text he continues, 'She, through her shut lids is conscious of a new world, as expressed in the last words of the *Vita Nuova*.' Throughout his life as painter/poet, Rossetti displayed his obsession with the works of Dante.

The idea for this picture probably followed on from the three panels he painted in 1859, to decorate a settle in Morris's rooms in Red Lion Square. Their theme was the love of Dante for Beatrice, *Dantis Amor*, the central panel being the most notable. He made also six replicas of the *Beata Beatrix*.

14 For Rossetti's and Janey's life with the children at Kelmscott, see Life WM, pp225–39, Doughty, chap X, pp469–85, 'Kelmscott, 1871', and chap XIV, pp542–68, 'The Return to Kelmscott, 1872–74'.

15 In 1851 at Ewell, near Surbiton, Surrey, Millais was painting the background of *Ophelia* (Elizabeth Siddal as model), and Holman Hunt was busy completing the landscape setting for his *Hireling Shepherd*. In both pictures the Pre-Raphaelite concern for meticulous transcription of nature in detail, 'selecting nothing, rejecting nothing', is paramount. In Millais' painting we see a bank of the River Ewell, also a tributary of the Thames, depicted in all its richness of wild flower and weed. Unfortunately Rossetti never shared Ruskin's and the P.R.B.'s obsession with recording the minutiae of nature, so Kelmscott's river banks go unrecorded during his time there. We can see the setting however in the vivid descriptions of Morris recorded by Mackail (Life WM, pp226–31).

16 See Doughty, pp486–504 for an account of the attacks on Rossetti and Swinburne as leaders of the 'Fleshly School of Poetry', especially that launched by the journalist and 'poetaster', Robert Buchanan, under the pseudonym of 'T. Maitland', in the *Contemporary Review* for October 1871. He also gives an interesting account of the hypocrisy over sexual matters that was so characteristic of Victorian Society.

17 Throughout his life Rossetti was plagued by an absence of 'tin', which at times obliged him to prepare pictures with their potential for sale as a major consideration. It also forced him, when especially 'hard up', to employ rather unethical tactics in approaching clients (see No 28a Fine Art). For Morris, therefore, meeting Rossetti was to be a very expensive encounter in more ways than one.

18 Concerning Rossetti's last phase, John Gere writes (Introduction to DGR Cat. RA, pp14–15): 'As isolation grew his art became increasingly mannered and turned in on itself. In such pictures of the 1870s as *Astarte Syriaca* or *Proserpine*, Mrs Morris's features undergo their final transformation into an inhuman icon of narcissistic, obsessive sensuality.'

19 Burne-Jones exhibited his first picture, *The Beguiling of Merlin*, in Paris in 1878. In 1889 his *King Cophetua and the Beggar Maid* was shown at the Exposition Universelle and achieved considerable popular success. Burne-Jones was awarded the Cross of the Legion of Honour. The *Wheel of Fortune* was shown in 1891 and he continued to exhibit in Paris until 1896.

20 See *William Morris and the Art of the Book*, *William Morris: Book Collector* by Paul Needham, Pierpont Morgan Library, Oxford University Press, 1976. (See Catalogue of Books, pp165–183.) Needham quotes as follows (p41): 'For over a year before his death Morris suffered from a progressive weakness, different from his usual attacks of gout. It became more pronounced after the New Year, 1896, when he began to lose weight steadily. A succession of examinations by several doctors did not produce any conclusive diagnosis until the summer, when they finally affirmed that it was tuberculosis.'

'Dear William'

Martin Shuttleworth

Dear William

A mere third of a century after they buried you in Kelmscott Churchyard, a man called Auden wrote:

Private faces in public places
Are wiser and nicer
Than public faces in private places.

Kelmscott Manor was a very private place. You rented it in 1871 when you were 37. By that age you had published *The Defence of Guenevere, The Earthly Paradise, The Life and Death of Jason* and two translations from the Icelandic. When Wilfrid Scawen Blunt (who had not yet fallen for your wife, nor even met either of you) came home from Madeira that year and 'made a dash for Rosalind Howard . . . he realised that she had dressed up specially for him. Her style was something that he had never seen before – a green serge gown copied from drawings of Marguerite in Faust, with slashed sleeves, a looped skirt and a satchel hung on a chain from the waist. This, he later discovered, was the neo-pagan fancy of London town ladies, whose Bible was William Morris's *Earthly Paradise* and whose *Book of Hours* Rossetti's Pre-Raphaelite preachings. Blunt found Rosalind's "fantastic garb" unbecoming, but it excited him. He tried to kiss her after luncheon. She rebuffed him volubly – and then held out both hands in friendship . . .'

To mention this particular Rosalind (who had a walk-on part in your life too) and that butterfly Scawen Blunt is to remember that, by the time that you were 37, you were already a fashionable prophet. It was not entirely your own fault. You began by writing extremely well, harsh poems out of Malory and Froissart. As a child I loved them. At my preparatory school, a limping dominie crippled in the last days of the Kaiser's war used to make us get them by heart. In the rain beside the Severn, the crocodile of small boys would shout out in unison:

Swerve to the left, son Roger, he said,
  When you catch his eyes through the helmet-slit,
Swerve to the left, then out at his head,
  And the Lord God give you the joy of it!

And we would imagine, not very concretely, death in the tilt-yard, though there was more than one poem in that first collection of yours (*The Defence of Guenevere and other Poems*) that, then as now, strikes me as quite terrifying.

Had Froissart lived today he could have been on the payroll of both MI5 and the KGB and neither would have been quite sure for which he worked, while only those who have never read Sir Thomas Malory's *Morte D'Arthur* (which you quarried with a minute attention) imagine that Malory was a romantic. Malory lived at a time when the French had artillery and we had none to speak of; lived during that long, sordid fag-end of the Hundred Years' War when our defeated armies came home to destroy each other and England in the Wars of the Roses. To understand why these men who wrote of the breakup of the age of chivalry meant so much to you when you were a young man is to begin to understand you, for yours was a time super-ficially most unlike theirs; a time of great self-consciousness and bumptiousness in England. By the year 1850, when you were 16, 'Great Britain had triumphantly established herself both as the workshop of the world and as the shipper and trader of the world'.

I quote from the *Cambridge Modern History*, which is slackly unaware of your place in our history, or the world's. It does scant justice to your extraordinary achievements as a visual artist; fails to recognise that you were one of the greatest of all the dissenting Victorians; finds no place to mention that when you were 11 you were sent as a boarder to a preparatory school in Walthamstow, nor that, when you were 14 – the year your father died – you were banished from home and sent to Marlborough, where conditions for small and bullied boys were not unlike those in the dank England of the deep past where knights squelched in their rusting armour through the rain, and were treacherously set upon at the edge of the dark wood . . . or so it seems it could seem to an imaginative, rebellious small boy.

Much later on, when you were in your early fifties, you referred to your parents as 'two accidental persons', and asked: 'How is it possible to protect the immature citizen from the whims of his parents? Are they to be left free to starve his body or warp his mind by all sorts of nonsense; if not how are they to be restrained?'

Your parents, you wrote to another friend, 'did as all right people do, shook off the responsibility of my education as soon as they could; handing me over first to nurses, then to grooms and gardeners, and then to a school, a boy-farm I should say. In one way or another I learnt chiefly one thing from all these – rebellion.'

By the time that you wrote these two letters from which I have just quoted you had discovered Karl Marx and declared yourself a Socialist. You had written, in 1878, in your lecture on 'The Lesser Arts': 'I do not want art for a few, any more than education for a few, or freedom for a few.

'No, rather than art should live this poor thin life among a few exceptional men, despising those beneath them for an ignorance for which they themselves are responsible, for a brutality that they will not struggle with – rather than this, I would that the world should indeed sweep away all art for a while, as I said before I thought it possible she might do; rather than the wheat should rot in the miser's granary, I would that the earth had it, that it might yet have a chance to quicken in the dark . . .'

Fiery torrents choked with innumerable corpses seem to separate this from the slashed sleeves, looped skirt and satchel hung on a chain from the waist that Wilfrid Scawen Blunt had found both unbecoming and exciting when Rosalind Howard had dressed herself in a way that Burne-Jones's illustrations to your *Earthly Paradise* had made fashionable seven years before in 1871.

It was easy, from the first, for people to scent that what you were about was both bold and revolutionary, far less easy to see exactly what it was. Three years after Scawen Blunt made his unsuccessful pass, you went to stay with Rosalind Howard and her husband at Naworth Castle in Cumberland, and rather frightened her. She wrote in her diary: 'He was rather shy – and so was I – I felt he was taking an experimental plunge amongst "barbarians", and I was not sure what would be the resulting opinion in his mind. However he has grown more urbane – and even three hours has worked off much of our mutual shyness – A walk in the glen made me know him better and like him better than I fancied I should. He talks so clearly and seems to think so clearly that what seems paradox in Webb's mouth in his seems convincing sense. He lacks sympathy and humanity though – and this is a fearful lack to me – only his character is so fine and massive that one must admire. He is agreeable also – and does not snub one.'

The term 'barbarian' that she uses there was Matthew Arnold's. In *Culture and Anarchy*, which had come out in 1869, Arnold had called the new plutocracy 'Philistines' and the hereditary aristocracy of which Rosalind Howard and her husband were somewhat untypical members 'barbarians' with a small 'b'; all his life Arnold looked down on upper-class loutishness from a high Balliol window. There was rather a lot of it, he gathered, in Magdalen, Christ Church and the Houses of Parliament;

but he did not specifically object to people hunting foxes or fighting colonial wars, so long as they did not talk about their brutish activities in his hearing. Equally, the changes he envisaged for the country did not include the over-turning of the 'Philistines' – the replacement of a capitalist society by a socialist.

Nor, that summer of 1874 when you went to stay with the Howards of Naworth in your fortieth year, had you yet come to that clear-cut solution. You knew very well that a great deal was insupportably wrong with society, but you had as yet no clear solutions. That is why I have adopted this letter-form. You were a voice of troubled conscience in your own time, and you are a voice of troubled conscience still. It may seem ridiculous to write a letter to a man who would be 148 next March, but the majority of the problems that faced you and your age face us still and, besides, there are people still alive in Georgia and Kashmir who were toddlers when you were a toddler. If you had been born in some upland Asian valley and lived on yoghurt you might well be alive still. In the world's long history, a century and a half is not a very long time. A century and a half separated – say – Henry of Blois and William of Wykeham, but when you look at the walls of Farnham Castle and try to determine who built what, it's by no means obvious, even for the art historically trained: Blois' twelfth- and Wykeham's fourteenth-century masons were working within the same idiom. It is only when you get the pipe-rolls out on the microfilm reader (one of our latter-day doddles) that you come to grapple with the sheer number of the medieval years, the medieval generations from which moderns like you and us are separated by a gulf infinitely deeper than the succession of events which fall between nineteenth- and twentieth-century members of the British middle class.

The truth is that you, and we, belong to either the middle or the end of what it is proper to call the 'tele' age. That little Greek particle is the most unconjunctive of words. You learnt Greek at school so there is no need to tell you that it means 'distant' or 'afar off'. It first entered the European languages in modern guise in 1611 when Prince Cesi, the founder of the Roman Academy of the Linei, re-christened Galileo's *perspicillum* a *telescopio*. In 1834, the year of your birth, a French military engineer called Sudré invented what he called a 'telephonic system' so that military and naval commands might be communicated by means of a musical code across any distance. Since then we have hardly looked back. Each new invention as it has come along has had as much destructive as life-enhancing potential. The very latest, as I write, is a 'space-shuttle' that can be used not only to carry telescopes up above the earth's atmosphere but to destroy other less mobile craft already orbiting the earth.

Born into the 'tele' age like the rest of us, you had, from the first, a gut loathing of the unloving and unlovely society it had brought about. Your deepest instinct was to attempt to discover the nature of the bonds that might still keep mankind together. That is why your story still has so much meaning.

It is a story that does not end at your death, but must begin in your well documented childhood. According to your mother, you taught yourself to read before you were four. Your father died when you were still a schoolboy. There was something of him in you, and of you in him. He was a fairly rumbustious toughy. His London was the London of Thackeray's *Vanity Fair*, of Dickens's *Our Mutual Friend*, that favourite book of yours through which the Thames winds as it was to wind through your own life; which was to give you, in Mr Podsnap, the quintessen-

43

tially accumulative, amoral city man whose name you were to invoke whenever you wished to condense into one word all your hatred of your age. 'Was it all [you were to ask] to end in a counting-house on the top of a cinder heap, with Podsnap's drawing-room in the offing, and a Whig committee dealing out champagne to the rich and margarine to the poor in such convenient proportions as would make all rich men contented together, though the pleasure of the eyes was gone from the world, and the place of Homer was to be taken by Huxley?'

It was a London whose extreme contrasts of luxury and squalor appalled foreigners such as Doré, and the young Dostoevsky. Dostoevsky had no English. He could only report what he saw, and what he saw was that London was a suburb of hell, a city of marionettes picking each other up in the Haymarket, riding round in coaches, dying of starvation in the fetid gutters. For your more commonsensical father, it was just a place to make money. Then, as now, there were two ways to get to the top in the City: go to Harrow and make the right contacts young, or start at the bottom. 'Son William,' he said, 'start at the bottom and be sharper and brighter.' He burnt himself out even younger than you did. In your childhood, the forest came up to London's northern doorstep. Every morning, he would go in the 14 miles by stagecoach from Walthamstow to the City. By the time he was 43 and you were six, he was the commuting evening lord of Woodford Hall, a goodly manor house where your mother had her own brewery, laundry, buttery and bakery and you a shaggy pony, a toy suit of armour and the freedom of the forest.

You were always a child of that frontier; of most (though by no means all) of the other frontiers on which the thinking and the compassionate have to live. Although your father was not entirely immune to Podsnap's

disease (after all, he got the College of Heralds to run him up a coat of arms), he and you were always outlanders, brachycephalic endo-mezzomorphs of Welsh border stock, round-headed, Punch-sized barrels of energy with an inbuilt tendency to auto-intoxication. There may have been some inherited epilepsy. Your elder daughter was to develop it; Bernard Shaw thought that your 'lack of physical control when crossed or annoyed was congenital and not quite sane'. He diagnosed 'eclampsias' which comes from the Greek 'to shine forth', and which the Oxford English Dictionary defines thus: 'Epileptiform convulsions dependent on some actual disturbance of the nervous centres caused by anatomical lesion'. No-one else (so far as I know) maliciously diagnosed anatomical lesions, but there is no account of you which does not dwell on your phenomenal energy and powers of concentration; 'Whatever chanced to be Morris's goal of the moment', wrote Theodore Watts-Dunton putting briefly what many others wrote at length, 'was pursued by him with as much intensity as though the universe contained no other possible goal.'

If you urged your pony eastward into the forest, there were still impenetrable thickets of hornbeams, the oldest English tree; clearings with lodges royal hunters had once used. In one of them, very young, you saw a faded tapestry, and when you rode home, the sun setting at your pony's back, a loving mother and eldest sister would indulge and pamper you. Neither then nor later do you seem to have taken much notice of your other brothers and sisters. Emma, your eldest sister, you loved; your mother you respected, and were fond of, but between you and the rest of your siblings there was to intrude an icy chasm of indifference and disapproval, at least after you had all grown up. Henrietta, your second sister, who was also older than you,

Woodford Hall, Essex, where the Morris family lived from 1840 to 1848

poped (as they used to say), and died a difficult Roman Catholic spinster; Isabella married a naval officer who died young, trained as a nurse at Guy's, worked for years in South London slums, and became a deaconess (but was ostracised by the rest of the family for letting them down socially); Hugh became a gentleman farmer and bred pedigree cows; Alice married a banker who was killed hunting; Thomas was commissioned into the Gordon Highlanders; Arthur into the 60th Rifles; Edgar followed his father into the City but lacked the shrewd touch, lost all his capital and ended up working for you at Merton Abbey as a tally clerk.

Brand-newly armigerous, soi-distant gentle-folk, would-be upperlings modelling themselves on an upper class that ever allows entrance on its own terms to the conforming children of the newly rich, you embarrassed them, they you and you rejected not only them but all 'artifical' family ties: in your *News from Nowhere* – in the future as you would have it be – 'families are held together by no bond of coercion, legal or social, but by mutual liking and affection, and everybody is free to come and go as he or she pleases'.

You have reminded many writers of a child who never grew up: a God child whose pram was never big enough; a unique male child with two elder sisters, a father and mother and nurses to dote, driven into yourself further year after year as each new little Podsnap arrived and competed for your parents' love. You retreated on your pony into the forest, early came to know the names and the ways of the insects, flowers, birds and small animals. They even let you ride your pony to baby school. Southward, immensely distant to a child but fully visible on clear days from the edge of the forest, was the huge stinking 'wen', the smoking chimneys, the filthy streets, the spires and towers to which your father retreated every day by stagecoach to make money. At the moment, it was still only a presence, a menacing unknown. Eastward, in your childhood, the Essex plain still stretched away to the undrained marsh and sea; as you crouched in the saddle with your beaver up you could see, far away, the line of sails – rarely punctuated then by funnels – that marked the open Thames:

Forget six counties overhung with smoke,
Forget the snorting steam and piston stroke,
Forget the spreading of the town;
Think rather of the pack-horse on the down,
And dream of London, small, and white, and clean,
The clear Thames bordered by its gardens green.

What follows these lines is often mere knitting in a void but – for their first readers and still – these opening bars of *The Earthly Paradise* seem momentarily to carry a perception of the 'vision splendid'; the beauty and the glory of the childhood of the world matched only in our language, I think, by Wordsworth's ode to his own lost childhood. Yours, my dear William, came to a sudden (though, in the middle classes, not uncommon) end.

When you were 11, 'they' (those 'accidental' beings, your parents) sent you away to boarding school. It was quite close to home but you were up against other people, and a system. We do not know what happened when you gave vent to the sudden bursts of temper to which we know from so many witnesses you were prone. Since you were already big and strong (though always short and barrel-shaped) it is the common view of your biographers that you were spared the worst bullying, and that you were able to champion the weak. After three years there, your father suddenly died, at the age of 50, exhausted by his years of money-grubbing, travelling up and down from Essex in all weathers, playing the evening, week-end squire. In terms of money (which is not love) you were all left very, very well off indeed. He had put you down for Marlborough and there you went, rather late, just before your fifteenth birthday.

Marlborough was one of several very new 'boy-farms'; originally intended for the sons of the clergy, it was very quickly opened to any other children whose parents could pay the fees. When you got there they had fee-paying boys by the hundred, a chapel, a library (which was exceptionally good from the first), a few ready-made buildings adaptable to pack boys in and new buildings going up everywhere. The headmaster was one of those principals most of us have come across in our time: weak one moment, severe the next; slightly dotty, extremely cunning, largely disorganised and wholly disastrous. Very little teaching seems to have gone on. As much as possible, the boys were loosed upon the countryside to amuse themselves. You escaped as often as you could into an England already more meaningful to you and much older; to Savernake Forest and to Avebury, to Silbury and Stonehenge. There is extant an ecstatic letter to your sister Emma in which you tell her of your wanderings and discoveries, and of your longing to be home for the holidays. There is, too, a poem written later, but one of your very first, called 'The Three Flowers':

. . . three flowers grow for ever
On the flower-covered hill
But two flowers grow together . . .

The person closest to you – your beloved sister Emma – had gone and got herself married to a clergyman and they had not even invited you to come back in mid-term for the wedding.

One of your best twentieth-century biographers, Jack Lindsay, believes that this sudden loss of a sister provoked years later *The Defence of Guenevere* poems and foreshadowed your later acceptance of your wife's lovers. I do not know, but long before you had read Malory or Froissart, from the time that you had donned your infant suit of armour and begun to read Scott, the idea of the knight who would always fight the evil in the world was central to you. There are several poems and there is later prose of yours which are still as painful to read as it is painful to watch a lion hurl himself against the bars of his cage while his rival in the next cage sidles round the lionesses. But again and again in the agony that Rossetti later caused you, you shook off your own hurt and roared out the question which is implicit in *The Three Flowers* and blazes forth in *The Defence*: are women chattels for men to possess or share?

It was a question that had been in the air since the French Revolution, a question to which Mary Wollstoncraft and Shelley and Godwin had given their passionate attention, a question which – not long before – John Stuart Mill had brought up again in his essays, notably the one on 'The Subjugation of Women'. (Mill was one of the few Victorians who said publicly and repeatedly that his wife was cleverer than he was.) We know that you read most of what he wrote – and that you were extremely well and widely informed – but the chief reason that the 24

volumes of your own writings remain such a treasure trove is that, from the first, you had an inimitable ability to stumble over each of the major problems of the age on your own account and let out a great bellow. From the first, whether it was your sister Emma, or your imaginary Guenevere, or your own wife Janey, you would not have women judged by rules made by and for men, nor would you easily submit to any 'arbitrary' rules yourself.

There was a lot of bullying and stone-throwing in that school, and profound unhappiness. When you were 17, there was a full-scale rebellion, followed by floggings and 'sendings-home'. Dr Wilkinson was a shifty man. Without the authority of the School Council who were increasingly at loggerheads with him he had no power to 'expel' boys, so what he did was to 'send them home'. From him you early learnt the often Janus-faced, perfid ways of Albion's establishment. What part you played in the rebellion (most of whose leaders were younger than you) we do not know, but your mother took you away and put you in to a crammer home in Essex. Latin was never to your taste, but you snapped up Greek, especially the gory legends of the beginning of the world, the Homeric rumbustiousness.

When you were betwixt a boy and a man, we know that you were already rebellious: that you refused – for instance – to go up to town to see the Duke of Wellington's funeral; that you spent much time boating, and wandering in the forest, but that you were considerate to your mother and that – under her influence and Emma's – you determined to go into the Church. Afterwards, you looked back on this early ambition with amusement, and perhaps it was not very deeply held. From this time on, we hear more and more of your enormous energy. 'Just as in after years, in the thick of his work', Burne-Jones wrote, 'it was noticeable how he never seemed to be particularly busy, and how he had plenty of leisure for expeditions, for fishing, for amusement, if it amused him; he never seemed to read much, but always knew, and accurately; and he had a great instinct at all times for knowing what would not amuse him, and what not to read.'

What time you had over from cramming for Oxford or field marshalling your younger brothers and sisters, you seem to have spent punting, riding, swinging a single-stick, dipping into innumerable books or netting ... netting. At Marlborough, a contemporary noted that you were seldom if ever still and that if you could find nothing better to do, you would make endless nets out of string: a small red-headed godling rehearsing in a corner of Valhalla his future galaxies.

You had high hopes of Oxford. It was said, in those days, that the approach to Oxford by the Henley Road was the most beautiful in the world. 'Soon after passing Littlemore you came in sight of, and did not lose again, the sweet city with its dreaming spires, driven along a road now crowded and obscured with dwellings, open then to cornfields on the right, to unenclosed meadows on the left, with an unbroken view of the line of towers, rising out of foliage less high and veiling than after sixty years of growth today', wrote William Tuckwell in 1874 of the Oxford of 1814. Your own first biographer, Mackail, wrote: 'The Oxford in which Morris and Burne-Jones began their residence at the end of January 1853, was still in its main aspects a medieval city, and the name (in Morris's own beautiful words) roused, as it might have done at any time within the four centuries then ended, "a vision of grey-roofed houses and a long winding street, and the sound of many bells". The railway was there but it had not yet produced its far reaching effects ... the Oxford of 1853 breathed from its towers the last enchantments of the Middle Ages; and still it offered to its most ardent disciples who came to it as to some miraculous place, full of youthful enthusiasm, thirsting after knowledge and beauty the stony welcome Gibbon found at Magdalen, that Shelley had found at University ...'

It was, according to the most brilliant of its dons, Mark Pattison, 'a scurvy pond stagnant with sameness and custom'. The very year in which you went up, a Royal Commission was sitting which was to do its best to bring the university kicking into the nineteenth century, but the education that you received from your tutors was of the old, unreformed sort. No modern history was taught, nor modern literature, nor modern languages. The choice was Mathematics or Classics. Classics, which you chose, contained some ancient history, and both Plato and Aristotle, though there was no need for undergraduates who wished merely for a degree to grapple particularly hard with either. What science there was was not for undergraduate study; and theology was considered too dangerous a subject for students to dabble in until they had taken their first degree, whereupon those who were going to be clergymen were given a short, but not necessarily very sharp course.

All the dons – except for Heads of Houses and the odd privileged professor – were celibate clergymen of the Church of England; all the undergraduates had to attend chapel daily, listen to the University Sermon every week, take Holy Communion once a term and sign their formal acceptance of the Thirty-Nine Articles of belief of the Church of England before they were allowed to matriculate. Moreover the great majority of the colleges had long elected men into fellowships more for their 'soundness' and 'clubbability' than for their intellectual distinction – which sounds cripplingly parochial, yet there were solid reasons why the most powerful nation in the world had allowed both her ancient universities so to run down.

When you went up in 1853, Mackail, your first biographer, tells us that the undergraduates at Exeter (which was your college) 'were divided, more sharply than is now the case at any college, into two classes. On the one hand were the reading men, immersed in the details of classical scholarship or scholastic theology; the rest of the college rowed, hunted, ate and drunk largely, and often sank at Oxford into a coarseness of manners and morals distasteful and distressing in the highest degree to a boy whose instinctive delicacy and purity of mind were untouched by any of the flaws of youth . . .'

Be that as it may, not all the 'Gentlemen-Commoners' were sots. When you went up, the allotted task of the ancient universities was not to turn out speculative minds who might come up with awkward answers to the eternal question: *Quomodo sedet sola civitas?* – On what is founded all in which we are supposed to believe? Their task was to turn out English gentlemen, an unending supply of future Members of Parliament, clergymen, landowners, colonels, captains RN, bankers and what have you.

It was a task at which they had been successful throughout the eighteenth century, and well into the nineteenth. If, when you went up, there was still a large-bulking religious content to what passed for university education it was for two conflicting reasons. The first was that, at the end of the seventeenth century, when there was still a threat of Catholic invasion, and when religious dissent of the kind that had fuelled the mid-century civil war was still potent, the Church of England had been deliberately established 'as part of the Constitution; and the Prayer Book as an Act of Parliament which only folly or disloyalty could quarrel with'.

I quote John Keble, who was one of the earnest young men of the 1820s who were instrumental in shaking up that earlier eighteenth-century church. Historically, the success of that church had been multi-fold. Its great cathedrals and ancient parish churches (stripped long since of their medieval and often disturbing popish finery) had become as much part of our tousled inheritance as the cliffs of Dover or the brown Thames itself. In a relatively short life, the native church had conjured potent miracles of the word out of the English language: the King James Bible, the Book of Common Prayer, the half-whispered, comfortable words at Holy Communion. It was also allowing. It allowed communicants who were half way to Geneva, and communicants who were half way to Rome and, in an increasingly secular century, it had not stood effectively in the way of secular specu-lation, of secular development, nor had it very stringently nor consistently persecuted dissent.

That is why it had grown sleepy and stagnant, but that is also why it still survives, and with it a monarchy and two houses of parliament (despite your best efforts). The part of the college that 'rowed, hunted, ate and drunk largely' well understood that, and were not riled by the lip-service that they had to pay to dogmas in which they might or might not believe, but when Mark Pattison referred bitterly to the university as 'a scurvy pond stagnant with sameness and custom', he was referring not only to Old High Tory Oxford, but to Keble and his friends who – coming up in the decade after the French revolutionary wars – had seen that the England that had defeated the revolutionaries had itself become largely a secular power, its national church increasingly complacent and inept at bringing the Word of God to an ever-increasing population, and had decided to devote their lives, not to reforming it (for they had little use for the reformers of the sixteenth century), but to attempting to bring it back to the purity of the early church.

This not entirely obscurantist movement was part of a general reaction after the long wars and the French Revolution, a widespread search for meaning in the remote past which, in part, had been sparked off by that Revolution itself. It had a certain social concern associated with parts of it, sometimes. It was to influence you deeply. This particular bit of it became known as the 'Tractarian Movement' because of Keble's itchy habit of producing endless pious pamphlets, one after another. Newman, the most austere of the group, found that the deeper he looked into the credentials of his national church, the less they withstood his scrutiny, and went over to Rome. Keble did not follow him, perhaps only because he had got a job outside Oxford and married, and so could not remain a priest if he did. Returning to Oxford as a professor in the early 1830s, he was to become the moving force in an extra-ordinary attempt to halt the nineteenth century in its tracks, and return not only Oxford but the country to a gentle medieval theocracy of the mind. To quote Pattison again: 'It was soon after 1830 that the "Tracts" desolated Oxford life, and suspended, for an indefinite period, all science, humane letters, and the first stirrings of intellectual freedom . . .'

Nevertheless, when you went up, energetic ripples of the Tractarian Movement were still being felt both in Oxford and far from Oxford, especially in public schools such as the one from which you had just come. We know from your friend Dixon that when he first met you when you were in your second year you were still Morris 'the aristocrat', the feudally minded clergyman to be. Or were you? By 1854, it was not only the credentials of the Church of England that were openly under attack, but the

credentials of Christianity itself. It was not till 1859 that Charles Darwin was to publish *The Origin of Species* but, beneath the surface of the scurvy pool, not all was still. Officially, when you were up, the world began with Adam and Eve and the Garden of Eden, in the year 4004 BC, a date calculated in the 1640s by Archbishop Ussher. There had been doubts cast on it, and on the whole Eden story centuries before. Some of St Augustine's hottest invective is reserved for those Egyptian writers who persisted in his day in holding that their country was immensely old. In the sixteenth century Juan de Valdés got into hot water for suggesting in his edition of St Augustine's works that the Egyptians might have been right but it was not until 1830, when Charles Lyell published his *Principles of Geology*, that anyone was able to show quite conclusively that the world is infinitely older. For a little while Oxford was not unworried but, a year or so before, she had appointed a professor of Geology, a fellow called Buckland who had promised on his appointment that he would always do his best to reconcile Faith and Science. When Lyell's book came out, he promptly proved Lyell wrong, demonstrating quite conclusively that all the fossils that Lyell thought rather old had been thrown up in the mud left after Noah's flood. Whereupon Philip Shuttleworth, Warden of New College, let it be known:

Some doubts were once expressed about the flood,
Buckland arose and all was clear – as mud.

We do not know at exactly what point you ceased to want to be a clergyman, and ceased to believe in Christianity itself, but it was while you were still at university. We know that the formal curriculum soon began to bore you and that, from your first year on, you devoted more and more time to a small, close group of friends. Like you, these friends came mostly from families newly recruited into the middle classes. Charles Faulkner was a mathematician, William Fulford a universal genius in extreme youth who never fulfilled his promise, Cormell Price an embryo headmaster, Richard Dixon an embryo Canon of the Church of England, Ted Jones (who was shortly to become Edward Burne-Jones) a strange, shy youth already determined to become an artist.

A generation earlier, in 1829, Tennyson at Cambridge had early decided that 'none but dry-headed, calculating, angular little gentlemen can take much delight in the studies of the university' and promptly been inducted into the Apostles, the secret undergraduate debating society which – according to Harold Nicolson – even then had 'a troubled, militant, masonic atmosphere, as of some secret society which would reform the world'.

In your third year, you and your friends founded a somewhat similar 'Brotherhood' dedicated to a 'Crusade and Holy Warfare against the age'. It differed from the Apostles in that it was by no means secret; resembled it in that, in one form or another, it has existed to this day for – besides the official William Morris Society in this country – there are and have been, in most English speaking countries, groups who have gathered, in your lifetime and since, to remember you, and to attempt to honour what you were about.

It was at this time that what you were going to be about began to come clear, you had begun to find that you could write a vigorous and lyrical verse; you had discovered Ruskin, bursting into Burne-Jones's room one day with the news; you were already 'Topsy' to your friends.

'Topsy', the name comes down to us out of the past, jokey, ebullient. It has a touch of the Mad Hatter about it, though you weren't that shape. You were a quite terrifyingly talented, original, and privileged human being. On your twenty-first birthday, while you were still an undergraduate, you came into £900 a year.

This, in our money, is an enormous sum. You could get a housemaid for £25 a year, a governess for £60, the dons who taught you rarely drew more than £230; and when, some 30 years later, Matthew Arnold retired from the Schools Inspectorate, his pension – a special one 'conferred in recognition of his literary merits' – was only £250 a year.

The money that your father left you enabled you to do most of what you afterwards did. 'Give people cash,' wrote E. M. Forster 14 years after your death, 'for it is the warp of civilisation, whatever the woof may be. The imagination ought to play upon money and realise it vividly for it is the second most important thing in the world. It is so slurred over and hushed up, there is so little clear thinking – oh political economy of course; but so few of us think clearly about our own private incomes, and admit that independent thoughts are in nine cases out of ten the result of independent means. Money: give Mr Bast money, and don't bother about his ideals. He'll pick those up for himself . . .' Out of the woof of things, presumably? That is certainly where your ideals came from. The woof was all about you, from childhood on. The forest. The marsh. The distant wen. The rivers. The ponds. Stonehenge. Avebury. The behaviour to boys of both masters and boys. Walter Scott. Malory. Froissart. Dickens. The first sight and smell of drains, factories, slums; from the first you wanted for all the Basts in the world not just money, money would just allow them to join the Podsnaps in the middle class, become part of the warp in things. That is why first Ruskin and then Marx were to speak to you as Moses and Mohammed were spoken to in the wilderness by voices that could not be denied.

The words of Ruskin's that stunned you are in the second volume of his *Stones of Venice*. The copy in our college library was bequeathed us by a defunct bishop of Winchester. He got through the first volume but most of the pages of the second were still uncut. It was not that he lacked time to read the book. He was given it by an aunt on his eighteenth birthday and died a bishop at over 70. As I took a paper knife to them so that I could read them again in his lovingly bound birthday present, I wondered if he had known what effect they had had on you, and decided that safety was the best policy. From the first you were hyper-sensitive to poetry read out aloud, and to the printed page, but nothing that you read in your life – except, I think, Keats's 'La Belle Dame sans Merci'; Malory's *Morte d'Arthur*, some of Froissart's deadpan accounts of bloody ambuscades in the Hundred Years' War and, very much later on, *The Communist Manifesto* and *Capital* – had so much effect on your life as that chapter in *The Stones of Venice* which is called 'On the Nature of Gothic, and the Office of the Workman therein'.

I must not make too long a story of why that chapter so fired you, but also I cannot quite pass the matter over. Ruskin's was by no means a lonely or an early voice. The Gothick Revival began somewhere between Inverary Castle and Strawberry Hill as an aristocratic diversion, though the need for machicolation on remote fortresses had never quite died out. There is a sense in which the original Gothic never quite expired but was resuscitated, first as an eccentric if urbane Gothick, then as that portentous stuff: Gothic Revival; if the French Revolutionaries had seen themselves initially as ancient Romans who were bringing back Roman virtue to a diseased and decayed world, their opponents in England and Germany increasingly harked back to virtues and traditions of their own remote pasts when England and Germany had sprung into being. Rickman was the Dior of the movement, far away in Berlin the old wizard Schinkel quickly twigged that the neo-classic was now passé, started doodling turrets instead of stoas, and Prussia went suddenly and nightmarishly Gothic too.

What is so fascinating about this Gothicism is that it could either be a conservative theory or a very, very revolutionary one. When Pugin contrasted the supposed virtues of the thirteenth century (in a book which was in the library at Marlborough) with the squalors of the nineteenth, he was making a conservative point. When Théroigne de Méricourt got up on a barrel in her riding habit and told the working women of Paris: 'It is time at last that women should throw aside their shameful inactivity in which ignorance, pride and the injustice of men have kept them for so long. Let us return to the times when our mothers, the Gauls and proud Germans, spoke in the public Assemblies, and fought beside their husbands', the point she was making was certainly a revolutionary point though one may suspect that she had to read some Tacitus at school. (How well I remember when we first read the *Germania* in class, the gowned master pacing up and down explaining that although we must all relearn barbaric virtues, Tacitus did not actually mean quite what he said . . .) Tacitus has a lot to answer for. I think he influenced Marx, he certainly influenced you, and Wagner, and Nietzsche, and Hitler, but the desire to go back into the past was not only a desire of the ardent and the active. Rossetti (whom you were very shortly to meet) was never much of a revolutionary (his father was one, the sons of revolutionaries very seldom are) but the thesis of Pre-Raphaelitism is that everything went wrong at the Renaissance. Like butterflies making for the same waterhole as a rhinoceros,

THIS IS THE PICTURE OF THE OLD HOUSE BY THE THAMES TO WHICH THE PEOPLE OF THIS STORY WENT. HEREAFTER FOLLOWS THE BOOK IT-SELF WHICH IS CALLED NEWS FROM NOWHERE OR AN EPOCH OF REST & IS WRITTEN BY WILLIAM MORRIS

Frontispiece from News from Nowhere *(B21)*

Hobbits are furry little men who don't wear shoes and who live in burrows in an England which he called the Shire which comes straight from you: 'when we can get beyond that smoky world [of the hideous towns of the industrial revolution], there, out in the country we may still see the works of our fathers yet alive amidst the very nature they were wrought into, and of which they are so completely a part: for there indeed if anywhere, in the English country, in the days when people cared about such things, was there a full sympathy between the works of man and the land they were made for: – the land is a little land; too much shut up within the narrow seas, as it seems, to have much space for swelling into hugeness; there are no great wastes overwhelm-ing in their dreariness, no great solitudes of forests, no terrible untrodden mountain-walls: all is measured, mingled, varied, gliding easily from one thing into another: little rivers, little plains, swelling, speedily changing uplands, all beset with handsome orderly trees; little hills, little mountains, netted over with the walls of sheep-walks: all is little; yet not foolish and blank, but serious rather, and abundant of meaning for such as choose to seek it: it is neither prison nor palace, but a decent home . . .'

That was what you got from Ruskin: the notion that before the coming of capitalism, not only in Venice, but all over Western Europe, master builders sketched out cathedrals on the ground and then hundreds of free and happy craftsmen appeared with their mallets and chisels and each put his own creativity into his own bit of stained glass, vaulting, gargoyle, gutter and the Middle Ages were tee-to-tum till the breakdown of chivalry and the coming of capitalism . . .

If I am being unfair it is quite deliberate. The ruination of the countryside by modern greed and modern industry is one thing, to return to the

they were fluttering ahead of Marx's account of the breakdown of feudalism and the rise of the bourgeoisie. This is what, intuitively, took both you and Rossetti to the *Morte d'Arthur* and Froissart. Both Malory and Froissart are late writers. The cash nexus is already sabotaging old brotherly bonds, chivalry is breaking down . . .

I must admit that I do not find it easy to read that chapter of Ruskin's on how they built Venice, in the way that you read it. It has been spoilt for me by one of your most strange followers this century, a man called Tolkien. Tolkien invented creatures called Hobbits.

Middle Ages quite another; as Mark Pattison said, enforced returns to the Middle Ages, however idealistic, in fact desolate life, and suspend for an indefinite period all science, humane letters, and the stirrings of intellectual freedom . . .

Yet you were determined, and you had the means to do so, and the effort turned out to be quite extraordinarily painful, and quite extraordinarily fruitful: in your last long vacation, you and Burne-Jones visited the cathedrals of Northern France. 'Less than forty years ago,' you later wrote, 'I first saw the city of Rouen, then still in its outward aspect a piece of the Middle Ages: no words can tell you how its mingled beauty, history, and romance took hold on me: I can only say that, looking back on my past life, I find that it was the greatest pleasure that I have ever had . . .'

It is one of the ironies of modern literature that that Rouen of your beatific vision was the Rouen that Flaubert knew, even down to which was the cheapest and which the safest brothel, which he was at that moment in the process of realistically, and yet poetically, describing in his *Madame Bovary*; yet I do not think that when Mackail called you 'a boy whose instinctive delicacy and purity of mind were untouched by the flaws of youth' he was particularly close to the mark: you knew your way very well about in the real world. I think not only of violent early poems but also of a letter that you wrote late in life to your friend Faulkner. E. P. Thompson prints it in full. It is Flaubertian in its cold dissection of the actual relations of men and women in the real world. You were not a Romantic, except in the willed sense that both Marx and Luther were. You were something else, a prophet, a conscience. It is difficult to find the exact word, 'revolutionary' is not quite the *mot juste*.

That is why you were taken, for a time, as a fashionable prophet, but it is also why you became a great artist, and changed not only the nature of the arts you practised, but fore-notions of what was possible in them. It was Burne-Jones who showed you that a hoofing great ex-public school boy with no education at all in the visual arts, could at least make a fist at drawing. If thereafter you did not frequently soar as a draughtsman, there are drawings of yours, crucial to your work as a designer, that extend the limits of the perceivable. Gordian knots dreamt in childhood string, given enduring form. In 1861, at the age of 27, you started to make your own wallpaper, and designs. Among them are some of the most beautiful, and some of the most disturbing, patterns that men or women have ever made. They wind, they curl their plant flesh and shadows under coffered ceilings of leaves. The best are almost as alive and unpredictable as the forest itself. People should be wary of putting them in their nurseries. My acquaintance with you began when I was four or five. I know now that the wallpaper that used to frighten me very much is called 'Daffodil', and that those monsters are not snakes. But yet they are, in the half light of curtains drawn against a summer evening, or the grimmer caverns created in full dark by a small night-light. Snakes used to come out at me and hiss from a brown and gold jungle that belonged to a world far older and more mysterious than the world of grown-ups and children, or the ordinary English plants growing in the garden.

But I run ahead of your move from Oxford to London. On your last long vacation abroad, you decided to become an architect. When you went down you were induced to put some of your money into a new paper called *The Oxford and Cambridge Magazine*. After a year you got bored with the losses and allowed it to fold, but it employed your friends and it was a good nursery for your own first writings. Simultaneously you apprenticed yourself to the Oxford architect, G. E. Street; there you met Philip Webb, who was then Street's chief clerk. When Street moved to London, you moved with him. Topsy came to town bringing the Middle Ages with him, plenty of 'tin' (as your set called cash), lots of admiring friends, and you danced up to London vulnerable as an auto-intoxicated Hobbit on a spree.

Your friend Ted Burne-Jones had already apprenticed himself to Dante Gabriel Rossetti to learn painting from him. Rossetti had very little 'tin' but a reputation already (he was six years older than you) as a great man; and a marvellous ability, already, to borrow money, not only from women, much of it unpaid back at his death. Rossetti was fascinating, there is no doubt about that. Brilliant, there is no doubt about that, both as a verse-maker and as a painter. His letters reveal a literary intelligence of a very high order, but he was lazy, and a bit of a charlatan, and a bit of a couturier, creating and playing up to fashion, and he took you on as pupils, and promptly played Fagin, and you weren't the Artful Dodger. Like his Jenny, he was always looking for the easy guinea, always ready to fall into a daydream, or onto a passing 'stunner'.

Topsy had come to town to look for the Grail. Topsy was an easy touch. The word soon got around. The biggest gas was when you all went to paint the frescoes in the Oxford Union, and fooled about, and forgot to prime the walls.

That was in 1857, the year that Baudelaire published *Les Fleurs du Mal*; that Flaubert was prosecuted for the 'obscenity' of *Madame Bovary*; that Renan got his start as a writer; that Dickens was working on *The Tale of Two Cities*; that Thackeray was getting very boring, that Trollope was in full spate, and that Robert Baden-Powell, the founder of the Boy Scout Movement, was born.

In Oxford, you got stuck inside a suit of armour that you had had specially built for you so that you could paint it. Rossetti spotted a 'stunner' in a theatre and persuaded her to sit as a model, and be perpetuated on the Union walls.

Swinburne, who had become one of the gang, saw at once that you were a fool to think of marrying her. Rossetti never acquired the art of letting pennies lie long enough in the bank to turn there into capital, but the forest of his life was full of shrikes' larders. Just as that bird spears insects and leaves them to mature, and comes back to gobble them when it's hungry, so Rossetti liked to keep a lot of girls going at once so that if the current mistress died, or dropped him, or he wanted to give her the chop, he need not exert himself too hard to replace her, for there was someone else whom he had spotted and spiked in a far larder of the mind years before.

Thus was set the scene for the tragedy of your private life, whose long first act was to run from your marriage in 1858 to that May morning in 1871 when you handed over Kelmscott Manor in Oxfordshire to your wife and her lover and went off to Iceland. After that she was to have at least one other lover and it is impossible to visit Kelmscott now without thinking of the rascally Blunt: the soft, spoilt radical confiding to his diary: 'Mrs Morris slept alone at the end of a short passage at the head of the staircase to the right. The hall was uncarpeted with floorboards that creaked . . . To me such midnight perils have always been attractive.'

But your life as a whole was a life of epic strength, tragedies sustained and lived beyond. 'I have never known', you told a Glasgow audience late in life, 'what I fear many of you unfortunately have known – actual poverty – the pain of today's hunger and cold, and the fear of tomorrow's, or the dread of a master's voice, or the hopeless despair of unemployment. I have, I truly believe, lived as happy a life as anyone could wish to live, save for the misery of seeing so much cruel wrong and needless suffering around me. Yet I am no more entitled to that happiness than any of my fellows.'

In a passage that E. P. Thompson has made famous you were to write: 'We of the English Middle Class are the most powerful body of men that the world has yet seen . . . And yet when we come to look the matter in the face, we cannot fail to see that even for us with all our strength it will be a hard matter to bring about that birth of the new art; for between us and that which is to be if art is not to perish utterly, there is something alive and devouring; something as it were a river of fire that will put all that tries to swim across to a hard proof indeed, and scare from the plunge every soul that is not made fearless by desire of truth and insight of the happy days to come beyond . . .'

Did you cross that river William? I am not sure that you did, I believe that you stepped into it, and stepped back, and that that is part of your greatness.

Or perhaps there are two rivers. Within a decade of your death, Lenin was affirming that there are. The majority (*Mensheviks* in Russian) of nineteenth-century men who found the evils of existing society insupportable and were converted by Marx to Socialism remained, Lenin said, bourgeois-intellectual individualists. Only the minority (*Bolsheviks* in Russian) who accepted 'proletarian organisation and discipline' could cross the second river. It was not a thing a man could or can do of his own volition. 'All must regard themselves as agents of the (central) committee, bound to submit to all its directions, bound to observe all "laws and customs" of this "army in the field" into which they have entered and which they cannot leave without permission of the commander', any

more than you could get off Compulsory Chapel at Oxford in your day.

Engels called you a *Gemütlich*, that is to say a drawing-room socialist; he was pretty sure that you would never cross that second river. Other Marxists, E. P. Thompson and Miguel Abensour among them, have argued 'that Morris may be assimilated to Marxism only in the course of a process of self-criticism and re-ordering within Marxism itself'. Bully for them, but I wonder if you were not more of a Luther than a Marx? Nietzsche once wrote that there was a moment (it is highly doubtful if there was, but let that pass) a moment in the teens and twenties of the sixteenth century when, at the very centre of Christianity, in Rome itself, the Pope and the majority of his Cardinals were atheists, and Christianity might have passed peacefully away had not Luther attacked the Church and, in attacking, strengthened it. This, I believe, is very much what you have done for this peculiar society of ours in which – at least since the Renaissance – we have all had to live among the echoes and shadows of all that has gone before, and the centre is almost impossible to touch – *Quomodo sedet sola civitas*? – except, that is, by those who believe *l'humanité attend toujours le mot d'ordre de la pensée marxiste*, and count on the end of capitalism. The rest of us, less confident denizens of this distancing 'tele' age, seem to spend our lives as well as we can in a jungle that the muddled human race has somehow furbished over the centuries into a partly domesticated wood, where there are still to be found, if we look hard enough, the life-giving springs. You were one of them, and are still.

Yours from across the river.

'No Drawing Room Sort of Man'

Gillian Naylor

In March 1884, the same year as the formation of the Art Workers' Guild, William Morris gave two lectures on *The Gothic Revival*,[1] to the Birmingham and Midland Institute in Birmingham. Many of the ideas he was expressing had become common currency among British designers and architects. True Gothic, he said, was 'free, progressive, hopeful and full of human sentiment and humour', and its creations were 'the outcome of corporate and social feeling, the work not of individual, but collective genius'. The nineteenth-century revival of Gothic, on the other hand, was an 'intellectual revolt'. Both spiritual and social revolution, therefore, was necessary if its impetus was to be maintained; for without a total change in the means and motivation for production, the movement was doomed to become 'merely an aspiration of cultivated men seeking art through art, instead of seeking it through the life of the people'.

Such opinions were, of course, familiar to those who had followed the development of Morris's theories. What is interesting about these talks, however, apart from their reiteration of current aesthetic and moral convictions about the nature and history of design, is Morris's public and personal assessment of the Firm's contribution to the Gothic Revival:

'*I may also be allowed to mention*', he says in the second of the talks, '*that some of us thought that the revival might be extended to the accessory arts, and made I assure you desperate efforts to revive them: in which process we have at least amused and instructed ourselves a good deal, and even done what is called "lived on" our efforts; in other words have extracted a good deal of money out of the public by them: allow me to excuse ourselves for that brigandage by saying that the public will have these accessory arts, or some pretence of them, and if I am not quite blinded by vanity ours are at any rate prettier than those which went before them.*'

The tone is ironic, but the opinions are significant. The eventual financial success of the Morris Firm, and the continuing demand for the most accessible of its designs – wallpapers and fabrics – point to the fact that they do evoke a response and fulfil a need. It was, however, the nature of the public's response to the Firm's products which so agonised Morris. For the patronage which gave him personal freedom to work and experiment so challenged his integrity that he was forced to question the validity of his achievements. Two years before the Birmingham lectures, in January 1882, he had written to Georgiana Burne-Jones:

'*. . . I know that the cause for which I specially work is doomed to fail, at least in seeming; I mean that art must go under . . . It does sometimes seem to me a strange thing indeed that a man should be driven to work with energy and even with pleasure and enthusiasm at work which he knows will serve no end but amusing himself; am I doing nothing but make-believe then, something like Louis XVI's clock-making?*'[2]

The conviction that his life's work might add up to nothing more than 'make-believe' obviously tormented Morris. Throughout his career he was concerned, like the majority of the protagonists of the Gothic Revival, with 'reality'. Red House, for example, was to be no Strawberry Hill pastiche, Webb's vernacular and craftsmanship aspiring not to the picturesque, but to 'a common tradition of honest building'. And although the impetus for the formation of Morris, Marshall, Faulkner & Co may have come from convivial chats about 'the way in which artists did all kinds of things in olden times, designed every kind of decoration, and most kinds of furniture',[3] the Firm aspired, even at the outset, to authenticity – imitation of the past being meaningless: 'unfair', as Morris was to put it, 'to the old and stupid for the present'.[4]

They were helped, of course, by a growing body of research and scholarship that had contributed to both the theory and the practice of design and architecture in the nineteenth century. At the same time, however, apart from their experience in decorating and furnishing Red House, they were all more or less amateurs in the various skills they offered, and it was the ways in which they developed and demonstrated, and – in Morris's case – defended these skills, that were to become part of the canon of the Arts and Crafts Movement.

From the outset, they considered themselves artists – 'Fine Art workmen', as their first prospectus put it, 'in Painting, Carving Furniture and the Metals'. In the early years, however, they had to establish themselves in this role. After their success in the International Exhibition of 1862, they had a steady stream of commissions (the most prestigious being the decoration of both the Green Dining Room at the South Kensington Museum and the Armoury and Tapestry Room at St James's Palace). This work was obviously a strain on their time, ingenuity and resources, and although they no doubt 'amused and instructed themselves a great deal', they did not, at this stage, stop to consider the wider implications of their enterprise. The first person, it seems, to question their values, as well as the professionalism of the Firm, was George Warington Taylor, who succeeded Faulkner as business manager in 1865. In one of a series of letters to Webb, in which he complains about confusion in the accounts, and the haphazard approach to commissions, he writes: 'Just remember we are embezzling public money now – what business has any palace to be decorated at all?'[5] He was anticipating Morris's self-questioning by about ten years.

Warington Taylor had, however, misunderstood the nature of Morris's professionalism and his priorities. For, although deadlines had to be met and the accounts kept in some sort of order, Morris was obsessed by the need to communicate not only skills, but values. His values were both practical and aesthetic: he needed to understand the nature and potential of the materials he was working with, and to demonstrate this understanding through his work. This was to remain the corner-stone of his design philosophy. 'Never forget the material you are working with,' he wrote, 'and always try to use it for doing what it can do best'.[6] And again, in an interview with a *Clarion* reporter:

'I have tried to produce goods which should be genuine as far as their mere substances are concerned, and should have on that account the primary beauty in them which belongs to naturally treated substances; I have tried for instance to make woollen substances as woollen as possible, cotton as cotton as possible, and so on; I have only used the dyes which are natural and simple.'[7]

The difficulties of achieving and maintaining this authenticity and simplicity, however, forced Morris to redefine the nature of his commitment. For, by any definition, standards and perfectionism as well as respect for the past were of little account in an age of 'eyeless vulgarity'. So that, in spite of his modest financial success,[8] and his total absorption with the practical problems of his work, he was becoming increasingly depressed by his dependence on the patronage of the 'idle privileged classes'. It was, of course, the conviction that he might be producing 'nothing but dull adjuncts to meaningless pomp, or ingenious toys for a few idle rich men'[9] that drove him to political commitment; and as E. P. Thompson has pointed out:

'The transformation of the eccentric artist and romantic literary man into the Socialist agitator may be counted among the great conversions of the world.'[10]

Morris's political convictions, however, did not have any obvious influence on his practical work. He opened a shop in Oxford Street in 1877; the first hand-knotted rugs were produced in Hammersmith in 1878; a high-warp tapestry loom was set up in Merton Abbey in 1880; the Firm was working on new decorations for the Throne and Reception Room at St James's Palace in 1881, and the Kelmscott Press was founded in 1891. His justification for embarking on these enterprises was the threatened extinction of the various crafts involved. In his lecture on 'The Lesser Arts of Life' he describes how the art of tapestry weaving 'must now be spoken of in the past tense', and how the 'gift of harmonious colour is speedily dying out in the East before the conquest of European rifles and money bags'. His aim, therefore, was to revive the sensitivity and skills of the past and to work for their future survival.

By the 1880s he was not alone in his campaign for the revival and survival of craftsmanship. Mackmurdo, together with Selwyn Image and Herbert Horne, had founded the Century Guild in 1882; the Art Workers' Guild was established in 1884, the Arts and Crafts Exhibition Society held its first exhibition in London in 1888, and in 1896, the year of Morris's death, W. R. Lethaby was appointed first principal of the Central School of Arts and Crafts.

The efforts of the designers and architects involved in these enterprises led to the now legendary renaissance of British craftsmanship at the end of the nineteenth century, and to the prestige and emulation of British design in Europe and America. ('When English creations began to appear,' wrote Samuel Bing in 1898, 'a cry of delight sounded throughout Europe. Its echo can still be heard in every country.')[11]

In evaluating this renaissance, however, one must attempt to distinguish between the ideal

THE ATTITUDE OF THE POLICE.
(DEDICATED TO "THE FORCE," MR. SAUNDERS, AND THE SOCIALISTS.)

The Earthly Paradox, *1886*

and the achievement. The ideal, which had its roots in the ethics as well as the aesthetics of the Gothic Revival, was the recreation of a national and vernacular tradition, and with it a people's art. But, although we are still, quite rightly, celebrating the achievement, it fell far short of the ideal. 'We have made', C. R. Ashbee was to write, 'of a great social movement, a narrow and tiresome little aristocracy working with great skill for the very rich.'[12]

These nineteenth-century reformers faced dilemmas that their counterparts in the twentieth century no longer attempt to resolve. It is inevitable that the products of a pioneering design reform will reflect the values of the pioneers, rather than the people they are trying to serve. Nevertheless, although the brutality of the twentieth century has shattered any ideal of reform and regeneration, the myth still retains its potency. As Morris found out when he visited Iceland: 'Whatever solace your life is to have . . . must come out of yourself, or these old stories, not over-hopeful themselves.'[13]

The aim of the Firm in the early years was to establish 'some one place where (people) could either obtain or get produced work of a genuine and beautiful character'.[14] His success in achieving these aims, however, was little consolation to Morris once he had recognised their ambiguity. Having convinced himself that 'a reform in which art is founded on individualism must perish with the individuals who have set it going',[15] he became a socialist.

But in spite of the growing number of designers who professed a similar commitment, in spite of his influence on design education and some areas of design production, and in spite of his enthusiasm for the revival of the old methods of handicraft, Morris could never convince himself that his work had real meaning. 'I have spent, I know', he told Edward Carpenter, 'a vast amount of time designing furniture and wallpaper, carpets and curtains; but after all I am inclined to think that sort of thing is mostly rubbish, and I would prefer, for my part, to live with the plainest whitewashed walls and wooden chairs and tables.' 'He certainly was', adds Carpenter, 'no drawing room sort of man.'[16]

1 Reprinted in *The Unpublished Lectures of William Morris*, ed. Eugene D. Lemire, Wayne State University Press, 1969, pp54–93.

2 *Letters of William Morris to his Family and Friends*, ed. Philip Henderson, Longmans, Green & Co, 1950, p157.

3 J. W. Mackail, *The Life of William Morris*, London, 1899, vol 1, p121.

4 W. R. Lethaby, *Philip Webb and His Work*, OUP, 1935, p120.

5 Letter from Warington Taylor to Philip Webb (V & A Manuscript) dated December 1866.

6 *Arts and Crafts Essays*, Longmans, Green & Co, 1899, p38.

7 Quoted from *Political Writings of William Morris*, ed. A. L. Morton, Lawrence & Wishart, 1979, pp15–16.

8 'I believe', he wrote to Andreas Scheu in 1883, 'that if I yielded on a few points of principle I might have become a positively rich man.' Quoted from *William Morris: Selected Writings and Designs*, ed. Asa Briggs, Penguin Books, 1862, p31.

9 'The Lesser Arts', 1878, quoted from *William Morris*, ed. G. D. H. Cole, Nonesuch Press, 1948, p495.

10 E. P. Thompson, *William Morris: Romantic to Revolutionary*, Merlin Press, 1977, p243.

11 Quoted from Robert Schmutzler, *Art Nouveau*, Thames & Hudson, 1964, p153.

12 C. R. Ashbee, *Memoirs*, unpublished typescript, 1938, vol IV, Victoria and Albert Museum Library, p201.

13 Quoted from Philip Henderson, *William Morris: his Life, Work and Friends*, Thames & Hudson, 1967, p125.

14 The first prospectus of Morris, Marshall, Faulkner & Co; quoted from Henderson, *op cit*, p67.

15 From a letter to Andreas Scheu, Penguin Books, *op cit*, p32.

16 Edward Carpenter, *My Days and Dreams*, George Allen & Unwin Ltd, 1916, pp216–17.

'If I Can', designed and embroidered by William Morris c1857 (T1) ▶

William Morris and Victorian Decorative Art

Stuart Durant

William Morris had scant regard for Victorian decorative art. He declared on one occasion that 'whatever is worth considering' in modern design 'is eclectic and is not bound by the chain of tradition . . . whatever of art is left which is in any sense the result of continuous tradition is, and has long been, so degraded as to have lost any claim to be considered as an art at all'. These are strong enough words – what followed was stronger still. He insisted, 'the present century has no school of art'.[1] But in truth, Morris's own design is thoroughly Victorian.

George C. Haité (1855–1924), a successful designer for the trade, was, on the other hand, entirely satisfied with the Victorian decorative achievement. In an article 'On the Design and Designers of the Victorian Reign', which appeared in the *Architectural Review* in two parts in 1897, Haité presented a roll-call of Victorian designers, including Crace, Pugin, Matthew Digby Wyatt, Owen Jones, Bruce Talbert, E. W. Godwin, Eastlake, Dresser, Arthur Silver and Voysey. There is no homogeneity in the decorative work of these men but there is the diversity which demonstrates that the era Morris despised had vigour, if nothing else.

Of course Haité included Morris in his roll-call and went as far as to illustrate a printed cretonne of his. He observed that in the recent notices of Morris's death, the press had given his qualifications for recognition as 'poet, socialist and designer'. Only a few years earlier, Haité mused, the qualification 'designer' would have been omitted. The pioneering work by some of the men Haité lists was indeed crucial in Morris's own recognition as a designer.

Lewis F. Day placed Morris – at least Morris the designer – in a clear historical setting.[2]

◄ *Design for 'Small Barr' Hammersmith carpet by William Morris (or J. H. Dearle), after 1879*

'Morris was born just at the right moment: the way was prepared for him. Walter Scott, without really appreciating Gothic art, had called popular attention to its romance. Rickman had long since "discriminated" the styles of English Architecture. Pugin had established his True Principles of Gothic Architecture *and was designing all manner of medieval furniture; and by the time (Morris) came to take any heed of art, Gothic architecture was the fashion. Shaw [I assume Day means Henry Shaw, whose* Dresses and Decorations of the Middle Ages *appeared in 1843] and others had published books on medieval antiquities and Viollet-le-Duc his famous dictionary; even Owen Jones, the orientalist, had cleared ground by creating a reaction of taste against mere naturalism pretending to be design. Fergusson, Semper, Wornum, Digby Wyatt and above all Ruskin had been writing about art until people were beginning to listen. Men like William Burges and E. W. Godwin were hard at work already . . . the times were ready for the man and that man was William Morris.'*

Day, like Haité, evidently saw Morris not as the sole crusader against philistinism, but rather as the culminating figure in a wider movement that had resolved to revitalise decorative art. Because of Day's own experience as both theorist and designer, his views have more than the value of mere contemporaneity.[3]

If we can accept that Morris was a representative of a movement it is important that we examine that movement's principal concerns. In his *Address at the Distribution of Prizes at the Birmingham Municipal School of Art* on 21 February 1894, which was to be published in 1898, Morris offered advice to students on how to avoid becoming 'mannered' in their work. The passage is worth reproducing, for here, with characteristic clarity, Morris sets out the options open to the designer who sought inspiration and who desired to produce work that was more resonant than the historical pastiche.

'The corrective to overmuch manner is, first, diligent study of Nature, and secondly, intelligent study of the work of the ages of Art. The third corrective is infallible if you have it . . . it is imagination.'

Morris, it transpires, was saying nothing really new. Nature and 'the work of the ages of Art', as he characteristically puts it, had long been the preoccupation of those who were concerned with the welfare of decorative art. As for imagination and Morris, this is not an appropriate essay in which to discuss the theme. That his imaginative faculty was highly developed we know and that he strove equally to foster its growth in his fellows we know also.

First, to consider the issue of Nature as Sourcebook. The theme is topical enough even now and in the recent past designers as diverse as Buckminster Fuller, Le Corbusier and Norman Bel Geddes – who saw streamlined forms as inspired by nature – have all deferred to nature as supreme mentor. In the 1840s and 1850s two painters – William Dyce and Richard Redgrave – taught students at the new Government School of Design how to transform botanical drawings into ornament, thus making official the cult of nature as supreme designer. Pugin, in *Florinated Ornament*, 1849, an elegant collection of ornamental sprays and the like, asserted: 'it is impossible to improve upon the works of God' – meaning, of course, botanical nature. (Pugin, in fact, took his nature not from the hedgerow, but from a well known late-sixteenth-century German herbal.) Owen Jones devoted a whole chapter of the monumental *Grammar of Ornament*, 1856, to illustrations of plants simply waiting to be re-cycled as ornament. For Jones 'true art' meant idealising, not copying, nature. Ruskin in *The Two Paths*, 1859, insisted that no

school of art had 'ever advanced far that did not have the love of natural fact as a primal energy'. Gilbert Scott once told an audience at the Architectural Association:

'Closely as we ought to study the finest works of the best periods of our art . . . I nevertheless assert that if we do this without reverting . . . to the works of nature as the great guides and suggestors of art, our efforts will produce mere lifeless results.'[4]

This could almost be Morris himself talking.

Now to turn to the second of Morris's Birmingham themes – the Museum as Source-book, for it was to the museum that Morris the tiro went to see the work of the 'ages of Art'. In June 1851, in *The Journal of Design* – shortly after the opening of the Great Exhibition – Owen Jones described the advantages and perils of borrowing from the past. The passage is so eloquent and its message so seductive that it warrants examination. I take Jones to be the most articulate exponent of the philosophy of ornament that was being evolved by the Government School of Design circle – for the most part civil servants who sought to re-educate the nation in matters of taste. Jones wrote:

'We possess the inestimable advantages of living in an age when nothing of the past remains a secret; each stone of every monument of every clime has told its tale, which is now brought within reach of our own fire-sides; yet, hitherto, how little we have shown ourselves worthy of this great privilege. The ease with which our knowledge might be obtained has made us indifferent to its acquirement, or led us to substitute an indolent and servile imitation for an intelligent and imaginative eclecticism.'

Certainly Morris, in this sense, was eclectic. But Morris did not merely borrow from the past. He related the products of the past to the societies that had produced them and saw in them – in the same way as Pugin and Ruskin had – certain moral pointers. Here is Morris on

Byzantine art and architecture, and let it be remembered that architecture in the nineteenth century subsumed decoration. The passage is taken from *The History of Pattern Designing*, 1882, from which I have quoted earlier:

'You have doubtless heard this art spoken of with contempt as the mere dregs of the dying art of the ancient world . . . but it was a death that bore new quickening with it; it was a corruption which was drawing to it elements of life, of which the classical world knew nothing: and the chief element that it gave expression to was freedom – the freedom of the many – in the realm of art at least . . . an architecture which was pure in its principles, reasonable in its practice, and beautiful to the eyes of all men, even the simplest . . . a thing, mind you, which can never exist in any state of society under which men are divided into intellectual castes.'

By comparison with Morris's analysis, Owen Jones's 'intelligent and imaginative eclecticism' appears arid.

One is reminded by Morris's utterance of certain strands of thought that permeate 'The Nature of Gothic', the great chapter in *The Stones of Venice*, 1852–3, in which Ruskin proclaimed that Gothic building had allowed the common craftsman to express himself. Out of 'fragments full of imperfection' – the petty carvings, the gargoyles, the foliated capitals and all the other humble manifestations of pride of craftsmanship – could rise up 'a stately and unaccusable whole'. The cathedral has become the metaphor for a whole society which, because it is hierarchical, is both stable and organic. With Morris, on the other hand, there was no call for the reinstatement of a society comprised of masters, no matter how just, and compliant servants. Morris called for a society of equals.

Morris's ideas on popular art – and by this he primarily means decoration – had wide reverberations. Godfrey Blount, a Christian

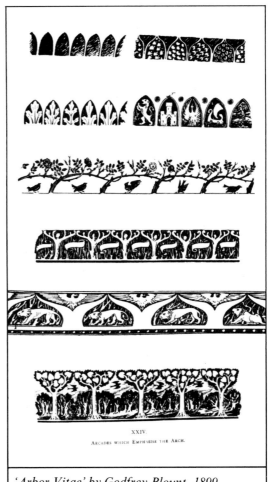

XXIV.
ARCADES WHICH EMPHASISE THE ARCH.

'Arbor Vitae' by Godfrey Blount, 1899

socialist, in *Arbor Vitae*, 1899, saw, like Morris, the restoration and, one could say, therapeutic potential of decoration. Blount's book, which perfectly enshrines the philosophy of the arts and crafts as applied to decoration, has been undeservedly neglected. Like Morris, Blount condemned mere aestheticism and believed that

'Designing Games' by W. R. Lethaby, 1929

'Something that will not drive us either into unrest or into callousness; something which reminds us of life beyond itself, and which has the impress of human imagination strong on it; and something which can be done by a great many people without too much difficulty and with pleasure.'[5]

No other designer attempted with such passion, such poetry, to explain the social role of art. This is of infinitely greater significance than all of Morris's lovely designs.

the machine diminished the imagination, while handicraft extolled it. W. R. Lethaby, in a little pamphlet called *Designing Games*, published by Dryad Handicrafts of Leicester in 1929, described various simple, game-like ways with the aid of which the layman, or the child, could take his first steps in decorative design. As had Morris, Lethaby wanted art to become 'a normal mode of activity'.

Ruskin, Morris, Blount and Lethaby all said that the industrial system had brutalised and estranged men. Morris understood the benign influence of the crafts in combating the tedium of the 'deadly rhythm of the production line'.

On the surface, Morris's decorative design does not differ quite as radically as is sometimes claimed from the work of the more accomplished designers of his generation. To say otherwise is to misrepresent him. At least such is the case in conventional art historical terms in which pictorial, or in this case ornamental, detail counts for all. In common with his contemporaries, too, Morris was preoccupied with the treatment of nature and the profitable exploitation of the past. But listen to Morris in his lecture 'Some Hints on Pattern Designing', delivered at the Working Men's College in December 1881. Here are some of his desiderata for good decoration. It should be:

1 See 'The History of Pattern Designing', published in *Lectures on Art, delivered in support of the Society for the Protection of Ancient Buildings*, 1882.

2 See *William Morris and His Art, Art-Journal Easter Art Annual*, 1899.

3 Another useful essay on the background to Morris's work is Walter Crane's *The English Revival in Decorative Art*, reproduced in *William Morris to Whistler . . .*, 1911.

4 Scott is here quoted by James K. Colling in *Art Foliage . . .*, 1865. This work itself confirms the importance of my theme 'Nature as Sourcebook'.

5 See *Some Hints on Pattern-Designing. A Lecture delivered by William Morris at the Working Men's College, London on December 10, 1881*, published in 1899. Morris was more specific in this lecture than he was anywhere else about the nature of decoration. Even so, the writings of Christopher Dresser, F. E. Hulme, Lewis F. Day, Frank G. Jackson, Walter Crane and James Ward, among contemporary British authorities, contain infinitely more on the mechanics of pattern design. Morris's lack of specificity can be seen as part of his concern that the individual should arrive at his own style of work, no matter if clumsy.

William Morris and his Interest in the Orient

Patricia L. Baker

By the time that Frederic Leighton, society painter and President of the Royal Academy, commissioned his architect and friend George Aitchison to construct an Arab Hall in his London home in 1873, the idle curiosity that had characterised the early fashion for *Chinoiserie*, visible in the Royal Pavilion at Brighton, had been tempered. Scholars at home and abroad provided material for the serious student. Translations of oriental literature and research papers on a wide variety of subjects were available, while reports of archaeological findings generated public excitement. Interest was further fanned by the awareness that British political influence was spreading in these lands.

It was this growing knowledge – however superficial it may now be regarded – of these cultures and societies of the Middle East, the Indian subcontinent and the Far East, that allowed parallels to be drawn concerning design and craftsmanship. Dissatisfied with the contemporary decorative repertoire, Augustus Pugin, Owen Jones and others found inspiration in the decorative motifs of the East. In them, Owen Jones saw the visual proof of his design principles. Decorative patterns, he held, should possess:

'. . . *a perfectly* flat *unshadowed character* . . . *Secondly the quantities and lines are equally distributed, so as to produce at a distance the appearance of* levelness'[1]

which in turn would be relieved by harmonious colouring. Marvelling at the unity and consistency in style of such patterns produced by the non-European craftsmen, he regretted that:

'*It is far different with ourselves. We have no principles, no unity . . . each craftsman runs each his independent course; each struggles fruitlessly, – each produces in art novelty without beauty, or beauty without intelligence.*'[2]

Such quality, it was thought, could only come from a living tradition as yet untrammelled by industrialisation, such as those found on the continent of Asia, safeguarded and enriched by the cohesive nature and self-sufficient character of communal life.

These ideas and conclusions found a ready disciple in William Morris. Whether his interest in the arts of Asia was first prompted by the apparent link between the contemporary Eastern artisan and the craftsman of medieval Europe, or by the styles of decorative pattern originating from these regions is not important, but clearly both aspects occupied his thoughts. He considered that this quality of the artisan's life, his craft and designs were already at risk. He anxiously watched the effect of nineteenth-century European commercial involvement on the traditional crafts of the East and warned the British public:

'. . . *this art of unconscious intelligence is all but dead; that what little of it is left lingers among half-civilised nations, and is growing coarser, feebler and less intelligent year by year; nay, it is mostly at the mercy of some commercial accident, such as the arrival of a few shiploads of European dye-stuffs or a few dozen orders from European merchants; this they must recognise, and must hope to see in time its place filled by a new art of conscious intelligence, the birth of wiser, simpler, freer ways of life than the world leads now, than the world has ever led.*'[3]

How this was to be achieved was not discussed, but then actualities of this sort often proved too uncomfortable to be considered in depth.

According to Morris, the individual character given by such craftsmen to their work was not to be found in the Far East, home of 'perfect ingenuity' and 'pretty toys', but in India and the central Islamic lands. Although Morris owned a personal collection of oriental blue and white porcelain, the technical perfection in body, glaze and painting of Chinese porcelain did not appeal to him, and he stated his preference for the wares of Persia, Turkey and Spain. To the ceramic student of today his reasoning is difficult to follow. The principles and guidelines he laid down for potters in 'The Lesser Arts of Life' are more immediately apparent in Far Eastern ceramics. The flowing lines of contour, the plastic nature of clay, the distinctive mark of the potter's hand in form and surface decoration, swift and yet decisive,[4] are rarely displayed in the moulded and turned frit-bodied wares of Persia and Turkey. But then these guidelines were never employed in the Morris workshop. And with the exception of a few pieces reminiscent in shape and decorative composition of the Tz'u Chou style, planned by William De Morgan,[5] the inspiration for the Morris and De Morgan ceramics, when non-European in origin, is to be found in Islamic pottery. The profiles, the decorative techniques, motifs and their arrangement are derived from the lustre wares of Seljuq and Qajar Iran, and from the underglaze painted vessels and tiles of sixteenth- and seventeenth-century Ottoman Turkey.

Interest in Islamic ceramics had been growing in fashionable circles since the 1860s. Introducing the 50 or so pieces of 'Persian' ware shown at the 1862 Special Loan Exhibition at the South Kensington Museum, J. C. Robinson commented:

'This very characteristic and beautiful variety of pottery has, within the last few years (only), become a very favourite category with amateurs and collectors.'[6]

In 1867, Frederic Leighton, one of the leading influences on British artistic sensibilities, had started forming his own collection. By 1871, the museum had purchased some 100 examples, including 49 pieces of Hispano-Moresque lustre wares, but its holdings were substantially augmented in 1876, when 823 items classified as 'Persian' ceramics were entered into the central register. That was the year that William Morris began his work at South Kensington as examiner for the Science and Art Department.

Morris was one of the 41 private owners who lent objects to the 1885 public exhibition of Islamic Art, organised by the Burlington Fine Arts Club, London. Most of the 13 pieces he lent were metalwork, but item 577 shows that his later interests ranged wider. It was an early-seventeenth-century copy of the *Shah-name* of Firdawsi, illustrated with 'Many miniatures of spirited design, with ornamentation similar in character to that found on Rhodian and Persian pottery.'[7] Two years earlier, Morris had been working on a translation (from the French) of this Persian epic, to complete the trio of the world's great epic cycles, but the manuscript was never completed.[8] His knowledge of oriental literature did not end there. The *Rubaiyat* of Omar Khayyam had already proved a favourite, as the personally penned and illuminated gift to Georgiana Burne-Jones showed.[9] Other Muslim works were no doubt brought to his notice when he met Wilfrid Scawen Blunt; we know that recent publications on the Middle East by European scholars and travellers were passed on from Blunt to the Morris family. He also read translations of the Indian epics for, in his list for the *Pall Mall Gazette* of books he considered literary works of art, he included the *Kalevala* and the *Mahabharata*.[10] Perhaps other friends, Wilfred Heeley and Sir George Birdwood of the East India Company, introduced Morris to these works and to Hindu art in general. In this he showed his independence of Ruskin who had little time for this 'distorted and monstrous' art form. Clearly he felt it did possess artistic and educational value, as in 1869 he presented to the South Kensington Museum a thirteenth/

fourteenth-century South Indian or Sinhalese bronze figure of Hanuman, monkey god and hero of the *Ramayana*.[11] However, this interest in Hindu art is not reflected in Morris's own designs.

Morris's lecture given to the Birmingham and Midlands Institute in March 1884 defines his views of Indian art, and also of Middle-Eastern art, Pre-Islamic[12] and Islamic.

'... we can note that the art of Byzantium proper on the one hand much influenced by the kindred development of Persian art spread all over the Mussulman East, producing everywhere an architecture of nearly complete unity of style which can in fact otherwise only be named from the countries or among the tribes where it is found, as Indian, Arab, and the like; for as to Indian Art, outside the Brahman architecture which is a survival of early Arian work obviously even amidst its lack of beauty akin to that of Greece, and outside also Buddhist art, which takes the impress in some places of other families of man who fell under the sway of that great religion, there is no art peculiar to the peninsula. While as to Arab art, except that the race has impressed a sense of its turn for number, order and repetition, a sort of poetry of arithmetic upon the Byzantine-Persian ornament, which shows in its elaborate geometrical interlacements and the like, except for this, there is no trace of any prepossession towards any form of art among the Arab people.*

'So one may say that the first and most obvious branch of the new Free Art is traceable in the Architecture of the Mussulman East.'[13]
One cannot agree with his thesis today. But late-nineteenth-century opinion held that the Indian and the Arab were as children, in dire need of direction in all matters, political, economic and social. The Turk was a threatening barbarian, but yet held responsible for his actions. Constantinople may have been four centuries

under Ottoman control, but to the British scholar, poet and politician, glimpses of the old order could still be caught. As for the Persian, his land held the secrets of civilisation.

To Morris and his colleagues, all that was beautiful in Islamic art unquestionably owed its inspiration, if not production, to Persia.
'To us pattern-designers, Persia has become a holy land, for there in the process of time our art was perfected, and thence above all place it spread to cover for a while the world, east and west.'[14]

William Morris revelled in Islamic or 'Persian' textiles,[15] their designs 'fertile of imagination and lovely in drawing'[16] and colours. In the same year that the South Kensington Museum acquired its first Middle-Eastern carpet, Morris was describing his London house as possessing an Arabian Nights' atmosphere, with so many 'Persian' textiles. He was soon acknowledged as an expert, and his opinion was sought when expensive purchases were being considered, for example an early Mughal carpet, now housed in the Museum of Fine Arts, Boston, and the 'Ardabil' carpet in 1893. Thomas Armstrong brought Morris into the arena to support his proposal for its purchase, which Morris did in an official letter, arguing:
'... this is the chief reason that I wish to see it bought for the public, the design is of singular perfection; defensible on all points, logically and consistently beautiful, with no oddities or grotesqueries which might need an apology, and therefore most especially valuable for a Museum, the special aim of which is the education of the public in Art.'[17]

It was of course Islamic pattern – whether on pottery or in textiles – that intrigued him, the creation of tension and rhythmic harmonies, the independence and interdependence of motifs, the interweavings and superimposition of layers in two dimensions:

'. . . *in all patterns which are meant to fill the eye and satisfy the mind, there should be a certain mystery. We should not be able to read the whole thing at once, nor to desire to do so, nor be impelled by that desire to go on tracing line after line to find out how that pattern is made, and I think that the obvious presence of a geometrical order, if it be, as it should be, beautiful, tends towards this end, and prevents our feeling restless over a pattern.*'[18]

The exact nature of the debt that William Morris and his colleagues, especially William De Morgan, owed to oriental art cannot be considered here. Without turning his back on European decorative tradition, he enthusiastically recognised the possibilities of abstract shape and colour offered by non-European art. He was not alone in this enthusiasm. Such open-mindedness was a characteristic of late-nineteenth-century aestheticism.

1 Owen Jones, *Journal of Design and Manufacture*, 1852, vol VI, p110.

2 Owen Jones, *The Alhambra Court in the Crystal Palace*, London, 1854, p16.

3 William Morris, 'The Decorative Arts', lecture delivered about 1878, as published in A. Briggs ed. *William Morris*, London, 1962, p92.

4 William Morris, 'The Lesser Arts of Life', lecture, as published in *Lectures on Art*, 1882, pp189–90, 192, 194–5.

5 Berger Collection (Morris & Co Archives) entries no 28 and 29 in *Morris & Co. Catalogue*, Stanford, 1975.

6 South Kensington Museum *Catalogue of the Special Exhibition . . . 1862*, London, 1863, p284.

7 Burlington Fine Arts Club *Catalogue of Specimens Illustrative of Persian and Arab Art*, London, 1885.

8 William Morris's letter dated 28 February 1883 as published in P. Henderson ed. *The Letters of William Morris*, London, 1950, p165. The unfinished manuscript is now held in the British Library (English Ms. Add. 45317); it begins with the story of Gayumars and ends with the tale of Zahhak.

9 British Library English Ms. Add. 37832; an unfinished page is bound in Cockerell, *English Handwriting*, (Victoria and Albert Museum English MS. 86.444, item 5).

10 William Morris's letter to the Editor, 2 February 1886, as published in P. Henderson, *op cit*, pp245–6.

11 J. Irwin, 'A Gift from William Morris' *Victoria and Albert Museum Bulletin*, London, vol I (i), 1965, pp38–40.

12 The enthusiasm for Pre-Islamic art may have been fired by Henry Middleton, an expert on Greek and Persian art, Islamic carpets and textiles, whom Morris first met in 1873.

13 William Morris, 'The Gothic Revival', lecture delivered in March 1884 as published in E. D. Lemire, *The unpublished lectures of William Morris*, Detroit, 1969, pp58–9.

14 William Morris, 'History of Pattern Designing', lecture as published in *Lectures on Art*, 1882, p144.

15 For example, see A. F. Kendrick and C. E. C. Tattersall, *Hand-woven Carpets, Oriental and European*, London, 1922, vol I, p43; Pope ed. *A Survey of Persian Art*, in ed. 1938, in which many items known to have been produced outside Iran are classified as Persian.

16 William Morris, 'The Lesser Arts of Life', *op cit*, p205.

17 Victoria and Albert Museum Textile Department Archives, nominal file of Vincent Robinson.

18 William Morris, 'Making the Best of it', lecture as published in *Collected Works of William Morris*, 1914, vol XXII, p109.

Tiles designed by William De Morgan (C5)

Charger designed by William De Morgan (C6)

Reverse of charger (C6)

'Good Citizens' Furniture': William Morris and the Firm

Helen Snowdon

Looking back on the contribution made by his Firm to the conflict with the 'philistinism of modern society',[2] William Morris bitterly concluded that he had wasted this part of his life in 'ministering to the swinish luxury of the rich'.[3] Some of his most outspoken lectures on 'the present system of commercialism and profit-mongering'[4] date from the very period when Morris & Co had become commercially successful for the first time:[5] indeed, it was partly *because* of the form that this success took, that Morris became deeply involved in the public debate about socialist ethics and public aesthetics from the late 1870s onward. The apparent contradiction between the specific intentions of the Firm ('reforming all that'[6]), the working methods it symbolised, and the market its products reached, was not only felt by Morris (and some of his charmed circle), but has also informed the terms in which some recent commentators have presented this stage in his career: Morris the guild socialist, whose clientele included 'enterprising men of wealth and nostalgic parsons',[7] a clientele which seems actually to have enjoyed being abused by this uncompromising artist; Morris the opponent of fussy 'style of design',[8] whose Firm produced decorative furniture in the eighteenth-century mould complete with gilt painting and brass inlay;[9] Morris the leader of a 'revolution in Victorian taste',[10] whose work, when it was not conservative, often relied heavily on other people's ideas which were 'of his age';[11] Morris the enlightened craftsman who sought to break down the distinction between mental and manual labour[12] but whose Firm depended on paper designs drawn by famous architects or painters of the day,[13] as well as on the practical skill of cabinet-makers from the furniture trade;[14] and,

perhaps most contradictory of all, Morris, who 'belonged to the well-to-do classes and was born into luxury',[15] informing the workmen of England that 'I ask much more of the future than many of you do',[16] and exhorting them to 'have nothing in your houses that you do not . . . believe to be beautiful'.[17]

The terms of this debate – based largely on Morris's later writings, even when applied to the period 1861–74 – have tended to relegate his 'creative work' to a marginal role,[18] in sharp contrast to the more old-fashioned art histories which ignored his politics altogether. They have also put considerable pressure on any future studies of the Firm's output for there is a strong temptation to overload the patchy evidence with a significance which it can never have had at the time: in other words to ask the questions which Morris only came to formulate after the event. This is the case, whether the historian is researching the contributions of individual artist-designers, the division of labour in the workshops, the financing of the Firm, the marketing of the products, the relationship with the rest of the furniture trade, or even the range of goods listed in Morris's and Rossetti's brochures.

We do not know precisely what Dante Gabriel Rossetti's contribution was or Ford Madox Brown's, or even Philip Webb's. No one yet knows the parts that were played by Curwen the Bloomsbury cabinet-maker in the early 1860s, or by George Campfield the foreman. There is still a very great deal to learn about what roles precisely were taken, in the 1870s, by 'the men from Camden Town' and the 'boys from Euston Road'[19] – and we still do not entirely understand how Warington Taylor operated as business manager from 1865 to 1869.[20]

How did the way that the Firm conducted its affairs compare with other informal business

◄ *The Tapestry Room, table by Philip Webb (F1)*

arrangements of the time such as Owen Jones and Associates or Christopher Dresser and Co? Or with other furniture companies such as Waring and Gillow?

We do know that the relationship with the mainstream trade was sometimes openly hostile,[21] but we also know that there were borrowings on each side. As yet these borrowings have not been fully charted. Even the history of the Firm's marketing policy – from individual ecclesiastical commissions[22] to showrooms and other retail outlets[23] – has yet to be written.

One of the problems is that Morris's lectures and papers have survived in abundance, as have assorted memoirs and letters by members of his Brotherhood, while evidence of the day-to-day running of the Firm – who made the furniture? who bought it? how much did it cost? how far was it distributed? – is notoriously difficult to track down. So, it is all too easy to make a little historical material go a very long way.

Consider the claims to significance opposite. They were made at different times by various associates and contemporaries. Together they form a kind of history of ideas about the Firm.

The history of the Firm has often been pieced together from these and other statements made at the time – the fairy-tale history of a small brotherhood of romantic artists who alone took on the Victorian furniture trade, refusing to compromise either their design philosophy or their belief in the value of pre-industrial modes of work. Since supporting documentary evidence is so scarce, the written intentions of the Brotherhood have often been treated as synonymous with their historical significance as innovators. To take the most obvious case: very few examples of Madox Brown's 'artisan' furniture have survived; is this because they sold so well to 'artisans', or because only a few of them were made, for Brown's personal use? If we

Washstand by Ford Madox Brown (F3i)

accept the claims to significance made by Morris & Co, then we must assume they sold very well to a wide market, but if we look closely at the artefacts that assumption seems more and more dubious. Or take the famous case of what Morris liked to call his 'Cottage', 'Workaday', or 'Good Citizens'' furniture – the Sussex range. Like the adjustable 'Morris' chair (an adaptation, with turned stretchers to make it look more 'medieval', of a country regency design which had first been made in the 1820s), the 'Sussex' chair was indirectly derived from earlier spindle and bobbin chairs like the Windsor range, which had been around at least since the 1750s and which, suitably refined, appear to have been fashionable with picnicking Londoners during the Regency.[24] Warington Taylor asked his

74

'One evening a lot of us were together, and we got talking about the way in which artists did all kinds of things in olden times, designed every kind of decoration and most kinds of furniture, and some one suggested – as a joke more than anything else – that we should each put down five pounds and form a company . . . It was a mere plaything at business, and Morris was elected manager – because he was the only one among us who had both time and money to spare.'
D. G. Rossetti (quoted in *The Athenaeum*, 10 October 1896)

'Up to this time, want of artistic supervision, which can alone bring about harmony between various parts of a successful work, has been increased by the necessarily excessive outlay consequent on taking one individual artist from his pictorial labour. The Artists whose names appear above hope by association to do away with this difficulty . . . They have established themselves as a firm, for the product by themselves and under their supervision of – Furniture, either depending for its beauty on its own design, on the application of materials hitherto over-looked, or on its conjunction with Figure and Pattern Painting.'
First Prospectus of the Firm probably drafted by Rossetti (Aymer Vallance, *William Morris*, London, 1898, p58)

'The announcement of the Firm came with the provocation and force of a challenge, and dumbfounded those who read it at the audacity of the venture . . . Had it been possible to form a ring and exclude Messrs Morris, Marshall, Faulkner and Co from the market, the thing would infallibly have been done.'
Aymer Vallance (*The Studio*, 70, 1917)

'Light and boisterous chats among themselves and something like dictatorial irony towards the customers, were the methods by which this singular commercial firm was conducted, and was turned, after a longish period of uncertain probation, into a flourishing success. There was no compromise. Mr Morris, as the managing partner, laid down the law and all his clients had to bend or break. The goods were first rate, the art and workmanship excellent, the prices high . . . You could have the things such as the Firm chose they should be, or you could do without them.'
William Rossetti (*The Furnisher*, III, 1900–1, pp61–2)

Contemporary estimates of the Firm's aims and ideals

'Madox Brown held that utility and simplicity were the two desiderata for domestic furniture, united with solidity of construction. Veneer, so beloved of the philistine in early Victorian days, was abhorrent to him. 'Let us be honest, let us be genuine, in furniture as in aught else' was his motto. 'If we must needs make our chairs and tables of cheap wood, do not let them masquerade as mahogany or rosewood; let the thing appear that which it is; it will not lack dignity; if it only be good of its kind, and well made.'
E. M. Tait (*The Clarion*, 19 November 1892, p100)

'I have tried to produce goods which should be genuine so far as their mere substances are concerned, and should have on that account the primary beauty in them which belongs to naturally treated natural substances . . . all this quite apart from the design in the stuffs or what not.'
William Morris ('The Lesser Arts of Life')

'In the main, it was a revival of the old medieval spirit (not the letter) in design; a return to simplicity, to sincerity; to good materials and sound workmanship; to rich and suggestive surface decoration, and simple constructive forms . . . The simple black framed old English Buckinghamshire elbow-chair, with its rush-bottomed seat, was substituted for the wavy-backed and curly-legged stuffed chair of the period, with its French polish and concealed, and often very unreliable construction.'
Walter Crane (*Scribner's Magazine*, July 1897)

'So I say our furniture should be good citizens' furniture, solid and well made in workmanship, and in design should have nothing about it that is not easily defensible, no monstrosities or extravagances, not even of beauty lest we weary of it. But besides this kind of furniture there is the other kind of what I call state furniture which I think is quite proper even for a citizen: I mean sideboards, cabinets, and the like, which we have quite as much for Beauty's sake as for use . . . these are the blossoms of the art of furniture.'
William Morris ('The Lesser Arts of Life')

'The earliest furniture made for William Morris was massive in form and decorated with paintings of figures or subjects from the romances. Some of that which was made by the Firm in its infancy was also painted, notably a Gothic canopied sideboard designed by Mr Philip Webb and repeated more than once. By degrees, however, the cabinet work began to take the place of carpentry, and side by side with oak or stained ash furniture of a somewhat severe Feudal type, the Firm produced rich inlaid cabinets and suites of fine construction and design, mostly by Mr Webb and his successor Mr George Jack. In its finish, the cabinet work of Morris and Company will bear close comparison with the best productions of Chippendale and Sheraton . . . Without sinking to the common craze for more antiquities, Morris and Company have reproduced some of the best forms of the Chippendale and Queen Anne period, especially in regard to carved drawing room and dining room chairs . . . William Morris's work, however, appeals to middle class life, quite as much as to such stately surroundings, and middle class needs were prominently in his thoughts in designing (the products) which have so widely influenced public taste. Those who think that work to be good must necessarily be costly will find that it is not always so. Morris liked to sell his wares cheaply, so long as they paid to make; and wished them to be in everybody's reach . . . not only 'cheaper in the long run' as good work must always be, but actually cheaper in many respects to buy than ordinary trade productions which have to be produced in the first instance to cover profit for the middleman who sells (or sometimes only handles) the goods, as well as for the manufacturer who produces them . . .'
Fiftieth Anniversary Sketch of the Morris Movement

'In spite of all the success I have had, I have not failed to be conscious that the art I have been helping to produce would fall with the death of a few of us who really care about it, that a reform in art which is founded on individualism must perish with the individuals who have set it going . . . Art cannot have a real life and growth under the present system of commercialism and profit-mongering.'
William Morris (*Letters*, p187)

'Artisan' bed designed by Ford Madox Brown (F3iv)

'artistic supervisors' to adapt and develop the prototype – a mixture of 'Sheraton Fancy' and 'Country' styles – which only seems 'simple' in comparison with the more fussy designs which had dominated the market from the 1830s onwards. Since Morris professed to be less interested in 'the design or what not' than in truth to materials and the circumstances of the making – at least, when he was writing to his socialist comrades – this should not matter: but the Sussex chair was also ebonised (Sheraton-style), a technique used to disguise cheap woods, and involved some very complex cabinet-making skills (carving the arms, shaping the back supports), as well as good old medieval joinery. So William Morris's 'good citizens' furniture' relied on Sheraton and Regency designs, a 'country' look, *and* the most sophisticated

processes the furniture trade could offer, depending on skill specialisation and the division of labour: a far cry from 'naturally treated natural substances' and 'simple constructive forms'. One commentator has even suggested that some of the shaping and carving on Morris & Co's furniture in this period was machine assisted.[25] Later in the Firm's history, when the catalogue proudly advertised reproduction pieces, fine inlay work and 'genuine old antique furniture' – as well as boasting of commissions for the Royal Family and the New England aristocracy – the break between Morris's claims and the products on offer was to become complete: in the 1860s and 1870s, by contrast,

Easy chair covered in 'Peacock and Dragon'
design fabric (F10) ▶

78

Morris did actually manage to convince his wealthy clients that they were buying something that was very *avant-garde*.

Of course, it would be surprising if Morris & Co had 'revolutionised' Victorian furniture design overnight. His 'supervising artists' were clearly in touch with both the latest development in design, *and* classic design ideas which had not been particularly fashionable for about 30 years – which they were commercially astute enough to revive. In short, William Morris was really the 'great classical designer of his age',[26] a synthesiser rather than an innovator. Hermann Muthesius (1903) reckoned that the Firm's main contribution was to bring Chippendale and Sheraton 'back into fashion' – a challenge to the dominance of 'pompous Victorian furniture'.

But the historian of design has to look closely at the Firm's products – rather than at the justly influential manifestos which surrounded them – in order to come to this commonsense conclusion.

Egyptian armchair by D. G. Rossetti (F4)

1 The phrase 'Good Citizens' Furniture' comes from Morris's lecture 'The Lesser Arts of Life', delivered on 23 January 1882. See *Collected Works*, ed. Mary Morris, London, 1914, vol 22.

2 See E. P. Thompson, *William Morris*, revised edition, London, 1977, pp90–8, and Perry Anderson, *Arguments within English Marxism*, London, 1980, pp157–75. The opening section of this article owes a great deal to the debate between these two commentators, and to the contribution of Raymond Williams's *Culture and Society*, Middlesex, 1975, pp137–61, *The Country and the City*, London, 1975, pp320–1, 326–9, *Politics and Letters*, London, 1979, pp102–5, 116, 128–30.

3 See E. P. Thompson, *op cit*, pp250–1.

Daybed designed by Philip Webb (F7)

4   See *The Letters of William Morris*, ed. Philip Henderson, London, 1950, p187.

5   See E. P. Thompson, *op cit*, pp96–8.

6   See *The Letters of William Morris, op cit*, p186, E.P. Thompson, *op cit*, pp93–4, and Perry Anderson, *op cit*, pp162–4.

7   E. P. Thompson, *op cit*, p98.

8   *Ibid*, pp99–100.

9   As early as 1903, Hermann Muthesius pointed out the eighteenth-century origin of much of the Firm's 'original' output; more recently, Simon Jervis (in *Furniture History*, 10, 1974, p99) has discussed this thesis with specific reference to the 'Sussex' range.

10 E. P. Thompson, *op cit*, pp763–4.

11 See especially Peter Floud's two articles on 'William Morris as an Artist' and 'The Inconsistencies of William Morris', in *The Listener*, 7 and 14 October 1954.

12 See, among many other references, William Morris, 'Useful Work Versus Useless Toil' in *Selected Writings*, ed. Briggs, London, 1977, pp117–36.

13 See, for example, the pages from Philip Webb's book of accounts transcribed in W. R. Lethaby's *Philip Webb and his Work*, reprint, London, 1979, pp40–3.

14 See, among other references, Paul Thompson's *Work of William Morris*, London, 1967, pp66–7, 75.

15 Perry Anderson, *op cit*, pp164–5.

16 Morris's *Society of the Future*, cited by Anderson, p163.

17 This famous Morris aphorism was used as an epigraph in the anonymous *Brief Sketch of the Morris Movement*, 1911, held in the Victoria and Albert Museum library.

18 See pp763–71 of *Postscript* to E. P. Thompson, *op. cit*.

19 See J. W. Mackail, *The Life of William Morris*, London, 1899, vol 1, p153; Paul Thompson, *op cit*, pp15–16, 66–7, also the comments on Morris & Co in Gillian Naylor's *The Arts & Crafts Movement*, London, 1971, and Ray Watkinson's *William Morris as Designer*, London, 1967.

20 Chapter IV of Lethaby's *Philip Webb, op cit*, pp47–62, provides some intriguing clues, but much work still needs to be done.

21 This process was noted as early as 1898 by Aymer Vallance, in *William Morris*, pp58–9; Walter Crane commented on the 'fashion' for the Firm's designs, in *William Morris to Whistler*, London, 1911, pp51–5; and, more recently, E. P. Thompson, *op cit* pp96–8, has suggested possible directions for further research.

22 See, for example, the suggestions of E. P. Thompson, pp96–8, Paul Thompson, pp66–82, and W. R. Lethaby, pp32–46.

23 Which we have to reconstruct from *catalogues* which were not even issued until some 50 years later.

24 See Simon Jervis '"Sussex" Chairs in 1820', in *Furniture History*, 10, 1974, p99.

25 Elizabeth Aslin, in *Nineteenth Century English Furniture*, London, 1962, p58.

26 Peter Floud, 'William Morris as an artist: a new view', in *The Listener*, 7 October 1954.

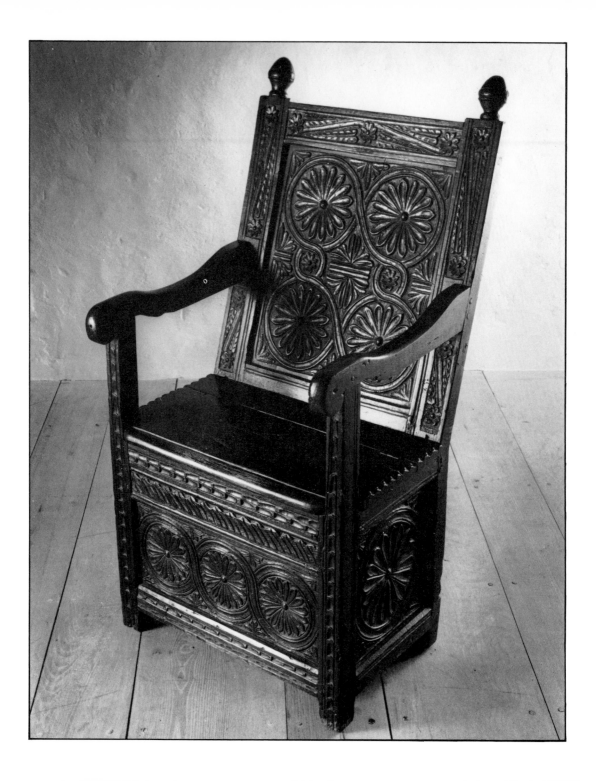

Traditional Furniture and Personal Items from Kelmscott Manor

Dorothy D. Bosomworth

Like any home, Kelmscott Manor has had a variety of occupants, creating an amalgam of taste. Any selection of items of furniture with the intention of conveying something of the ambience in which Morris and his family lived has certain inherent difficulties. However, three distinct phases may be distinguished in the history of the house's occupation, from the start of Morris's tenancy in 1871. The first lasts until Morris's death in 1896; the second ends with the death of May Morris in 1936; the third lasts from then until the present.

It would be foolish to imagine that the house's present furnishings are an accurate record of its appearance during Morris's life, or that they are only the result of his own purchases. Dante Gabriel Rossetti, a co-tenant with Morris from 1871 until 1874, brought with him a number of items, the majority of which he subsequently chose to give to Jane Morris. Other pieces were transferred to Kelmscott Manor from Kelmscott House, Hammersmith, following Morris's death. The strongest influence on the house's present appearance derives, however, from May Morris and her companion Miss Lobb. The extent of the catalogue of the sale held at Kelmscott, following Miss Lobb's death, reveals, by comparison, how crowded the house's contents must have been before May Morris's death.

Evidence about the appearance of Kelmscott Manor's interior during Morris's lifetime is provided by Aymer Vallance,[1] whose book on Morris quotes the latter's article in the 1895 volume of *The Quest*, the magazine of the Birmingham Guild of Handicraft.[2] Neither Vallance nor Morris is as informative as one

◄ Janey Morris's oak chair constructed in sixteenth-century style, with hinged lid to book box seat (TF8)

might wish. Vallance illustrates a drawing of Morris's bedroom, which shows in surprising juxtaposition Morris's four-poster bedstead with the Chinese chair.[3] Morris, in his article, describes the Tapestry Room, which he refers to as being 'our best sitting room now, though it was once the best bedroom'.[4]

Further evidence about the ownership of the house's contents emerges from the correspondence between Dante Gabriel Rossetti and Jane Morris.[5] Rossetti's departure from Kelmscott Manor in 1874 is followed by a succession of letters to Jane Morris in 1878, discussing the return of items of furniture which he had left at the Manor. Ultimately, he assigned almost all of them to Jane, but the size of his initial list, citing 22 entries, some of which contained more than one item, accentuates the impact of his presence on the household.

Looking at the traditional furniture as a whole, several conclusions can be drawn, one of the most obvious being their eclecticism. Some are English, some Eastern, and others European; their dates range from the fifteenth to the nineteenth centuries. If any common denominator can be identified, it is their use of surface pattern and texture, together with a certain richness of the materials themselves. Frustratingly, no information has as yet emerged which throws any light on the purchase of these items. Only the tapestries illustrating scenes from the life of Samson are known to have been already in the house when Morris's tenancy began.

If one discounts the items that were brought from Kelmscott House after 1896, it is impossible to accept Wilfrid Scawen Blunt's comment that the house was extremely primitive. Describing the inconvenience of the house's arrangement, where the Tapestry Room on the upper floor opens directly out of Morris's

The winds on the wold · and the night is a cold · and thames runs chill · and the old house here · and thames runs chill · of the bed · strait smites & smiling · with all ~~~
twixt mead & hill · but kind & dear · is the old house here · rest then & rest · and think · ~ in the town of the live ~~~ you & no one · and guest ~~~
and my heart is warm · midst winter's harm · rest then & rest · and think of the ~~~ more weleath · gifts love · the fale away · or the old ~~~

Chinese Huang Hua Li chair (TF4)

bedroom with its oak four poster bed, he stresses Morris's personal insensitivity to discomfort and inconvenience.[6]

Morris's own views on house furnishings express this philosophy of reduction to essentials. In a lecture he stated:

'Simplicity is one thing, needful in furnishing, of that I am certain. If only our houses were built as they should be, we should at all events take as our maxim the less, the better; the excess of furniture destroys the repose of a lazy man, and it is in the way of an industrious one; and besides, if we really care for art, we shall always feel inclined to save on superfluities that are forever in our way; but make work for servants and doctors. If you want a golden rule that will fit everybody, this is it: "Have nothing in your houses that you do not know to be useful, or believe to be beautiful."'[7]

The quality and character of the traditional furniture does, I think, stand the test of this maxim. The processes of selection of the house's contents that have gone on since May Morris's death have, in fact, proved positive. But now the mixture of older items and the products of Morris & Co on show in the house do create a most attractive and welcoming, peaceful atmosphere.

1 Aymer Vallance, *William Morris, his art, his writings and his public life*, George Bell and Sons, London, 1897, chap 7, 'Kelmscott Manor', pp183–92.
2 William Morris, 'Gossip about an old House on the Upper Thames', in *The Quest*, no IV, November 1895, pp5–13.
3 Vallance, *op cit*, p188.
4 Morris, *op cit*, p12.
5 *Dante Gabriel Rossetti and Jane Morris, Their Correspondence*, edited with an introduction by John Bryson in association with Janet Camp Troxell, Clarendon Press, Oxford, 1976.
6 *Wilfrid Scawen Blunt, My Diaries; being a personal narrative of events, 1888–1914*, Martin Secker, London, 1919–20, vol I, p28.
7 Quoted by Vallance, *op cit*, pp437–8.

◀ *William Morris's four-poster bed (TF10)*

The Importance of Philip Webb

John Brandon-Jones

In any study of the work of the Morris Firm it is essential to remember that its successes were due to the close collaboration of a group of like-minded men of very varied talents. Every member of the group put in what he could and the enthusiasm and energy generated by Morris himself supplied the impetus that kept them moving. But this company of strong-willed individualists required co-ordination and control and it was here that Philip Webb was able to make his special and unique contribution. Rossetti, writing in 1862, said:

'Morris and Webb the architect are our most active men of business as regards the actual conduct of the concern; the rest of us chiefly confine ourselves to contributing designs when called for.'

Years later, Webb remarked to Lethaby:

'The best of those times was that there was no covetousness; all went into the common stock – and then we were all such boys.'

Philip Webb and William Morris first met in the Oxford office of George Edmund Street in January 1856. Morris had decided to apprentice himself to Street because he took him to be 'a good architect as things go now, and he has a good deal of business, and always goes for an honourable man'. This choice of master shows good judgement on the part of Morris, for Street was certainly one of the most brilliant designers of his generation; he was also thorough and painstaking and well versed in all the crafts connected with building, his metalwork designs are particularly fine. Webb was only three years older than Morris, but he had already become Street's chief assistant, he was an able and conscientious man, quiet and unassuming, but firm and fearless when any question of principle was involved. The two young men soon became

◀ *Red House, Upton, Kent*

close friends, they shared an interest in outdoor pursuits, riding and rowing and walking and swimming, as well as a love of old buildings and a desire to leave the world a better place than they found it. They also shared an admiration for Ruskin. Even before his meeting with Morris, Webb had spent a whole month's wages on the purchase of the *Stones of Venice*.

Webb had been born and bred in Oxford, he knew and loved the old city and its colleges. During his apprenticeship in Reading he had been encouraged by John Billing to visit and sketch the churches in the neighbourhood; these activities were continued while he was working for Street and, no doubt, he was accompanied by Morris on many of his expeditions, absorbing the atmosphere of the old buildings and sketching the masonry and carpentry. The early, chunky details, characteristic of Red House and its furniture, probably owe much to these studies but, by 1871, when Morris became tenant of Kelmscott Manor, Webb had already begun to veer away towards a greater elegance of his mature designs. Part of the attraction of the Manor may have been that it seemed to give to Morris and his friends a chance to escape back to their earlier, more carefree days.

A few months after Morris became his pupil, Street decided to move his practice to London where he took an office in Montague Place, Bloomsbury; Webb and Morris moved with him. Burne-Jones was already established in London and Morris joined him in his rooms in Red Lion Square, while Webb found accommodation nearby. From this time forward, the trio began to work together on various projects. Webb made designs for furniture to be decorated by Jones and Morris and, in 1857, he spent his weekends and holidays with the group of young artists who undertook the decoration of the Oxford Union. Webb stayed with Street until 1859 but Morris,

Philip Webb *by C. F. Murray, 1873*

influenced by Rossetti, soon gave up architecture in favour of painting. According to Webb, an important reason for this change was that Morris became impatient when he realised that an architect must work through drawings and written instructions, trusting others to bring his ideas to fruition, whereas in painting and the crafts a man could carry out his designs with his own hands.

Webb had become increasingly disillusioned with the Gothic Revival, he realised that it was absurd for a nineteenth-century architect to try to act the part of a thirteenth-century master mason and, when Morris married, he was glad to give up his post with Street to undertake the

building of Red House. This is an interesting experiment in which the architect and the decorators worked hand in hand from the start. Red House has been described as 'revolutionary', but in fact it was a direct descendant of the parsonage houses of which its designers had had first-hand experience in Street's office. It also owes something to Butterfield, with whom Webb had established friendly contact. Webb's arrangement of rooms has been frequently criticised by careless historians who have seen the plans published years later in *Country Life* but have not taken the trouble to look up the original drawings in the V&A collection. The north-facing rooms on the ground floor were not intended as sitting rooms, the small room beneath the studio was a dormitory for bachelor friends who could sit up late and make as much noise as they liked without disturbing the Morris children at the far end of the house. Anyone who read Georgiana Burne-Jones's lively account of the pranks played by Morris and his friends will understand the necessity for this arrangement! It has also been said that Webb made a mistake in giving west-facing windows to the kitchen, but it should be remembered that this room was also the servants' sitting room and the aspect was chosen to give them a pleasant view over the gardens.

Webb's share in the design of Red House was not limited to planning and structural matters; he also designed furniture, window glass, metalwork and table glass for Morris. Thus it came about that when the Firm of Morris, Marshall, Faulkner & Co was set up in 1861, several of its members had already had experience of working together; they also had a promise from the architect G. F. Bodley, that when they were sufficiently organised he would find work for them in making stained glass and executing painted decorations for his churches.

Hall and staircase at Red House, Upton

Bodley proved as good as his word, and within a few years the Firm was employed by him in churches at Selsley, Brighton, Scarborough and Cambridge. At this time, Webb was a close friend of Bodley and stood in for him during a period of illness in 1869, supervising and making some of the drawings for an interesting group of houses at Malvern. In later years, Bodley's work became increasingly conventional and his friendship with the Morris group was broken when the Society for the Protection of Ancient Buildings criticised him for some of his church restorations.

From the beginning, it appears that Webb played a part second only to that of Morris himself. Lethaby tells us:

'Webb, as a trained architect, was invaluable in first organising and then generally supervising and co-ordinating the stained glass work. He planned the general lay-out of the windows, prepared small coloured sketches, arranged the disposition of the irons, insisting on thick bars from the first.'

A. C. Sewter, in his comprehensive work on Morris glass, also lays great stress on the 'controlling influence of Webb' in the early designs for glass, and Webb's account book shows that he was involved in many other branches of the Firm's work.

During the 1860s, Webb made drawings for chairs and tables, bookcases and cabinets as well as many smaller items such as candlesticks, heraldic tiles and a glass decanter. He was in charge of the redecoration work at St James's Palace and, according to Lethaby, the Green Dining Room at the Victoria and Albert Museum was entirely Webb's work, except for the figures designed by Burne-Jones. Webb was a keen naturalist, interested in animals, birds and plants: his sketch books contain numerous studies made on the farm or in the zoo; he seems to have been particularly fond of cats and his drawings range from the domestic tabby cat to the majestic lion. It is said that Burne-Jones based Circe's Black Panthers on sketches by Webb and it is certain that his drawings were used whenever birds or animals appeared in designs for tapestries, textiles or wallpapers. Among these are the 'Trellis' wallpaper, the 'Brother Rabbit' printed cotton and the 'Bird' woven wool fabric, hung by Morris on the walls of the Long Drawing Room at Kelmscott House and also used at the Manor.

In 1867, when the affairs of the Firm seemed to be getting out of hand, Morris's manager, Warington Taylor, wrote to Webb:

'In order that I may get a living, that Morris may get extra money, it is absolutely necessary to appeal to you from time to time on these matters of business. We could not move another step without your professional assistance, and therefore if you will not be paid the Firm must come to a stop –

because sponging on you is degrading.'
And again in 1869 Taylor wrote:
'Is everybody to be allowed to do as he likes? Ned, W.M. and Gabriel egg one another on to every kind of useless expense. How long do they intend to play boy? What is absolutely necessary to save the Firm from ruin is this: Someone must see the books weekly or fortnightly. We want vigorous stern action, if the Firm is to be saved. If you do not act, no one else will. Everyone treats it as a joke.'
Webb was always willing to help, but with such unruly partners, discipline was hard to maintain and it was probably as a result of a letter from Webb to Morris that the Firm was reconstructed on a more businesslike footing in 1875.

In later days, when Webb's architectural practice was on a scale that made it impossible for him to give so much time to the work of the Firm, younger architects, including George Jack, W. R. Lethaby, and W. A. S. Benson, became the principal designers of furniture and metalwork for Morris & Co. It was Lethaby who had charge of the work at Stanmore Hall, and his drawings can be seen in the RIBA Collection.

In 1877, Webb joined Morris in the foundation of the Society for the Protection of Ancient Buildings and, once again, it was Webb's firm grasp of practical matters that led to the success of the venture. It was all very well for Morris to shake his fist at the bishop or vicar, but the protests would have been far less effective if they had not been backed by realistic alternatives to the destructive proposals for 'restoration' put forward by distinguished architects. Webb was, by this time, well known and respected by members of his profession, his reports carried weight and he helped Morris to draft the Society's letters to the press and to influential individuals. Repairs carried out by Webb himself and by younger architects under his general direction set a new standard for the care of old buildings. Anti-Scrape, as Morris called the SPAB, continues the good work to this day.

Although Anti-Scrape was set up for the protection of old buildings, it was through the Society that Morris and Webb eventually exerted an influence over the design of new work carried out by a younger generation of architects. To quote Lethaby again:
'The SPAB was itself a remarkable teaching body. Dealing as it did with the common facts of traditional building in scores and hundreds of examples, it became, under the technical guidance of Philip Webb, a real school of practical building – architecture with all the whims which we usually call "design" left out.'
Young architects who later became leaders in the Arts and Crafts tradition learned from Morris and Webb in the Committee Room of the SPAB, among them Thackeray Turner, Lethaby, Gimson and the Barnsley Brothers, as well as members of the architectural staff of the LCC who applied Morris's ideals in their designs for housing and schools.

The Art Workers' Guild founded in 1884, inspired by the spirit of Morris and Webb, aimed to bring together architects, painters, sculptors and craftsmen. The architects included men such as Prior, Newton, Champneys, Jackson, Voysey and Ashbee, and there were artists and designers of the calibre of Heywood Sumner, Lewis Day, Hamo Thornycroft, Walter Crane and Henry Holiday. The Guild, with its offshoot the Arts and Crafts Exhibition Society, did much to promote good design and fine craftsmanship in building and in furnishing and decoration. (Like the SPAB, the Guild is still alive and still standing for the unity of the Arts.)

Webb was a welcome guest at the Manor and was consulted about repairs and improvements. Some letters to him from Mrs Morris have survived, in one of them she writes:

Design for 'St George and the Dragon' stained glass window by D. G. Rossetti, (P24)

'Dear Webb

I am getting the fireplace set straight in the dining-room, the one with the broken mantelshelf, perhaps you remember, and I think it would look well with tiles. Would you be so kind as to see about these at Queen Square for me? 6 dozen would be enough, 5 inch ones; they are to go in this way, 2 rows on each side and a single row along the top, the rest for the inside of the fireplace which will be an open one. Will they look best of various patterns or all alike? They must be blue. The mantelpiece is stone I find, so I am making the masons scrape off the former drab paint. The next thing to be thought of is a grate, I should like one like our dining-room in Queen Square, but I am afraid it would be too large, the space is 3 foot 7 inches, if you were to send me the measurements of it (and that of the one in the blue room too as I suppose Topsy will be taking out some of the others) I might judge, or perhaps Stennett has one, but this is giving you a lot of trouble, still you told me to write if I wanted anything, and I really want this seen to very badly.

Jenny and Mary send love they are a little out of temper with the weather, we have a deal of rain.
Yours affectionately
Janey'

The following week she wrote again:
'Dear Webb

Many thanks for your taking so much trouble about things for me. Are you quite sure you can use Barkentin's grate anywhere else? If not you must let me have it. I will never pull another fireplace down as long as I live, I feel inclined now to leave it till Topsy comes back, for there are no competent workmen in the place, however the masonry is nearly finished and they cannot make any great mistake provided I stand by to show them which is the right way up of each tile.

I enclose a little drawing I found when I opened your books, and which I ought and intended to have sent long ago, I ask your pardon for not having done so, and hope you have not been inconvenienced in any way by its temporary loss.
Yours affectionately
Janey'

Two other letters are of interest, though not directly connected with work on the Manor:
'Dear Webb

I shall never dare ask you for any design again, I had not expected anything half so elaborate or beautiful, thank you very much for it, I shall work it carefully in fine wool on blue serge I think, taking care to get different shades of blue for the flowers.

91

I have no news of Topsy yet, is not it rather odd?
You don't say how you are, I wish you would.
Good bye, Jenny & May send love –
  Yours affectionately
    Janey'

'*Dear Webb*

I told you I would write a line sometimes – I am already so much better that you would scarcely recognise me, I have actually got some suspicion of red in my face, and am feeling quite a different creature, I get down to breakfast comfortably with Jenny and May at half past eight. So much for my state of health.

I have been to Lechlade, I want to ask you about the church there. Is the spire as old as the church itself? And do you happen to remember if Shelley was living in the town at the time he wrote his poem in the churchyard?

The country I find is not so beautiful after one gets away from the river, though it is all delightful and home-like to me, and I love it, still I can well understand others not being much impressed with it, who are not used to it; every field is lovely by itself, and every house, but somehow when one looks far out, there is a sameness, a bareness of trees, which makes one begin to want more, but of course I am only speaking of the few miles in the immediate vicinity.

I have nearly finished "Elective Affinities", I think with all due respect to Goethe it is a most unsatisfactory book. What! Is nothing real? Must everything that is delightful change and leave nothing behind? I can't believe it; one begins by liking his characters very much, then they change, and one can no longer look upon them as real people. I still feel like little Margaret at the play when she asked me if May was really sewing.

Jenny and May send love.
  Yours affectionately
    Janey'

Etching of Morris's tomb in Kelmscott churchyard by Philip Webb, 1897 (P52)

Unfortunately these letters are undated, but they were probably written while Morris was in Iceland during the summer of 1871.

When Morris died in 1896, his wife asked Webb to design his tombstone in Kelmscott churchyard – 'a roof for the old man', Webb called it; and his last work before retirement was the building of a pair of memorial cottages not far from the Manor. Explaining his plan to Janey Morris, he wrote: 'the *broader* in effect the two cottages could be made, the less upstart in character would result'. For the centre gable he designed a panel, carved by George Jack, in which Morris is portrayed seated under a tree filled with birds – a final tribute to his lifelong friend.

Pugin and Ruskin, antagonistic though they were, had provided a theory and an ideal. Morris and Webb showed how the ideal could be applied in everyday practice.

The Socialism of William Morris

Larry Baker

The pronouncement of William Morris's family doctor that his patient 'died a victim of his enthusiasm for spreading the principles of Socialism', is symptomatic of the embarrassment which has afflicted both his own contemporaries and subsequent writers when they have attempted to account for the place socialism played in Morris's life and work. It is instructive to compare the entries on Morris in the 1910 and 1978 editions of the Encylopaedia Britannica. The more recent article by Philip Henderson states:

'Since the mid-twentieth century, it is as a designer and craftsman, rather than as poet or politician, that Morris is valued most, though future generations may *esteem him more as a social or moral critic, a pioneer of the society of equality.'*

By implication, the writer himself does not consider Morris's political ideas of major contemporary significance. The 1910 article, written by Arthur Waugh, although perverse in some of its judgements, for example asserting that:

'Morris indeed, was not primarily interested in men at all, but in objects.'

is less reticent in its ideological rejection of Morris's socialism:

'His socialism, though it made a brave show at times, was at heart, a passionate enthusiasm for an inaccessible artistic ideal.'

and more revealingly:

'His poetry deals, it is true, with human passions, but the emotion is always seen as in a picture, he is more concerned with the attitude of the group than with the realisation of character.'

The writer's assumption that art and politics are two separate self-contained worlds of experience with little profitable intercourse between them echoes a widely held Victorian belief, castigated by Matthew Arnold in his introduction to *Culture and Anarchy*, where he refers to

Frederick Harrison's assertion that:

'Culture is a desirable quality in a critic or professor of belles lettres, but as applied to politicians it simply means a term for small fault finding, love of selfish ease and indecision in action.'

Morris's attempt to heal the dissociation between art and life involved him in an attempt to analyse how that dissociation had come about. He found the answer in the development of capitalism which, through the division of labour, had alienated man from his work and culture. Arthur Waugh's criticism shows that the class struggle is present even in Morris's poetry.

However, although critics of a liberal and conservative persuasion may have underestimated the significance of Morris's socialism, his retrospective enfoldment into socialist orthodoxy by some historians and critics of the Left, has done him an equal disservice. Morris derived many of his ideas, it is implied, from private access to works of Marx and Engels, as yet unpublished. Not only can this influence not be proved, but a consideration of Morris's work for the 'Anti-Scrape' movement indicates that he was drawing on an earlier English tradition of radical criticism of Utilitarianism.

In 1880 he wrote:

'So the life, habits and aspirations of all groups and classes of the community, are founded on the economical conditions under which the mass of the people live, and it is impossible to exclude socio-political questions from the considerations of aesthetics.'

And this when he had never heard of Marx. The debt to Ruskin was obvious and acknowledged. Similarly when in 1884 he spoke of:

'Inchoate order in remotest time . . . moving forward ever towards something that seems the very opposite of that which it started from, and yet the earlier order never dead, but living in the new,

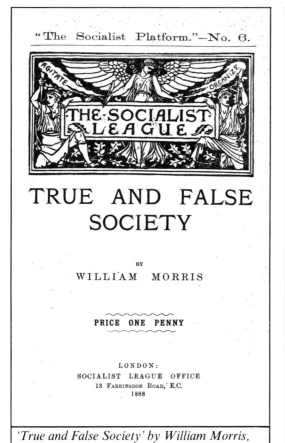

'True and False Society' by William Morris, The Socialist League pamphlet No 6, 1888

'Vive la Commune!' by Walter Crane for a socialist pamphlet, 1890

and slowly moulding it to a recreation of its former self.'

The indebtedness to both Marx and Ruskin was accepted, yet the discovery of the dialectic was Morris's own. His achievement in building upon and ultimately transforming the radical critique of capitalism within the Romantic movement is majestically charted by E. P. Thompson in his biography of Morris (first published 1955).

Morris's vision receives its most coherent expression in *News from Nowhere*. Though frequently dismissed as an escapist fantasy, readers inclined to join in this condemnation would do well to consider the final sentence of the work:

'. . . and if others can see it as I have seen it, then it may be called a vision rather than a dream.'

As A. L. Morton has commented in *The English*

94

Utopia, News from Nowhere is really the least Utopian of all idylls of that name. Not only the narrator but also the other actors in the dream are reminded at regular intervals of the distance travelled between the new world they inhabit and the nineteenth-century industrial civilisation out of which it evolved dialectically. Unlike many of the socialists he worked with, both in Hyndman's Social Democratic Federation and his own Socialist League, Morris retained a sense of the moral superiority of communism over capitalism, a moral superiority which was not to be compromised by either the scientific pretentions of orthodox Marxism, the palliatives of Fabian parliamentarianism, or the desperate and bloodthirsty ideas of his Anarchist colleagues. Indeed it is ironic that at the very time *News from Nowhere* first appeared in *Commonweal*, Morris's own influence within the Socialist League was being eclipsed by an Anarchist faction. Undoubtedly, the vision of *News from Nowhere* was considerably influenced by the ideas of Kropotkin, then resident in London, but the gentle and idyllic anarchy which the narrator finds in a transformed London should not anaesthetise the reader to the coherent statement of political theory which underpins the work. There is, for example, analysis of imperialism being the inevitable result of over-production of goods in capitalism, which sounds very familiar until one realises Hobson's *Imperialism* was published in 1902, and Lenin's *Imperialism, The Highest Stage of Capitalism* in 1916. Morris's Utopia convinces by its acknowledgement that even in an ideal society, elements of unhappiness will remain; sexual maladjustment, even violent crime, are to be found in *News from Nowhere*. There is a price to be paid in achieving happiness: interest in history, particularly among the young, wanes. Morris, with his immense interest in the past, particularly the Middle Ages, would have

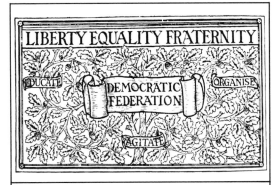

Membership card of the Democratic Federation, designed by William Morris

regretted this. Paradoxically, it is the awareness of the processes of historical change that compels the reader's attention. When the dream fades, one is made to realise how the understanding of history sustains the vision of *News from Nowhere*, and enables Morris and others to
'Go on living while you may, striving with whatsoever pain and labour needs must be, to build up little by little the new day of fellowship, rest and happiness.'

men went byrny-less, and were furious as dogs or wolves, and bit on their shields, and were as strong as bears or bulls: menfolk they slew, and neither fire nor steel might deal with them: and this condition is called bear-serks-gang.

NOW Odin would change his shape; his body would lie there as of one sleeping or dead, while he himself was a fowl, or a wild beast, or a fish, or a worm, and would go in the twinkling of an eye to far away lands on his own errands, or those of others. Moreover he knew by his craft how to slake the fire or still the wind and the sea with one word, or how to turn the wind to whichso quarter he would. Odin had a ship called Skidbladnir where-with he would fare over mighty seas; and that same ship would he fold together as a very napkin. Odin had Mimir's head ever by him, and that told him many tidings from other abodes; and whiles would he wake up dead men from the earth, or sit down under men hang-ed; wherefore was he called the Lord of the Dead, or

The Kelmscott Press
A Cornerstone of Modern Typography

Ray Watkinson

Morris once set out the general ground on which he, or we, might account for his remarkable achievement in the productions of his Kelmscott Press, at which in so few years over 50 books were printed before it closed in 1898, two years after his death. At the same time we might consider in the light of this statement in *Some Thoughts on the Ornamental Manuscripts of the Middle Ages*, how it was that it took him most of his life to set that press up and to give himself to the designing of type and the making of books.

'If I were asked to say what is at once the most important production of Art, and the thing most to be longed for, I should answer, a beautiful House; and if I were further asked to name the production next in importance and the thing next to be longed for, I should answer, a beautiful Book. To enjoy good houses and good books in self respect and decent comfort, seems to me to be the pleasurable end towards which all societies of human beings ought now to struggle.'

These seem very limited aims of life, but when we remember that for Morris a house is the setting in which life is to be lived with the loved living, and that a book is the setting of the life of the worthy dead whose ideas and passions we cherish as enriching our own life – that books were for him as for Milton, against whose writings he had one of his strongest dislikes: 'the precious life-blood of a master spirit' – we may see them not so simple, but very far-reaching indeed. They were thus expressed towards the end of a life of the most various and energetic creation, and they were given another form of expression in the book which more than any other brings together all Morris's ideas about life and his love for life – *News From Nowhere*, in which he has something

◀ *Manuscript of* The Story of the Ynglings, *translated from the Icelandic and illuminated by William Morris (B10)*

specific to say of the making of books and their use in living.

Yet until he began to control the design, and then the actual printing and production, of his books in the last seven or eight years of his life, his many volumes of poetry and prose, his lectures and pamphlets, and the newspaper *Commonweal* which he edited and subsidised for most of a decade, were published in a dress at best ordinary, and sometimes downright bad – true examples of all that he hated. He seems, until about 1888, to have been indifferent to this, and it is usual to say that he was inspired to see things in a new light by the lecture given on the occasion of the Arts & Crafts Exhibition by his friend, neighbour and fellow member of the Socialist League, Emery Walker.

Like so much that is repeated of William Morris, this is so simplified as to be a mis-representation, though it is true that Walker gave that lecture and that it was in talking with him afterwards that Morris decided to set up his own press. But the lecture was only the last in a chain of pressures towards that decision. Morris, though remotely, had begun moving towards it in the 1860s, when with Burne-Jones he projected a sumptuous edition of *The Earthly Paradise* on which he was then working: it was to be designed and adorned by Morris, with illustrations by Burne-Jones. But it was not very firmly, that is to say, practically, conceived and it came at a crisis in Morris's life, and was put aside in the interests of the rapidly growing work of the famous Firm. It went no further than a few ornaments and a couple of trial pages. Then, in a short time, the impetus towards the making of the book beautiful set Morris practising and exploring the art of calligraphy; medieval manuscripts had been a passion with him almost as early as architecture, and his first essays in formal writing and illumination had been made in the late 1850s

97

while he worked in the office of G. E. Street. But it was the 1870s that saw him begin a recreation of calligraphy of a very different, non-imitative kind, which at last resulted in the extraordinary flowering of the art at the hands of Edward Johnston.

The story of the Kelmscott Press has been told by Morris's son-in-law, Halliday Sparling, the first Secretary to the Press: additional information and insights are to be had from May Morris in her editing of the *Collected Works* and the supplementary volumes of *William Morris: Artist, Writer, Socialist*; from S. C. Cockerell, who succeeded Sparling as Secretary to the Press; from W. H. Bowden, who succeeded his father William Bowden as the printer; from Lethaby and others. What follows here is a summary of fact and a statement of value. The facts may be checked against these indicated sources; the values against the productions of the Kelmscott Press and the whole working life of its founder.

On all occasions when Morris meddled with the production of his books, they were printed at the Chiswick Press of the Whittingham family. Founded in the year of the French Revolution, it was one of the most distinguished of the new presses that recreated English printing at that time and was, for the whole of the nineteenth century, one of the best book-printing houses.

Morris's first published work was not, as we assume, the 1858 volume, *The Defence of Guenevere*; it appeared in the *Oxford and Cambridge Magazine*, set up by him with his Oxford friends at the end of 1855 and running for 12 monthly issues from January 1856. Morris funded the magazine, was at first its editor, and published in it several remarkable stories and poems and, what is rarer, a critical article on Browning. It was marketed (rather than strictly published, for they bore none of the cost) by

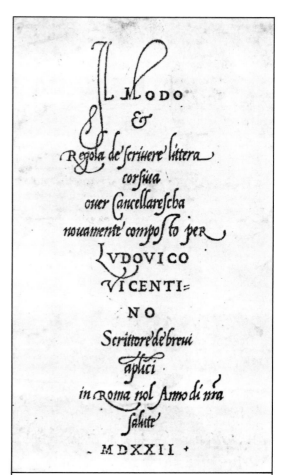

Page from a sixteenth-century writing book in William Morris's collection (B1)

Bell and Daldy; it was printed by Charles Whittingham of Tooks Court, Chancery Lane. When in 1858 Morris published his *Defence of Guenevere* – again marketed by Bell and Daldy – he took it likewise to Whittingham. When eight years later he was projecting the illustrated

98

Frontispiece from The Herball *by John Gerarde, 1633 (B3)*

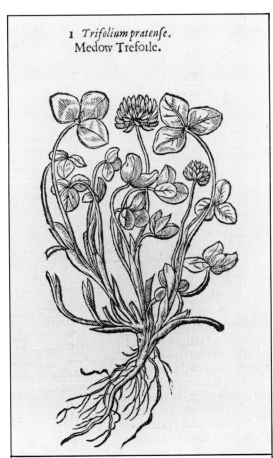

'Medow Trefoile' line drawing from Gerarde's Herball *(B3)*

edition of his yet unfinished *The Earthly Paradise*, it was the Chiswick Press again that printed the trial pages and the few completed ornaments. Now in all this, Morris was strictly his own publisher, and he alone was responsible for the choice of the Chiswick Press – on what advice we have I think no kind of knowledge.

Only after the success of the first edition of *The Life and Death of Jason* in 1867 did Bell and Daldy change their role from that of distributor to publisher; but thereafter, from 1868, Morris's bookseller friend F. S. Ellis became his publisher. And took Morris's books to very indifferent printers.

'The Musicians' designed by Edward Burne-Jones for The Earthly Paradise *(B28)*

The Nature of Gothic

ing, not adding to the generic forms. ❡ Now there are three good architectures in the world, and there never can be more, correspondent to each of these three simple ways of covering in a space, which is the original function of all architectures. And those three architectures are pure exactly in proportion to the simplicity and directness with which they express the condition of roofing on which they are founded. They have many interesting varieties, according to their scale, manner of decoration, and character of the nations by whom they are practised; but all their varieties are finally referable to the three great heads:

a, Greek: Architecture of the Lintel. b, Romanesque: Architecture of the Round Arch. c, Gothic: Architecture of the Gable.

Fig: XI.

a   b   c

98

Page from 'The Nature of Gothic' by John Ruskin, 1892 (B16)

In 1871–2, at the height of the relationship between Jane Morris and Rossetti, at the time of the taking over of Kelmscott Manor and of Morris's first journey to Iceland, Morris again projected a fine ornamented and illustrated edition of his new poem 'Love is Enough': again a few trials were made, again the scheme abandoned. Not for nearly 20 years did Morris again concern himself with typography and printing: his creative concern for books went into the making of a series of important manuscripts, many made for friends, notably Georgiana Burne-Jones.

It was in 1884 that Emery Walker became a friend of Morris's, and as they were neighbours,

fellow socialists, and shared a deep passion for books and history, the friendship became very close indeed. There can be no doubt that the two discussed the making of books and the principles of their design long before the setting up of the Kelmscott Press at the end of 1889: in December of that year Morris had already decided to set up his own press, and invited Walker to be his partner in the enterprise – which, it must be said, was no part of Morris & Co. Walker declined this; but his enormous expertise was at all times there for Morris to call upon. At the time, Morris was still pouring out some hundreds of pounds a year for the printing and publication of *Commonweal*, though he was soon to be ousted from the journal by the Anarchists, and did not at first contemplate more than a small office where he might design books, have them set, and then turn them over to Walker for actual printing. In the meantime he had been meddling to some purpose with the printing of two books at the Chiswick Press: *The House of the Wolfings* (1889) and *The Roots of the Mountains* (1890). He spent much time at the Press, discussing the format and the production of these books, using for them the same Basel type, revived half a century before by Whittingham, which he had used for the trial pages of *The Earthly Paradise*. Now, in rather a square format, both books were printed in this type and with title pages of pure typography, without ornament, and the first had already gone to press *before* the lecture was given by Walker – for whose illustrations Morris provided many of the originals from his growing collection of fine and early printed books, Walker's own firm making lantern slides from their pages.

It seems to have been the sight of these early letterforms and types blown up so big on the screen without loss of beauty and dignity that finally convinced Morris that he must not only print, but also design, his own types. When he set to work on the first of these types, 'Golden', he worked from photo-enlargements made for him by Emery Walker, modifying and reshaping not merely to get from each letter a satisfying form, but to ensure, as a type designer must, that all should work together in all combinations. The punches were cut by Edward Prince, who also cut those for the 'Troy' and 'Chaucer' which followed it, and were more Gothic in kind, but by no means black-letter. A fourth type on which Morris began work, making designs for only the lower case letters before serious ill health made him abandon it, was based on the 'Subiaco' type of Sweynheim and Pannartz, and the 'Golden' was based on the roman of Nicholas Jenson of 1476. It is interesting that when Morris went to Joseph Batchelor for his paper, the model he took was a Bolognese paper of three years earlier than this – so strongly did Morris feel that the best printing was that of those early days when the manuscript book was the life-experience of the men who made the new black art. It had been in real existence for little more than a quarter of a

'Cupid reviving Her' drawing (B36)

'Cupid reviving Her' woodcut (B36)

The Love of the Earth friend, this is what I came out for to see: this many-gabled old house built by the simple country-folk of the long-past times, regardless of all the turmoil that was going on in cities and courts, is lovely still amidst all the beauty which these latter days have created; & I do not wonder at our friends tending it carefully and making much of it. It seems to me as if it had waited for these happy days, and held in it the gathered crumbs of happiness of the confused and turbulent past." ❡ She led me up close to the house, and laid her shapely sun-browned hand and arm on the lichened wall as if to embrace it, and cried out: "O me! O me! How I love the earth, and the seasons, and weather, and all things that deal with it, & all that grows out of it, as this has done!" ❡ I could not answer her, or say a word. Her exultation and pleasure were so keen and exquisite, & her beauty, so delicate, yet so interfused with energy, expressed it so fully, that any added word would have been commonplace and futile. I dreaded lest the others should come in suddenly and break the spell she had cast about me; but we stood there a while by the corner of the big gable of the house, and no one came. I heard the merry voices some way off presently, & knew that they were going along the river to the great meadow on the other side of the house and garden. ❡ We drew back a little, & looked up at the house: the door and the windows were open to the fragrant sun-cured air; from the upper window-sills hung festoons of

292

▲ *The Golden Type*

I any the more: though it would indeed be hard if there were nothing else in the world, no wonders, no terrors, no unspeakable beauties. Yet when we think what a small part of the world's history, past, present, & to come, is this land we live in, and how much smaller still in the history of the arts, & yet how our forefathers clung to it, and with what care and

▲ *The Troy Type*

▼ *The Chaucer Type (See Note 1, p182)*

not see how these can be better spent than in making life cheerful & honourable for others and for ourselves; and the gain of good life to the country at large that would result from men seriously setting about the bettering of the decency of our big towns would be priceless, even if nothing specially good befell the arts in consequence: I do not know that it would; but I should begin to think matters hopeful if men turned their attention to such things, and I repeat that, unless they do so, we can scarcely even begin with any hope our endeavours for the bettering of the Arts. (From the lecture called The Lesser Arts, in Hopes and Fears for Art, by William Morris, pages 22 and 33.)

century when Jenson's Pliny was printed, from which Morris took his first steps as type-designer. From these same books too, modelled directly as they were on the MS tradition, he took his canons of proportion and the principle of the spread page as the unit of design.

A lot has been made of the use of ornament in the books of the Kelmscott Press, and there is a persistent general idea of them as over-decorated, 'Gothic' and unreadable, an anti-quarian diversion, out of place in the development of modern design, of book-production for the twentieth century which, after all, was only four years away when Morris died. In a note written for an American lecturer, Morris set out his typographical principles thus:

'I began printing books with the hope of producing some which would have a definite claim to beauty, while at the same time they should be easy to read and not dazzle the eye, or trouble the intellect of the reader by eccentricity of form in the letters. I have always been a great admirer of the

calligraphy of the Middle Ages, and of the earlier printing which took its place. As to the fifteenth century books, I noticed that they were always beautiful by force of the mere typography, even without the added ornament, with which many of them are so lavishly supplied. And it was the essence of my undertaking to produce books which it would be a pleasure to look upon as pieces of printing and arrangement of type.'

Did Morris practise what he preached? The answer is, emphatically, yes. Most of those who have ascribed to him a passion for overloading his books with ornament have in mind only the great *Chaucer*, the biggest and most magnificent of the Kelmscott productions; they entirely ignore the many other, simply dressed books, from the Press. Nor do they really look at this sumptuous book analytically. It has 554 pages. Of these, 87 bear illustrations by Burne-Jones, each set in a magnificent border. Twenty-nine other pages without illustration have borders, some with very large initial letters. The solidly patterned title page from Morris's hand makes, with the rest, 117 decorated to 437 plain pages. Two pages in 13 are illustrated and bordered. Two in 37 have borders only. In every 19 pages, 15 are plain. And this is a great ceremonious table-book. Nor, on grounds of price, can the usual criticism of the Kelmscott Press productions be sustained. These books, of the finest materials and workmanship, not intended for the open market, but in the first place in small editions of 20 or so, as gifts for friends, were far from dear. Several were priced at 30 shillings, two at seven shillings and sixpence, two at ten shillings. Morris's own lecture on *Gothic Architecture*, half a crown.

And lastly, far from least, the influence of Morris's work at the Kelmscott Press, inspiration though it was to the other private presses that followed it – Ricketts, Pissarro,

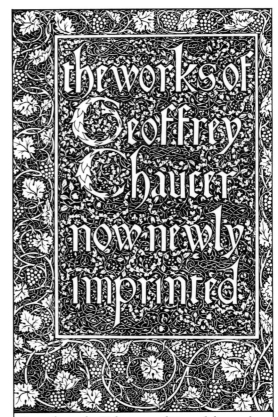

Page from the Kelmscott edition of the works of Geoffrey Chaucer (B26)

Ashbee, St John Hornby and, of course, Emery Walker and Cobden Sanderson with their Doves Press – was very real in commercial printing. It was, though, the enterprising and most modern printers of the USA and above all of Germany who saw what Morris was up to, and who began to follow his example on the large commercial scale.

103

Textiles at Kelmscott, an Introduction

Jacqueline Herald

The collection of textiles at Kelmscott Manor represents a wide range of designs and techniques executed by Morris himself, his family and friends, and the Firm. It includes printed cottons, examples of machine-woven and hand-knotted carpets, embroidered panels and tapestries, as well as lengths of woven fabric – an area considered by Morris to be far nobler and of greater importance than the chintzes and wallpapers which have received more scholarly and popular attention. Acquired from a variety of sources and over a considerable span of time, the collection registers the range of Morris's involvement in textile design. For instance, though conceived by one and the same man, the early hanging repeatedly patterned with his motto 'If I can' and embroidered by Morris in about 1857 belongs to a world far removed from the pieces of textile sold from Morris and Company's shop in George Street, Hanover Square. Examples of the latter, bought in the late 1920s and now at Kelmscott, are frequently inferior to the originals produced by the Firm during Morris's lifetime. Also to be found at Kelmscott are modern printings of wallpapers and chintzes; they are generally evocative of Morris's love of pattern, though the colourways and the redrawing of blocks on to screens for printing are sometimes unfaithful to the original.

This sense of distance between the designer and the maker is an issue about which Morris passionately struggled. Some of his feelings are expressed in the following letter, written by Morris to an American lady admirer of his work: *'I have tried to produce goods which should be genuine as far as their mere substances are concerned, and should have on that account the primary beauty in them which belongs to naturally treated natural substances; have tried, for instance, to make woollen substances as woollen as possible, cotton as cottony as possible, and so on; have used only the dyes which are natural and simple, because they produce beauty almost without the intervention of art; all this quite apart from the design in the stuffs or what not. On that head it has been, chiefly because of the social difficulties, almost impossible to do more than to insure the designer (mostly myself) some pleasure in his art by getting him to understand the qualities of materials and the happy chances of processes. Except with a small part of the more artistic side of the work, I could not do anything (or at least but little) to give this pleasure to the workmen, because I should have had to change their method of work so utterly that I should have disqualified them from earning their living elsewhere. You see I have got to understand thoroughly the manner of work under which the art of the Middle Ages was done, and that that is the only manner of work which can turn out popular art, only to discover that it is impossible to work in that manner in this profit-grinding society. So on all sides I am driven towards revolution as the only hope, and am clearer and clearer on the speedy advent of it in a very obvious form, though of course I can't give a date for it.'*[1]

The process of selecting textiles for the Farnham exhibition was quite rigorous. For, rather than attempt to present a comprehensive survey of Morris's work in this field, as was done in Birmingham in April 1981, two specific aspects were chosen – namely, his use of red and blue and his impressions of birds in their design context. The articles which follow shall, it is hoped, offer new ways of approaching Morris through very specific channels.

1 J. Leatham, *William Morris Master of Many Crafts. A Study*, Deveron Press, Turrif, 4th ed, 1934, pp51–2.

'Bullerswood' type pile carpet (T6) ▶

104

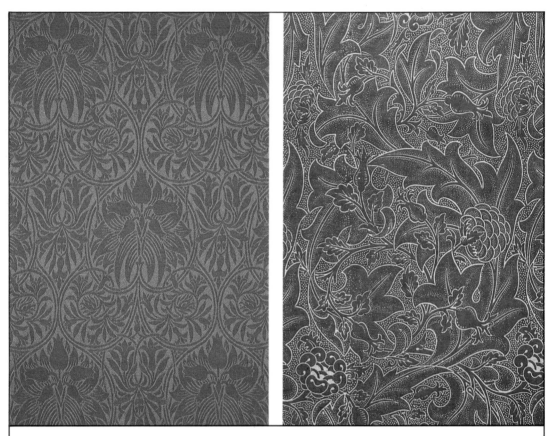

Above left: The red worsted damask 'Crown Imperial' is woven in two tones of madder. Designed in 1876, it was based on a fifteenth-century Rhenish block-printed linen, the paired birds of which have been substituted by the crown imperial flower (T14). Above right: The design for 'Lea' was registered in 1885, though this piece postdates 1917 for it was sold from the company's showrooms in George Street, Hanover Square. It is a resist-dyed mid-tone indigo and bears a label with the number 3015, which corresponds with a recipe in the Merton dyebook (T23)

'Red and Blue'

Deryn O'Connor

'"*Red* and *Blue*" he used to say in his full-blooded way.'[1] So Walter Crane remembered.

These colours seem to represent richness, generosity and honesty for Morris. After playing a major part in his stained glass they became for him the great colours, as he involved himself in work on textiles and learnt the properties of dyes and fibres. They presented him with enormous problems, his greatest struggle being the achievement of his choice of red and blue in his printed cottons. In this article an attempt is made to elucidate what led to the production of such cloths as 'Strawberry Thief', 'Wandle' and 'Evenlode'.

Although it was not until at least 1883 that Morris mastered the use of red and blue in his textiles he had early on shown a feeling for these colours produced by the dyes he was later to use himself. 'I remember', he said, at the opening of the Manchester Art and Industrial Exhibition in 1882, 'when I was first setting up house 23 years ago, and two or three friends of mine were in the same plight, what a rummage there used to be for anything tolerable. On the whole I remember we had to fall back on turkey-red cotton and dark blue serge.'[2] These were everyday unsophisticated cloths within reach of everyone's purse. Turkey-red cotton was the plain full red cloth that can be seen enlivening nineteenth-century patchworks, a colour produced from madder dye by a long and complicated series of processes. Blue serge was the simple indigo-dyed worsted cloth made for ordinary suitings. The serge wall-hangings that Janey Morris and friends embroidered for the main bedroom at Red House survive at Kelmscott Manor. Morris himself wore indigo-dyed wool, cotton and linen almost as a uniform. Mackail reports: 'In his suit of blue serge and soft felt hat, he had something of the look of a working engineer and something of a sailor', and refers to 'the blue cotton shirts

which, in later years, became his invariable dress and almost of the essence of his appearance'. There is mention of his 'French workman's blouse'.[3] The members of our generation whose uniform is blue jeans are instinctively wearing them for the same reasons that William Morris wore his blue – partly social and partly aesthetic. They are the hard-wearing clothes of work, and they are dyed with indigo which gives a particularly sympathetic blue even when it loses strength through use. It was these dyes, indigo for blue and madder for red, which became the most important for Morris and with which he had the greatest tussle.

At the height of his career, Morris said:
Do not fall into the trap of a dingy, bilious-looking yellow-green, a colour to which I have a special and personal hatred, because (if you will excuse my mentioning personal matters) I have been supposed to have somewhat brought it into vogue. I assure you I am not really responsible for it.[4]
In the 1880s, the textiles produced in Morris's own workshops increasingly exploited the use of red and blue. The Hammersmith hand-knotted rugs and carpets often have blue as the background in the central area and red for the ground in the borders. This arrangement can be seen in the huge carpet now in the attic at Kelmscott Manor. In 1893, Morris wrote:
On the whole, in designing carpets, the method of contrast is the best one to employ, and blue and red, quite frankly used, with white or very light outlines on a dark ground, and black or some very dark colour on a light ground, are the main colours on which the designer should depend.[5]
His hand-woven wool furnishing fabrics of the 1880s also depend to a great extent on red and blue. 'Tulip and Net' plays on varying tones of blue, 'Violet and Columbine' red and blue, while 'Bird' comes in a blue version and a red version. In connection with the chintzes, Morris said:

'In the many-coloured printed cloths, frank red and blue are again the mainstays of the colour arrangement, these colours softened by the paler shades of red, outlined with black and made more tender by the additions of yellow in small quantities, mostly forming part of brightish green, make up the colouring of the old Persian prints, which carry the art as far as it can be carried.'[6]

The dyes on which Morris came to rely were traditional: the plant dye madder and the insect dyes cochineal and kermes for red shades, and the plant dye indigo for blue. These at different strengths formed the basis of a wider palette produced by overdyeing or overprinting with each other or with the addition of the plant dye weld, which gives varying shades of yellow. It took him, however, from about 1874, when he became seriously involved in dyeing, until 1883 to master these dyes, or rather to learn to work with them. 'The art of dyeing is a difficult one, needing for its practice a good craftsman, with plenty of experience', he wrote in 1889.[7] Morris chose to use processes that were tedious and tricky rather than to employ the newer synthetic dyes of easier application that were being accepted in industry in the 1870s and 1880s. The easier dyes included not only those which rapidly followed Perkin's discovery of mauve in 1856, referred to by Morris as aniline dyes and today as basic dyestuffs, but also Prussian blue obtained from potassium ferro-cyanide and much used since the 1830s, as well as a treated form of indigo known as indigo carmine, which was used for level dyeing on wool. There were also pigments used for printing, such as ultramarine for blue and lead chromate for orange and yellow. All these suffered from one defect or another, particularly poor fastness to light or washing.

It should be remembered that many of the dyes from plants and woods that had been in use in Europe for generations were also fugitive. In the old dyebooks that Morris consulted, these were referred to as the Lesser Dyes. He would have none of them. He wanted the best, so he limited himself to using what were known as the Great Dyes. That meant using the best dyestuffs available and the best methods for achieving a fast colour on yarn or cloth, even though this might involve difficult processes. In general the dyes used in Morris and Company's textiles have lasted well, although where the printed cloths have been in position for some time, as with 'Kennet' and 'Strawberry Thief' at Kelmscott Manor, the indigo blue has faded from a dark to a medium blue. Morris was aware that this would happen but he liked the gentler blue that indigo becomes on fading. Although Morris chose to use traditional dyes he did not ignore contemporary developments in chemistry, as will be seen when indigo is discussed. Morris's first excursion into dyeing was with embroidery silks and wools, but before long he learned a number of lessons – which all dyers have to learn – concerning the differences in behaviour towards dyes and chemicals of fibres of different origin. In his day the main division was between those derived from animal sources – wool and silk – and those of vegetable origin, such as cotton and linen. The dyes he chose for red illustrate this well. Silk and wool yarns readily take up metallic salts such as alum, a process known as mordanting, which is the necessary preliminary before dyeing in madder, kermes or cochineal, and also in weld for yellow. Even so he wrote from Leek in March 1876: 'I am dyeing yellow and reds: the yellows are very easy to come by, so are a lot of shades of salmon and flesh colour and buff and orange: my chief difficulty is in getting a deep blood red.'[8]

Cotton and linen are a different matter. Cochineal and kermes have never found great use on these fibres: madder is the dye for red which spans all natural fibres, whether of animal or vegetable origin. Even so cotton and linen need considerable persuasion to take up the necessary amounts of metallic mordants to build up a good red shade. To produce the colour of the Turkey Red cloth Morris had bought when setting up house, the method was to treat the cloth repeatedly in an emulsion made from olive oil and a weak solution of soda; then to hang the material for hours in a hot chamber between each treatment to dry and 'age', prior to dyeing in the madder bath. There is no record that Morris used this process on cloth himself.

There are additional problems to be faced when printing madder. This was still the accepted dye for achieving red on cotton, as it is exceptionally fast to light and washing. When Morris began to commission printed cloths from Thomas Wardle in 1875, the first design, 'Marigold', was printed in monochrome, including alum madder red. One of Wardle's men was an expert: 'Kay is a madder printer and knows nothing about steam colours', wrote Morris.[9] He spent much time at the print works watching the various processes in order to understand them, but as far as can be ascertained he did not carry them out himself. Much additional skill is involved in printing madder because the mordants must be applied only where the design is required. The whole cloth is then dyed in the madder bath. There is no direct way of printing madder. One great problem is to ensure that loose mordant does not lead to staining of the ground during the dyeing. Great care is therefore necessary before dyeing to clear any unfixed oil and alum from the cloth. The technical term for this is dunging, and the word describes the process: the cloth was traditionally passed through a succession of baths made from cow dung let down with water. Morris did not dislike a tinge of creamy pink in the grounds of his red prints and in a letter to Wardle he took

issue with Bancroft, an early-nineteenth-century authority on dyeing: 'The other point he has at heart is the clearing of the grounds to a bright white which would naturally destroy our cloth to our ideas.'[10] Later, when Morris came to print velveteens at Merton Abbey, he deliberately used a red print on a pale red ground to give a rich effect. Several tones of red in one cloth can be simply achieved by using different strengths of alum mordant.

In 1869 the colouring matter of the madder plant, known as alizarin, was synthesised and ten years later this was being used in industry. The processes described are still necessary to produce the fastest colours. Direct printing developed by steaming eliminated the dyeing, but in this case the finest results required the preliminary preparation of the cloth in oil. Alizarin gave greater constancy of shade. All vegetable dyestuffs vary with soil and climate. In the years of Morris's greatest involvement with dyeing at Merton Abbey madder only was probably used but the anniversary booklet of 1911 states: 'The best alizarin dyes have been adopted by Morris and Company for some years past, but only as an addition to, not as a substitute for, the older vegetable dyes, which continue to be used by them for dyeing all the silks and wools used in their woven fabrics and embroideries.'[11]

The position regarding blue in textiles in the 1870s was different from that of reds. Indigo, as has been implied with reference to serge, was regularly used for dyeing wool blue but it was going out for silk. In 1862 Nicholson had discovered an easily applied acid dye which gave a brighter blue than indigo. In March 1876, in a letter from Leek, where he was learning to dye with Wardle, Morris wrote:

This morning I assisted at the dyeing of twenty pounds of silk (for our damask) in the blue vat: it was very exciting, as the thing is quite unused now and we ran a good chance of spoiling the silk. There were four dyers and Mr Wardle at work, and myself as dyer's mate: the men were encouraged with beer and to it they went, and pretty it was to see the silk coming green out of the vat and gradually turning blue; we succeeded very well as far as we can tell at present: the oldest of the workmen, an old fellow of seventy, remembers silk being dyed so, long ago.[12]

The old French and English dyebooks which Morris read abound with recipes for indigo on different fibres. Indigo dyes most natural fibres, although it is a faster dye on wool than it is on cotton. Special vats were advocated for different purposes, for example, for light blues. By the 1870s greater knowledge of chemistry had begun to alter certain practices. The use of sodium hydrosulphite as a reducing agent in the indigo vat was replacing some of the older methods. In the same letter quoted above Morris wrote:

'Tomorrow I am going to Nottingham to see wool dyed blue in the woad vat, as it is called.'[12]

This was a survival of an old method in which some woad was used with indigo to assist in 'setting' the indigo vat.

Indigo works in a completely different way from madder, cochineal and kermes. As we have seen, in order to make these reds the cloth or yarn has to be mordanted with metallic salts. Indigo and woad (which are chemically allied) need no mordants, but the fibres must be immersed in dye when it is dissolved in a vat in a reduced state. The dye fixes on the yarn or cloth and turns blue when oxidised in the air. The 'setting' of the vat is the dissolving of the indigo by various means to produce the reduced state. The vat is never stable, but always slightly changing its nature and the dyer must watch and adjust it. Morris wrote in 1875:

'We dyed a lock of wool bright blue in it, and left the liquor a clear primrose colour, so all will be

ready for dyeing tomorrow in it. Though, by the way, if you are a dyer, you must call it her.'[13]

In March 1876, he wrote with less confidence to Mrs Burne-Jones:

'We have set a blue vat for cotton, which I hope will turn out all right tomorrow morning: it is nine feet deep and holds one thousand gallons: it would be a week's talk to tell you all the anxieties and possibilities connected with this indigo subject; but you must at least imagine that all this is going on in very nearly the same conditions as those of the shepherd boy that made a watch all by himself.'[14]

A remark in a letter from Padua two years later, while he was on a visit to Italy, makes clear how involved Morris was with the complexities of indigo dyeing:

'A dyer's hand-cart came by us with a load of blue work (cotton) just done: I was so sorry I could not talk with one of the men, who looked good-tempered and intelligent.'[15]

By that time Morris had tried dyeing cotton, silk and wool in indigo and knew about the vagaries of hot vats, cold vats, woad vats, hydrosulphite vats and so on, including one he referred to as *'Cuve d'Inde'* which used bran and madder in the vat. Morris wrote characteristically at one point: 'I utterly distrust the cold vat and his ways and works.'[16]

It was, however, indigo in relation to printed textiles that caused him the most anguish and frustration, yet this led him to the great achievement of his multi-coloured indigo discharge chintzes. When he gave his first commission for printed cottons to Clarksons, he discovered that the current practice there was to use Prussian blue – on its own for blue and also as the basis for greens. He came to dislike this on two counts: that the greens were ugly and that the Prussian blue was not fast to alkalis and therefore did not stand severe washing. It seemed logical that if indigo could be used to dye cotton, it should be possible to apply it by printing. Because of his dissatisfaction with Clarksons, Morris transferred his problem to Wardles. One can almost hear Thomas Wardle and his men telling Morris that indigo could not be printed because the dye oxidised too quickly before meeting the cloth in a printing process. Morris refused to be put off. He found various recipes to try as in the past indigo had been used for some printing. He made trials himself at Queen Square and proudly presented his samples to Wardle with the remark:

'I suspect Kay don't know as much on the subject as the present writer, who now sendeth you a piece of cloth pencilled in (nothing will do but the chewed willow twig) by his own hand!'

Later in the same letter he added: 'I should say that I consider my pencil-blue as a good colour to go with the madders, and I am sure very good greens could be got with it. I should mention that I have used it unthickened, and that it is the glucose receipt that seems the best I have tried yet.'[17]

He made Wardle try out this method of printing indigo and in August 1876 asked him for a 'fent of African Marigold with the blue in indigo'.[18] Later in the month Morris wrote to Wardle: 'The indigo printing seems quite a success now and I am very pleased and congratulate you on it.'[19]

But there is often a difference between what can be done on samples and what can be produced on a large scale. Knecht and Fothergill wrote in their classic book on textile printing:

'These processes were very difficult to control – the rapid oxidisation of the indigo-white rendering it almost impossible to obtain regularity of shade – and, although certain of them were, to some extent, employed in practice, they were never satisfactory, and one and all became obsolete immediately upon the publication in 1883, of Adolf

Schlieper's glucose process.'[20]

There is evidence from the Merton Abbey Dyebook[21] in the Berger collection that Morris tried having 'Brother Rabbit' and 'Bird and Anemone' printed in indigo when he set up his own print workshop. But it was not plain sailing. Morris wrote on 19 December 1882:

'As to our printing, we are really not quite straight yet: I am quite ashamed of it: however they are doing Brother Rabbit successfully, and the Anemone will go on now, and when we are once out of this difficulty, I really think we shall have seen the worst of it.'[22]

One cannot conclude that Morris was referring to the indigo print as there are samples of 'Brother Rabbit' in the Merton Dyebook printed in madder and buff, but it does emphasise that there were printing problems and it is significant that before long Morris had settled on another method of achieving a pattern in blue: indigo discharge.

Morris had looked with more knowledge at the patterned cottons from India and Persia that he so much admired. In the East the traditional method of producing blues and greens, still to be found among some of the Indian cottons being imported into England today, was to resist areas to be kept undyed before dipping the whole cloth into indigo. Waxes and starch pastes of various kinds have been used. Morris realised that dyeing in indigo was the answer but chose to use in the main a chemically more sophisticated method of patterning – the discharging of the colour after the cloth had been dyed in the indigo vat. He was tapping the scientific developments of his own time and not relying on ancient methods. There is evidence again from the Merton Abbey Dyebook that certain designs, including 'Lea', were also printed using a printed resist prior to dyeing in indigo.[23]

Indigo was synthesised in 1880 and produced

commercially after 1897, but as with madder the methods used to produce the colour on cloth remained the same.

The final move in both technique and design for the chintzes was to unite the processes for achieving blue and red on the same cloth with yellow superimposed to give the richness of colours Morris enjoyed in the Indian palampores. He excluded a feature common in the eastern cloths: outlines in black. An iron mordant is printed on cloth soaked in tannic to give a black. Iron tends to dirty the reds and to discolour the ground so that the blue is less clear. By careful designing, Morris made his blue background serve as his outlines, so keeping the clarity of his reds and blues and reducing the number of processes.

The full process used to produce the multi-coloured chintzes such as 'Strawberry Thief', 'Wandle' and 'Evenlode' is described by Morris and Company in their anniversary booklet of 1911:

'The cotton cloth is first dyed to a uniform dark shade of blue in one of the large indigo vats, and is printed with a bleaching reagent which either reduces or removes the blue colour as required by the design. Mordants are then printed on the white parts, where the red has to come, and the whole cloth is dyed a second time with madder. The process is repeated a third time for yellow, the three colours being superimposed on each other to give green, purple, or orange. All loose colouring matter is then cleared away, and the colours are set by passing the fabric through soap at almost boiling heat. The final treatment is to spread the cloth on the grass with its printed face to the light, so that the whites may be purified and all fugitive colour removed in nature's own way. This process is called "crofting", and the meadows round the

◀ *'Wandle' designed by Morris in 1884 (T22)*

works in fine weather are bright and gay with long strips of many-coloured material stretched upon the buttercups and daisies.'[24]

By now the reader of this article may understand why the writer of the 1911 booklet preceded this description by saying:

'In these days, when hand-printed cottons are common, and many of them good, the difficulties which attended Morris's first efforts are not easy to realise. But for some years they were a source of considerable expense and loss which was only by degrees made up.'[24]

One can picture the situation that provoked Morris to write on 28 February 1883:

'We are not getting on quite as fast as we should with the printing: it is very tough work getting everything in due order, the cloths seem to want so much doing to them before they can be printed, and then so much doing to them after they are printed.'[25]

One can also understand how heartfelt was Morris's opinion on the art of designing for printed textiles:

'As to the craft among ourselves, it has, as a matter of course suffered grievously from the degradation of dyeing, and this not only from the worsening of the tints both in beauty and durability, but from a more intricate cause. I have said that the older dyes were much more difficult to use than the modern ones. The processes for getting a coloured pattern on to a piece of cotton, even a short while back when I was a boy, were many and difficult. As a rule, this is done in fewer hours than it was in days then . . . The natural and healthy difficulties of the old processes, all connected as they were with the endeavour to make the colour stable, drove any designer who had anything in him, to making his pattern peculiarly suitable to the whole art, and gave a character to it – that character which you so easily recognise in Indian palampores, or in the faded curtains of our grandmothers' time, which

still, in spite of many a summer's sun and many a strenuous washing, retain at least their reds and blues. In spite of the rudeness or the extravagance of these things, we are always attracted towards them, and the chief reason is that we feel at once that there is something about the designs natural to the craft, that they can be done only by the practice of it; a quality which, I must once more repeat, is a necessity for all the designs of the lesser arts. But in the comparatively easy way in which these cloths are printed today . . . there are no special difficulties to stimulate the designer to invention; he can get any design done on his cloth; the printer will make no objections, so long as the pattern is the right size for his roller, and has only the due number of colours. The result of all this is ornament on the cotton, which might just as well have been printed or drawn on paper, and in spite of any grace or cleverness in the design, it is found to look poor and tame and wiry. That you will see clearly enough when someone has had a fancy to imitate some of the generous and fertile patterns that were once specially designed for the older cloth; it all comes to nothing – it is dull, hard, unsympathetic. No: there is nothing for it but the trouble and the simplicity of the earlier craft, if you are to have any beauty in cloth-printing at all. And if not, why should we trouble to have a pattern of any sort on our cotton-cloths? I for one am dead against it, unless the pattern is really beautiful; it is so very worthless if it is not.'[26]

1 Walter Crane, *William Morris to Whistler*, London, 1911, p4.
2 J. W. Mackail, *The Life of William Morris*, London, 1901, 2nd edition, vol 1, p311.
3 *Ibid*, p217.
4 William Morris, 'Hopes and Fears for Art', quoted in Morris and Company Decorators Ltd, London, *Decoration*.
5 William Morris in *Arts and Crafts Essays*, London, 1893, p26.
6 *Ibid*, p32.
7 William Morris, 'Of Dyeing as an Art', in the catalogue of the second exhibition of the Arts and Crafts Society 1889.
8 J. W. Mackail, *op cit*, vol 1, p326.
9 William Morris, *Letter to Thomas Wardle*, 3 August 1875. Unpublished MS in Victoria and Albert Museum, London.
10 *Ibid*, 3 September 1875.
11 Morris and Company, *A Brief Sketch of the Morris Movement*, London, 1911, p30.
12 William Morris in a letter to Mrs Coronio in J. W. Mackail, *op cit*, vol 1, p326.
13 *Ibid*, vol 1, p318.
14 *Ibid*, vol 1, p325.
15 *Ibid*, vol 1, p369.
16 William Morris, *Letter to Thomas Wardle*, 10 July 1877. MS in Victoria and Albert Museum, London.
17 *Ibid*, 23 November 1875.
18 *Ibid*, August 1876.
19 *Ibid*, 24 August 1876.
20 E. Knecht and J. B. Fothergill, *The Principles and Practice of Textile Printing*, 2nd edition, London, 1924.
21 Berger Collection (Morris & Co Archives) entry no 50 in *Morris & Co Catalogue*, Stanford, 1975.
22 J. W. Mackail, *op cit*, vol 2, p88.
23 Berger Collection (Morris & Co Archives) entries no 53 and 54 in *Morris & Co Catalogue*, Stanford, 1975.
24 Morris and Company, *A Brief Sketch of the Morris Movement*, 1911, p41.
25 J. W. Mackail, *op cit*, vol 2, p100.
26 William Morris, 'Arts and Crafts Essays' quoted in Aymer Vallance, *William Morris His Art His Writings and His Public Life*, London, 1897, p101.

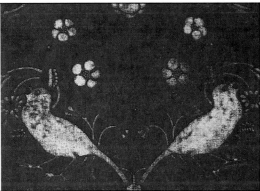

Above left: The right side of 'Strawberry Thief', a design registered in 1883. The fabric, first dyed in indigo, was then printed with two strengths of discharge to achieve mid-blue and white areas (indicated on the reverse, above right), and subsequently with three other colours to yield a vivid polychromatic effect (T19)

Embroidered serge curtains designed by William Morris circa 1859, worked by Janey Morris and helpers for the main bedroom at Red House, Upton, Kent (T2)

On Designing Textiles with Birds

Jacqueline Herald

To be reminded 'of the swallows sweeping above the garden boughs towards the house-eaves where their nestlings are, while the sun breaks on them',[1] or of the vine-trellis on the banks of the Nile, of wild woods and streams with dogs panting beside them, is surely better than 'having to count day after day a few sham-real boughs and flowers, casting sham-real shadows on your walls, with little hint of anything but Covent Garden in them'.[2] Morris claimed that ornamental art – the real art, the art of the people – through the observation of nature and the patterning of suggestive rather than imitative forms, should remind us 'of the outward face of the earth'.[3]

Such impressions of nature were particularly appropriate to the decoration of the walls of a room. 'Bird', a woven cloth produced in 1878, was one of Morris's favourite designs and the Firm's first textile pattern to include a bird motif. It was used in the same year in his drawing-room at Kelmscott House, Hammersmith – a first-floor room 40 feet long with five windows at one end overlooking the river and through which, on a sunny day, reflections of the water would be directed across the ceiling. Harmonising with the blue carpet on the floor, the walls were hung with 'Bird' – 'a perfect blue with pale gleams of colour in the birds and foliage'.[4] It was hung from within two feet of the ceiling to the skirting. 'The cloth is hooked to the top rail, and is but slightly plaited – only just enough modulation of the surface being allowed to just break the pattern here and there. The beautiful effect of a long wall hung in this way is quite inconceivable, and we much regret that we have not space for showing this use of the material', stated the brochure of

◀ Detail of 'Bird', the treble cloth designed by William Morris in 1878, and which hung in his drawing room (T8)

Morris and Company at the Boston Foreign Fair in 1883.[5]

Birds were extremely important to Morris; he delighted in studying their habits, movements and songs. In the Red Lion Square days of the late 1850s he occasionally amused himself by visiting the Zoological Gardens. After observing some of the 'greater' birds, he would return home and 'imitate an eagle with considerable skill and humour, climbing onto a chair and, after a sullen pause, coming down with a soft heavy flop'.[6] Later, in a letter to Lady Burne-Jones probably written in 1889, Morris included one of the many refreshing descriptions of the birds he habitually watched in the Upper Thames Valley while at Kelmscott Manor. The shape of wings, sense of movement and patterns of plumage were all features to which Morris alluded in his bird designs.

'The birds were very beautiful about us; I have been of late so steeped in London that it was a quite fresh pleasure to see the rooks about, who have been very busy in this showery weather. There was no lack of herons in these upper waters, and in the twilight the stint or summer snipe was crying about us and flitting from under the bank and across the stream: such a clean-made, neat-feathered, light grey little chap he is, with a wild musical little note, like all the moor-haunting birds . . .'[7]

He was never at a loss for words to describe birds in their natural surroundings, yet the portrayal of them in designs did not come easily to Morris. The 'green trees with gaily-coloured birds among them'[8] of the embroidery 'If I Can' are now much faded. The birds are weakly drawn, but nevertheless demonstrate his determination to incorporate them in his patterns, their beaks and tail-plumes giving rhythm and direction to the repeat of the textile, their wings adding pattern and colour. Also important is the relationship between the birds and the plant forms. Morris did not, however, persevere with birds at this stage, and designated the task of drawing beasts and birds to Philip Webb in the early days of the Firm. The Japanese-style birds in the 'Trellis' wallpaper of 1862 were by Webb, superimposed on a somewhat awkward background grid drawn by Morris.

It was not until 1877 that Morris showed signs of a real attempt to incorporate his own drawings of birds in a textile design. In a letter to Thomas Wardle he mentioned: 'I am studying birds now to see if I can't get some of them into my next design.'[9] The result was 'Bird' – a far more controlled, informed and sophisticated design than the embroidered hanging of 20 years earlier. In the meantime, Morris had learned much about dyes, particularly those used for red and blue. The earlier piece, being embroidered, was unimpeded by mechanical necessity to conform to repeats, but nevertheless shows a desire to master pattern. But one significant difference between the two textiles lies in the arrangement of the birds. In the first, the birds all face in one direction. In the second, the diagonal line of the bird's body and the alternation of bird and plant remain evident; but the whole is much more carefully drawn and, most significantly, the birds appear in pairs. This mirror image, constituting a 'turnover' pattern, is an emphatic feature of the textiles designed from 1876 to 1883 – Morris's most prolific period of pattern design, in which 11 wallpapers and 22 chintzes were produced. These formal mirrored repeats mark a strong contrast to the small number of flowing, spontaneous and naturalistic designs of his early phase of chintz production – 'Honeysuckle' of 1876 being one example. They are a result of Morris's studies of textiles in the South Kensington Museum (particularly after 1876 when he became an examiner there), and

especially of woven fabrics which are easier to point and set up on a loom if arranged in a 'turnover' manner.

It was in the later 1870s that Morris began to express great interest and excitement in the prospect of producing carpets and woven textiles. In the letter mentioned above[10] Morris exclaimed: 'I am dazzled at the prospect of the splendid work we might turn out in that line'; but first he had to trace skilled weavers who would help implement his plans. Employed for a year in 1877–8, a Frenchman named Bazin, found through a contact of Wardle's, helped him set up jacquard looms, after which time Morris possessed considerable technical knowledge of figured weaving and even more enthusiasm for the subject.

This is evident in one of Morris's notebooks,[11] datable to about 1879, in which he lists some of the textile pieces acquired by the South Kensington Museum. He was sifting his way through a number of boxes which contained 432 specimens of textiles. His scribbled remarks pinpoint the purposes for which he might use his findings. 'One piece of figured stuff of use educationally' probably refers to a North Italian silk of the thirteenth or fourteenth century. Such a textile would feature pairs of animals or birds, the same design convention appearing in those net and peacock patterns of the early sixteenth century on which Morris remarked. One, he considered, bore an 'early feeling in a late piece of stuff', while the other was noted as 'a useful pattern' and in very good condition. Another piece of figured textile in the same collection, 'green and gold with queer cutting on it', and probably dating to the late seventeenth century, is described as 'remarkable but not good to be imitated'.

Morris claimed that pattern-design was 'the ornamentation of a surface by work that is not imitative or historical, at any rate, not principally or essentially so'.[12] Nevertheless, a comparison of some of his textile designs with examples belonging to the South Kensington Museum offers striking parallels in the arrangement of pattern repeats and in the use of birds. The most common link is the pairing of birds, either facing or turning away from each other, the outline of their bodies and tails defining the lines of the 'net' – a repeat composed of rows of lozenges. The birds give shape to the pattern and thus a degree of order and restfulness; at the same time, because they contain interest of colour and form in themselves, they help disguise the formula by which the net has been assembled. This is evident in 'Bird'; but a more complex combination of mystery and clarity appears in 'Peacock' of the same year (1878).

'Crown Imperial', a worsted damask first produced in 1876, is interesting because it does not contain birds. The design is based on a fifteenth-century block-printed Rhenish linen,[13] itself a cheap version of a woven fabric produced in the preceding century. It features pairs of birds; but these are abandoned by Morris and substituted with the crown imperial flower. The explanation for this is twofold. First, Morris lacked confidence in the drawing of birds, for he was to make conscious efforts in 1877 to remedy the situation before producing 'Bird'. More significantly, however, the rendering of birds in a monochrome damask weave would not have enhanced their form, because it would have required the subtlest shading and spotting of wing and feather features in the construction of the weave, and the resulting textile would have fallen into the category of fussy eighteenth-century brocades which to Morris typified unnecessary and distasteful design.

In propounding his hopes and fears for art in a paper entitled 'Making the Best of It' (c1879),

Morris demonstrated his preference for the woven silks of the early Renaissance:

'Compare, for instance, those Sicilian and other silk cloths I have mentioned with the brocades (common everywhere) turned out from the looms of Lyons, Venice and Genoa, at the end of the seventeenth and beginning of the eighteenth centuries. The first perfectly simple in manufacture, trusting wholly to beauty of design, and the play of light on the naturally woven surface, while the latter eke out their gaudy feebleness with spots and ribs and long floats, and all kinds of meaningless tormenting of the web, till there is nothing to be learned of them save a warning.'[14]

Far more effective than such multi-coloured brocades are the weave structures used for the rendering of birds in 'Peacock', a heavy twill, and in 'Bird', a treble-woven cloth. The former is large enough in scale to offer bold areas of colour and to demonstrate the weight and texture of the wool. The forms are bound by a very firm outline, emphasised by the strong contrasts of colour between one area and the next. In the latter, the nature of the weave is such that where the warps cross to change colour, a slight contour is created around each area within the repeat, and so offers relief to the design. 'Mechanical weaving has to repeat the pattern on the cloth within comparatively narrow limits; the number of colours is limited in most cases to four or five. In most cloths so woven, therefore, the best plan seems to be to choose a pleasant ground colour and to superimpose a pattern mainly composed of either a lighter shade of that colour, or a colour in no very strong contrast to the ground; and then, if you are using several colours, to light up this general arrangement either with a more forcible outline, or by spots of stronger colour carefully disposed.'[15] In 'Bird', a lighter shade of indigo is superimposed on the deeper ground, while details of the birds' eyes, breasts and wings offer the opportunity to add spots of stronger colour.

The designs for chintzes, on the other hand, may be approached in a different way. As the surface of printed fabric is stiffer and duller than the light-reflecting woven patterns, the designs may include more detail and can be effective on a smaller scale. The pattern depends less on the striking use of large areas of colour (difficult to print in any case) and more on the drawing and cutting of blocks. The printed designs however are by no means divorced from the woven ones. In each case, the pattern arrangement is taken from historical sources; 'Brother Rabbit' and 'Strawberry Thief' of 1882 and 1883 respectively make the same use of pairs of birds as in Morris's woven designs of a few years earlier. They, and many other chintzes, imitate the introduction of bands of colour across the weft of figured woven textiles. In 'Strawberry Thief' the alternate rows of birds differ in colouring. In 'Brother Rabbit' the smaller birds appear against a dominant background and the larger rabbits are discharged in a bolder way, leaving less indigo ground to be seen; the whole effect creates alternating negative and positive bands of design.

The pattern of 'Bird and Anemone' is constructed differently. Designed in 1882 and produced as a wallpaper at almost the same time, each repeat is contained within a narrow vertical oblong. The birds are perched on stems in such a way as to emphasise the flow of movement and that essential sense of growth of the stems which sway to right and to left of the vertical axis. Yet their bodies and wings raised in preparation for flight effectively interrupt the lines of the stems which, if left bare and their direction of movement uncontended, would be far less suggestive of rambling nature; besides, the formation of the repeat would appear too obvious. The strong diagonal element in the movement of the stems gives way to the group of chintzes produced from 1883 to 1890. 'Kennet' of 1883 (hung around the walls of the green room at Kelmscott Manor) shows how the growth of flowers from each side of the main branch adds interest and a diversion to the pattern in the way that the birds did in 'Bird and Anemone'.

A similar relationship between birds and branches, and the crossing of a major stem with a subordinate one is a feature of the large attic carpet at Kelmscott, similar to the 'Bullerswood' carpet designed in 1889 and now in the Victoria and Albert Museum. Morris's textiles of the 1880s reflect his general interest in carpets, particularly those of Persia. As an adviser on the acquisition of textiles for the Museum, Morris was responsible for inspecting and reporting on those which came up for sale. In February 1883, Messrs Myers of Bond Street offered two Persian carpets to the Museum. The smallish carpet, which – despite Morris's recommendation – was not purchased, was described by him as 'on a dark blue ground, covered with a curious net pattern mingled with bold sprays partly of the wholly conventional type and partly semi-naturalistic, and also with figures of birds, one of which is Chinese in character'.[16] Similar exotic birds and vase designs would be seen in other Persian carpets at the Museum and could have been among the retail stock of Morris and Company by this date. They are the sources for the fiery-tailed phoenixes (often incorrectly described as 'dragons') featured in the 'Peacock' woven furnishing textile. Chinese-type birds also appear in the large attic carpet, their beaks craning to peck at bunches of grapes. However, the birds are not intended to represent literally a particular species for, 'owing to the comparative coarseness of the work' in carpets, 'the designs should always be very elementary in form, and

'Peacock', a composite twill designed by William Morris in 1878–9 (T9)

Unlike carpet-weaving, tapestry lends itself to 'soft gradations of tint'.[18] With tapestry, 'You really may almost turn your wall into a real rose-hedge or a deep forest, for its material and general capabilities almost compel us to fashion plane above plane of rich, crisp and varying foliage with bright blossoms, or strange birds showing through the intervals.'[19] The 'Woodpecker' tapestry in the William Morris Gallery, designed entirely by Morris in 1885, conforms to that Gothic crispness of detail. A similar use of foliage appears in the 'Vine and Acanthus' tapestry now at Kelmscott Manor, woven by Morris himself in 1879. But here the little birds are very different from those in the 'Woodpecker'; with details of wings highlighted in silk, they betray elements of the rather over-elaborate details of sixteenth-century tapestries, and even of those Gobelins of the eighteenth century which Morris so despised. At the same time, they relate closely to the types of bird that appear in 'Strawberry Thief', 'all made up of spots and stripes and flecks of broken colour'[20] – the kinds of thing we seem to desire in printed surfaces.

If Morris was so interested in birds, why did they not appear more frequently in his designs? In the way that the drawing and arrangement of plant forms must suggest interminable growth, so Morris's birds must give the impression that they can almost fly away, or eat the fruit they peck. At the same time, they are not meant to be realistic; they have a function to perform within the pattern. The shape and form of a bird is important only in so far as it assists the design; and yet it must relate to the surrounding foliage, twigs or branches and fruit, sufficiently credibly in order that one's imagination might be reminded of the real world of the countryside. Flowers and leaves are made from many different structures: the lines of their veins and branches

suggestive merely of forms of leafage, flowers, beasts and birds'.[17] Considering the scale of the knotting in the hand-woven Morris carpets and the length of the tufts used to make the quality of the wool visible, there is no way that a Morris carpet could approach the fineness of detail of the Persian originals.

The scale of the weave in tapestries, on the other hand, allows for more subtle contrasts of colour and texture in the portrayal of birds.

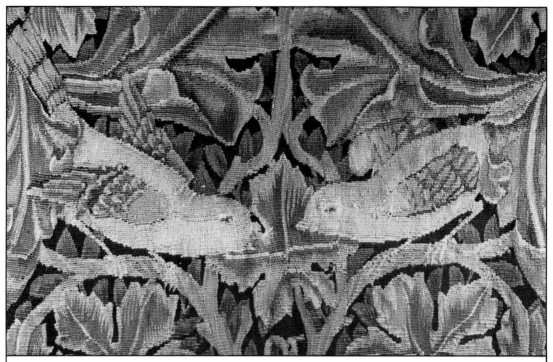

'Vine and Acanthus' tapestry, designed and woven by William Morris in 1879 (T3, see cover)

are far easier to manipulate into flowing curves than ever a credible bird would be. Nevertheless, among all Morris's textile designs incorporating beasts, birds receive far greater attention than the rabbits, squirrels or other animals of field or forest.

Acclaimed as one of the greatest masters of pattern, William Morris has received considerable attention in the history of textiles. Yet, despite the volume of writings by Morris himself and by his biographers, the common impression of Morris textiles is somewhat misguided and taken out of context.

Most studies have been restricted to those designs confidently attributed to Morris himself, thus ignoring the considerable quantity of patterns designed by other people but produced by or sold through the firm of Morris and Company. In order to get things made Morris had to look beyond the workshops of Merton Abbey, and contracted not only the machine-weaving of carpets but also the production of woven furnishings and other textiles to outside firms. His personal efforts in embroidering, dyeing and weaving textiles supported many of his theories. Ultimately they enabled him to direct his firm with perception and a clear understanding of what he could expect others to produce for him.

In considering his most prolific period of textile design, the textiles are invariably viewed in isolation, for direct parallels with concurrent design projects in other media or with his politics or writings are rarely drawn. A man as engrossed as Morris was in many creative fields could not divorce textile design from, for example, the stained glass or the poetry of the same period. One field of interest complemented and offset another; his involvement in textiles was an integral part of a lifestyle, his approaches to pattern and use of motifs evolving gradually. Nevertheless, all too often historians pinpoint individual events as moments of conscious artistic development. One such, in respect of Morris's textiles, is the year 1883 when a certain fifteenth-century Italian velvet was acquired by the South Kensington Museum; this moment is said to mark the beginning of a new phase in Morris's textile designs – that is, the use of a very strong diagonal emphasis to the main branching stem in the design. The fifteenth-century piece may have acted as catalyst; but the designs shortly preceding that year had already displayed new tendencies in the structures of pattern.

In addition, today's responses to Morris's original concepts of pattern and colour have been numbed by the superabundance of Morris-type reproductions and imitations in furnishings. Undoubtedly, Morris's textile designs have been influential, as have his theories about pattern and colour. Morris was not so intent on reinstating the ideal of the medieval craftsman that he became blind to the world about him – quite the contrary. One must also consider the extent to which Morris assimilated contemporary influences of fashion and taste as well as the historical precedents for his patterns.

The complexity of the subject of Morris textiles is increasingly apparent. It now remains for far more critical research to be undertaken.

1 Morris, *Some Hints on Pattern Designing*, Longmans, 1899, p6. Lecture delivered at the Working Men's College, London, 10 December 1881.
2 *Ibid*.
3 *Ibid*, p4.
4 P. Henderson, *William Morris, his life, work and friends*, Thames and Hudson, 1967, p188.
5 R. Watkinson, *William Morris as Designer*, Studio Vista, 1967, p52.
6 Mackail, vol I, p116.
7 Morris, *The Letters of William Morris to his family and friends*, ed. P. Henderson, Longmans, 1950, pp315–6.
8 Mackail, vol I, p159.
9 Typescript of letters written by William Morris to Thomas Wardle, Victoria and Albert Museum; letter of 25 March 1877.
10 *Ibid*.
11 Notebook containing information about tapestry, textiles, etc, in the Victoria and Albert Museum.
12 *Some Hints on Pattern Designing, op cit*, p1.
13 Victoria and Albert Museum, no T.7022–1860.
14 *Collected Works of William Morris*, vol XXII, Longmans, 1914, p106.
15 Morris, 'Textiles', in *Arts and Crafts Essays*, London, 1893, pp27–8.
16 Barbara Morris, 'William Morris and the South Kensington Museum', in *Victorian Poetry*, vol 13, nos 3 and 4, West Virginia University, Morgantown, 1975, p168.
17 Morris, 'Textiles', *op cit*, pp25–6.
18 *Ibid*.
19 *Collected Works, op cit*, vol XXII, p194.
20 *Some Hints on Pattern Designing, op cit*, p26.

Catalogue of
Paintings, Prints and Drawings

1

Mrs William Morris (Blue Silk Dress)
Painting by D. G. Rossetti
Oil

Size:	110cm × 90cm (43½ × 35½in).
Inscription:	Inscribed along the top of the canvas: 'Jane Morris AD 1868 D. G. Rossetti, pinxit conjuge clava poetâ et praeclarissima vultu, Denique pictura clara sit illa mea' (famed by her poet husband, and of surpassing fame for her beauty, now let her win lasting fame by my painting).
Provenance:	Mrs William Morris; May Morris; The Society of Antiquaries (Kelmscott Manor).
Reference:	S.372 p176.

The portrait seems to have been projected as early as June 1866, but not to have been properly in hand until the summer of 1868. It bears a close relationship to the studies for the oil painting *Mariana* that were in progress at the time.

Over half length, in a blue dress, turned to the right, seated at a table on which she leans her elbows; in front of her on the table are a pink carnation on an open book and a vase of roses and vine leaves.

Janey Morris's mysterious beauty, which fascinated Rossetti and so many others throughout her life, was never more powerfully revealed than in this portrait. Henry James also saw Janey within a year of its completion, and described her perfectly: 'a tall lean woman in a long dress . . . with a pair of strange, sad deep dark Swinburnian eyes, with great thick black oblique brows joined in the middle and tucking themselves away under her hair, a mouth like the "Oriana" in the illustrated Tennyson, a long neck without any collar in lieu thereof, some dozen strings of outlandish beads'. See Doughty pp371/2.

2

Jenny Morris
Drawing by D. G. Rossetti
Coloured chalks on pale blue-grey paper

Size:	44cm × 39cm (17¼in × 15½in).
Inscription:	Monogram and date lower right corner: '1871'.

◄ May Morris, painted by D. G. Rossetti in 1871 (P3)

Provenance:	Given by the artist to Mrs William Morris; May Morris; The Society of Antiquaries (Kelmscott Manor).
Reference:	S.360 p174.

Head of William Morris's elder child (b1861), turned three-quarters to right, looking down; dark hair worn in a fringe and falling upon the shoulders.

3

May Morris
Drawing by D. G. Rossetti
Coloured chalks on pale blue-grey paper

Size:	44cm × 39cm (17¼in × 15½in).
Inscription:	Monogram and date lower right corner: '1871'.
Provenance:	As for portrait of Jenny Morris (No 2).
Reference:	S.361 p174.

Head turned three-quarters to left; thick auburn hair worn in a fringe and falling on to the shoulders.

Rossetti loved the Morris children dearly, and he derived intense pleasure from their company during his time with Janey, Jenny and May at Kelmscott, talking, playing and joking with them and their animals during the happier months of Spring to Autumn from 1871 to 1874. He used them both as models, but especially May, his favourite. See Doughty, pp469/485, 542/568.

4

Sir Launcelot's Vision of the Sanc Grael
Study for the fresco painting in the Oxford Union Library
Pen and brown ink and pencil

Size:	23cm × 18cm (9in × 7in).
Date:	1857.
Provenance:	W. M. Rossetti; Fairfax Murray; Birmingham City Museum and Art Gallery (No 27204) S.93b p52. Cat. RA 135 p44.
Loaned by:	Birmingham City Museum and Art Gallery.
Reference:	S.363 p174, Cat. RA p276.

Study for Launcelot and Guenevere. Guenevere stands with extended arms beside the apple tree, an apple in her left hand. Launcelot is seated on the ground with bowed head and eyes closed.

Launcelot is drawn from the young Burne-Jones. The model for Guenevere is probably Jane Burden, whom Rossetti contrived to meet in an Oxford theatre at this time. She then began to pose for him, replacing Elizabeth Siddal, absent from Oxford. There is a close resemblance between the head in this drawing and Rossetti's drawing of her at the age of 17, from Kelmscott Manor (No 5).

5

Jane Burden
Drawing by D. G. Rossetti
Pencil

Size:	48cm × 33cm (18¾in × 13in).
Inscription:	Lower corner: 'D.G.R. Oxonial primo delt Oct 1857'. Upper left corner: 'J.B.AETAT XVII'.
Made at:	Oxford, the first known portrait head of Mrs Morris, when still Miss Jane Burden.
Provenance:	Mrs William Morris; May Morris; Kelmscott Manor Sale, 19 July 1939, (Lot 325); The Society of Antiquaries (Kelmscott Manor). (Presumably withdrawn from the sale in 1939, since it was listed by May Morris in her bequest to Oxford University.)
Reference:	S.363 p174, Cat. RA 276 p66.

6

Elizabeth Siddal
Drawing by D. G. Rossetti
Pen and brown and black ink

Size:	13cm × 11cm (5¹⁄₁₆in × 4⅜in).
Inscription:	Monogram and date lower left: 'Feb 6th 1855'.
Reference:	S.472 p191, Cat. RA 176 p50.
Loaned by:	The Visitors of The Ashmolean Museum, Oxford.

Head and shoulders facing the front with the eyes cast down under heavy lids. The loose hair hangs on the shoulders, curling inwards on the right side. Dress gathered into a narrow band at the throat.

Elizabeth Siddal ('Gug', 'Guggums') is shown full face. She was renowned for her famous hair 'which was a bright copper in colour'. Until her death in 1862, she sat for him for nearly all his pictures. 'One face looks out from all his canvases. One selfsame figure sits or walks or leans.'

7

Janey Morris
Drawings by D. G. Rossetti
Pencil

Size:	27cm × 26cm (10⅝in × 10⅛in).
Inscription:	Monogram and date right: 'Sept. 1861'.
Provenance:	Mrs William Morris; May Morris; The Society of Antiquaries (Kelmscott Manor).
Reference:	S.105 D, F, p59.

Studies for the head of the Virgin for painting *The Seed of David*, in Llandaff Cathedral. Mrs Morris is shown in profile to the left, the eyes looking down; a soft veil falls upon her right shoulder.

In 1856 Rossetti, with the help of Madox Brown and another friend, J. P. Seddon, was commissioned to paint a reredos for Llandaff Cathedral in the form of a triptych for the high altar (it has now been moved to a side chapel) – 'a big thing which I shall go into with a howl of delight'. Rossetti's description of it in his Papers, pp50–1, is as follows:

The picture shows Christ sprung from high and low, as united in the person of David who was both Shepherd and King, and worshipped by high and low (by King and Shepherd) at his birth.'

He began the painting in 1858, nearly finished it in 1861, finally completing it in 1864.

The head of the Virgin in the central 'Adoration' was originally taken from Ruth Herbert but Mrs Morris's was substituted in 1861. For King David in the right wing, crowned and wearing a black coat of mail under a richly embroidered tunic, the head is taken from Morris.

8

William Morris as David
Drawing by D. G. Rossetti
Pencil

Size:	25cm × 22cm (9¾in × 8¾in).
Reference:	S.105 J p60.
Loaned by:	Birmingham City Museum and Art Gallery.

Study of the head of David on the right-hand panel; taken from Morris. He is shown three-quarters to left, downturned wearing a small beard. (On reverse a pen and ink drawing of a man.)

9

Dante Gabriel Rossetti
Drawing (self portrait)
Pencil

Size: 25cm × 21cm (10in × 8⅛in).
Inscription: Monogram and date right: 'Oct. 1861'.
Reference: S.438 p185, DGR Cat. RA 246 p61.
Loaned by: Birmingham City Museum and Art Gallery.

This portrait was in the possession of Fanny Cornforth and C. Fairfax Murray before it was bequeathed by Murray to the City Collection at Birmingham.

10

William Holman Hunt
Portrait drawing by D. G. Rossetti
(So inscribed in the Birmingham Catalogue of Drawings)

Size: 13cm × 9cm (5in × 3½in).
Date: c1851.
Reference: S.340 p169.
Loaned by: Birmingham City Museum and Art Gallery.

On the back of the drawing, in the writing of W. M. Rossetti: 'I think this may be Holman Hunt's brother, done c.1851'. Head and shoulders, the head in profile to the left.

11

Sir John Everett Millais
Humorous drawing by D. G. Rossetti
Pen and ink (shaded with finger)

Size: 18cm × 11cm (7in × 4⅜in).
Date: c1851–3.
Reference: S.592 p208.
Loaned by: Birmingham City Museum and Art Gallery.

Millais is shown three-quarter length, standing in profile to left, his right hand raised with first two fingers and thumb extended. He is exclaiming 'slosh' to W. Holman Hunt who is shown in another humorous drawing exclaiming 'Of course' (S.591). 'Slosh' was one of Millais' characteristic expressions applied to pictures he disliked and the exchange echoes the youthful high spirits which accompanied all activities of the early P.R.B.

12

Algernon Charles Swinburne
Watercolour by D. G. Rossetti

Size: 18cm × 15cm (7in × 6in).
Inscription: Monogram and date upper right corner: '1861'.
Reference: S.523 p198.
Loaned by: The Syndics of the Fitzwilliam Museum, Cambridge.

This portrait drawing was made as pendant to the portrait of Browning. It was praised by Watts-Dunton, although regarded as an unsatisfactory likeness by Edmund Gosse.

Head and shoulders against an emerald-green ground, the head looking to the left; bushy auburn hair, slight moustache; dressed in blue coat, with yellow cravat and jewelled pin.

Swinburne went up to Balliol a year after Morris and Burne-Jones had arrived in Oxford. He soon became acquainted with and involved in the affairs of the 'Brotherhood'. His ebullient personality, poetic talent and lively wit soon made him a favourite, especially with Janey Morris and Lizzie Siddal. He was then 20 years old. However, by the mid-1860s he had become an embarrassment to most of his friends, ending many an evening so drunk that he was 'describing geometrical curves on the pavement' in Rossetti's words, and had to be sent home labelled, in a cab. In the 1870s he became with Rossetti a principal target for attack as a member of the 'fleshly school of poetry'.

13

Genevieve
Drawing by D. G. Rossetti
Pen and ink, arched top

Size: 27cm × 14cm (10¾in × 5½in).
Inscription: Monogram (G.C.D.R.) and date lower right: 'August 1848'. Inscribed with title lower left corner:
'She leaned against the armed man,
The statue of the armed Knight;
She stood and listen'd to my lay
Amid the lingering light'
('Love', S. T. Coleridge).
Reference: S.38 p9.
Loaned by: The Syndics of the Fitzwilliam Museum, Cambridge.

Designed for the Cyclographic Society as an illustration to Coleridge's poem in which the heroine is called Genevieve, an immature work by Rossetti which combines some of the stiffness of Nazarener drawing with the emotional medievalisation of subject matter characteristic of early Pre-Raphaelite painting.

14

The First Anniversary of the Death of Beatrice: (Dante drawing an Angel)
Pen and ink, enclosed within its own margin, curved top

Size:	40cm × 33cm (15¾in × 12⅞in).
Inscription:	Inscribed upper right: 'Dante G. Rossetti to his PR Brother John E. Millais'; above the curved top: 'Florence 9th June, 1291: the first anniversary of the death of Beatrice'; signed and dated lower left: '1849'.
Reference:	S.42 p12, DGR Cat. RA 85 p33.
Loaned by:	Birmingham City Museum and Art Gallery.

The quotation beneath describes the subject: 'On that day on which a whole year was completed since my lady had been born into the life eternal, – remembering me of her as I sat alone, I betook myself to draw the resemblance of an Angel upon certain tablets. And while I did this, chancing to turn my head, I perceived that some were standing beside me to whom I should have given courteous welcome and that they were observing what I did: also I learned afterwards that they had been there a while before I perceived them. Perceiving whom, I arose for salutation, and said: "Another was with me".'

See Dante's autobiography of his early life.

15

St Cecilia
Drawing by D. G. Rossetti
Pen and brown ink

Size:	9.7cm × 8.3cm (3⅞in × 3¼in).
Inscription:	Monogram lower right; '1856–7'.
Reference:	S.83 p48, DGR Cat. RA 126 pp41–2.
Loaned by:	Birmingham City Museum and Art Gallery.

Design for Moxon's edition of Tennyson's poems, to illustrate the lines from *The Palace of Art*.
'Or in a clear-walled city on the sea
Near gilded organ pipes, her hair
Wound with white roses, slept St. Cecily;
An angel look'd at her.'

Rossetti here has faithfully carried out the poet's intention. Madox Brown found the design 'jolly quaint, but very lovely'. In the woodcut, however, Rossetti according to his brother, 'has chosen to represent the subject from a more special point of view. He supposed Cecilia, while kept as prisoner for her Christian faith, to be taking air on the ramparts of the fortress; as she plays on her hand-organ an Angel gives her a kiss, which is the kiss of death. This is what Rossetti meant.'

This innovation appears to have been invented by Elizabeth Siddal.

16

St Cecilia
Wood engraving by the Daziel brothers for Tennyson's *Poems*, from a design by Rossetti (No 15)
First Edition, London, Moxon and Co, 1857

Reference:	DGR Cat. RA 155 p47.

There is a watercolour of the same subject dated 1853, now in the Ashmolean Museum, Oxford. This differs in design from the earlier composition. It was in respect of this watercolour that Ruskin wrote his first letter to Rossetti, saying how much his 'thoroughly glorious work' pleased him. It began a friendship which despite many hazards was of much value to both men.

17

How They Met Themselves
Drawing by D. G. Rossetti
Pen and ink and wash with some pencil

Size:	27 cm × 21cm (10⅝in × 8⅜in).
Inscription:	Monogram and date lower right: '1851–1860', 'The Bogie' drawing.
Reference:	S.118 p74, DGR Cat. 154 p47.
Loaned by:	The Syndics of the Fitzwilliam Museum, Cambridge.

18

Mary Magdalene at the Door of Simon
Drawing by D. G. Rossetti
Study for the head of the Magdalene in the oil painting of the same title
Pencil, pen and ink

Size:	21cm × 17cm (8⅜in × 6¾in).
Date:	c1858.
Reference:	S.109 I p64, DGR Cat. RA 118 p40.
Loaned by:	The Visitors of the Ashmolean Museum, Oxford.

Study of Mrs Crabbe (Ruth Herbert) turned three-quarters to the right. The hair, braided with a coil over the crown, is lightly sketched in.

Ruth Herbert is one of the first of Rossetti's 'stunners'. He writes to W. Bell Scott, in 1858: 'Blackfriars Bridge . . . I am in the stunning position this morning of expecting the actual visit of a model whom I have been longing to paint for years – Miss Herbert of the Olympic Theatre – who has the most varied and highest expression I ever saw in a woman's face, besides abundant beauty, golden hair, etc . . . O my eye! She has sat to me now.'

19

Design for painting 'Found'
Drawing by D. G. Rossetti
Pen and ink

Size:	23cm × 22cm (9¼in × 8⅝in).
Inscription:	Monogram lower right corner: 'c1855'. Inscribed along the foot of the drawing: 'I remember thee; the kindness of thy youth, the love of thy betrothal. Jerem II, 2'. Below is inscribed the title of the drawing.
Reference:	S.64A p29.
Loaned by:	Birmingham City Museum and Art Gallery.

A complete design for the picture, probably c1856, executed before his introduction to Fanny Cornforth as the female head is not from her.

There is a freedom in the drawing, for example folds of her dress, which indicates the increasing break with the severe Pre-Raphaelite style.

20

Study for painting 'Found'
Drawing by D. G. Rossetti
Pen and ink and slight ink wash

Size:	18cm × 20cm (7in × 7¾in).
Date:	c1859–61.
Reference:	S.64N p31.
Loaned by:	Birmingham City Museum and Art Gallery.

Finished study for the head of the woman, bust and shoulders indicated. The sitter is Fanny Cornforth.

Fanny became Rossetti's model in 1858 and her head figures in all the studies except No 19 and on the canvas itself.

Fanny Cornforth was born Sarah Cox, according to her own account, in Steyning, Sussex, in 1824, later taking her grandmother's name, Cornforth. She claimed that she was accosted by Rossetti, Jones, Brown and Price during a firework display in Surrey Gardens to celebrate the return of Florence Nightingale from the Crimea and they had deliberately knocked down her massed golden hair. Rossetti describes his first sight of her loitering in the Strand and 'cracking nuts with her teeth and throwing the shells about'. However, she soon agreed to model for Rossetti.

It is possible her own life as a 'simple country girl' was the source of the story of his painting *Found*. She was also modelling as a 'gay' woman for Stanhope.

'A pre-eminently fine woman with regular and sweet features, and a mass of most lovely blonde hair, light golden or harvest yellow', is William Rossetti's description of her.

During the 1860s and 1870s her image was to change; she now became the symbol of the new sensuousness in both Rossetti's verse and painting. He found her 'a superb thing, so awfully lovely', focusing upon her full-formed features as in the painting of 1860, *La Bocca Bacciata*, the oft-kissed lips described by Boccaccio, or again in the painting of 1864, *Lady Lilith*, Adam's beautiful witch wife before Eve.

By 1866, however, her reign as model was nearing its end. Rossetti was preoccupied with new beauty – Alexa Wilding and Jane Morris, the latter with a magnificence of hair, black and tumbling, new in his painting. Fanny was installed as his housekeeper in Tudor House, 16 Cheyne Walk, Chelsea, sharing both table and bed, and providing earthy companionship and stability in the rambling house with its disordered garden and private zoo.

By the 1870s Fanny was growing fat; Gabriel now referred to her as his 'good elephant' and made sure that he kept her away from Kelmscott, though he still needed her comforts occasionally – 'Old Rhinoceros is unhappy', he would write in invitation. He also rented her a house in nearby Royal Avenue, for her and her drunken husband, and when the latter died Fanny married her young lodger, Schott.

From the beginning she had been given various works by Rossetti, mostly drawings, but after this marriage and because of Gabriel's frequent incapacity to supervise matters, she used her own and her husband's influence to obtain a considerable number of his works. She had never been liked by the Rossetti family because of her coarseness and her hold over Gabriel; now they used their influence to keep her away from him as much as possible and eventually even to keep from her knowledge of his funeral, until it was too late for her to attend and, for some time after, to prevent her from seeing his will.

21

Mrs Beyer
Drawing by D. G. Rossetti
Pen and ink, sepia and wash

Size:	16cm × 11cm (6⅜in × 4⁷⁄₁₆in).
Date:	c1862.
Reference:	S.266 p157.
Loaned by:	The Syndics of the Fitzwilliam Museum, Cambridge.

The drawing is a study of Mrs Beyer, a German woman of whom little is known, but who according to W. M. Rossetti was the model for the oil painting *Joan of Arc*, dated 1863.

Rossetti wrote to Ellis Heaton from Paris in November 1864, 'I am much pleased that the *Joan of Arc* pleases you . . . the Joan was painted from a female model, and looks like nothing in the world but a female.'

We are again made aware of the appeal of the strong features and abundant hair of yet another 'stunner' drawn with the great skill and directness characteristic of Rossetti's early drawings from life.

22

Dante Gabriel Rossetti
Drawing by Charles Keene
Charcoal on grey paper

Size:	13cm × 12cm (5¼in × 4⅝in).
Date:	Undated.
Reference:	DGR Cat. RA 237 p59.
Loaned by:	The Visitors of the Ashmolean Museum, Oxford.

Rossetti is shown in a soft hat and wearing a cape.

23

Gardening
Study for a design by D. G. Rossetti
Pen and ink

Size:	13cm × 14cm (5¼in × 5½in).
Date:	c1861.
Reference:	S.132A p82, DGR Cat. RA 201 p53.
Loaned by:	Birmingham City Museum and Art Gallery.

About 1861 Rossetti made a design in watercolour for a minor panel in the Seddon cabinet, on the theme of Spring, this study is also for the cabinet.

A girl (Fanny Cornforth) is shown wearing a hood or sun-bonnet and holding a pair of scissors in her right hand, in the act of cutting flowering branches from a tree.

24

St George and the Dragon
Design for stained glass by D. G. Rossetti
Indian ink

Size:	50cm × 62cm (19⁷⁄₁₆in × 24½in).
Inscription:	Monogram lower right corner: '1861–2'.
Reference:	S.145–150 pp85–87.
Loaned by:	Birmingham City Museum and Art Gallery.

Six designs for stained glass were made by Rossetti for the Firm in 1861–2, to illustrate the story of 'St George and the Dragon'.

The subjects were as follows:
(i) The Skulls brought to the King.
(ii) The Princess Sabra drawing the Lot (this design was painted over with watercolour).
(iii) The Princess Sabra taken to the Dragon.
(iv) St George and the Dragon (design exhibited).
(v) The Return of the Princess.
(vi) The Wedding of St George.

25

Mrs William Morris
Drawing by D. G. Rossetti

Size:	24cm × 45cm (9½in × 17¾in).
Date:	Inscribed right: 'Aug. 12 1870'.
Provenance:	Mrs William Morris; May Morris; The Society of Antiquaries (Kelmscott Manor).
Reference:	S.381 p177.

Reclining whole-length on her left side; head and shoulders on the right supported by pillows; eyes looking down; arms crossed over the bust.

As Janey became more withdrawn and frequently ailing, she took regularly to her sofa. There are 16 drawings of her on a sofa, mostly reclining full length, recorded by Mrs Surtees as drawn over the four years 1869–73.

26

Mrs William Morris
Drawing by D. G. Rossetti
Pen and ink

Size:	6cm × 5cm (2½in × 1 9/10in).
Inscription:	Upper left corner 'To' and along the foot of the drawing 'from D.G.R. (in monogram) Xmas '73'.
Provenance:	Mrs William Morris; May Morris; The Society of Antiquaries (Kelmscott Manor).
Reference:	S.397 p179.

Drawn in the top-right-hand corner of the flyleaf to Burton's *Anatomy of Melancholy*.

Head and shoulders turned three-quarters to left, on an ink background, enclosed within its own line.

27

Mrs William Morris
Drawing by D. G. Rossetti
Pencil

Size:	28cm × 25cm (11⅛in × 9⅞in).
Date:	c1873.
Reference:	S.399 p180, DGR Cat. RA 279 p66.
Loaned by:	The Syndics of the Fitzwilliam Museum, Cambridge.

Janey is shown, over half length, reclining against cushions; head in profile to the left, hair upswept, her right arm raised to her head. She is wearing the upper part of an Icelandic costume with embroidery at the neck and on the sleeves.

28a

Water Willow
Portrait of Jane Morris by Charles Fairfax Murray, copy of painting by D. G. Rossetti
Oil

Size:	33cm × 27cm (13in × 10½in).
Date:	Original with monogram dated and inscribed, lower left corner: 'Kelmscott 1871'. Copy made in 1893.
Provenance:	Mrs William Morris; May Morris; The Society of Antiquaries (Kelmscott Manor).

Rossetti described his original painting thus: 'I have also got to work at a little picture with a river background from the neighbourhood here' (Rossetti's letters p969).

Mrs Morris (head and shoulders) is shown holding branches of willow in both hands. Behind her is the winding Thames, with Kelmscott on the left bank, on the right is Kelmscott church partly obscured by a tree, and a punt is moored by the river-bank.

Rossetti, hard pressed for money, touted the painting, unsolicited, to an old patron, the banker Rae for 300 guineas, but failed to sell it. It was bought after his death by Samuel Bancroft for his collection at Wilmington, Delaware, USA.

Returned to Britain for restoration and retouched in 1893 by Charles Fairfax Murray.

Charles Fairfax Murray was a shop boy who became a painter and a friend of William Morris. He was an assistant to Rossetti, and it was in Murray's studio that Morris drew from the life model. Murray rendered general assistance of all kinds, such as laying-in for Rossetti, copying for Ruskin, transferring drawings to wood-blocks and buying vellum in Rome etc for Morris. He owned Icelandic texts written and illuminated by Morris. He made a drawing of Morris just after his death (No 41). (Life WM, Vol I, pp123, 208, 299, 303, 319–320, Vol II, p257. See also Cat. *Morris and Company in Cambridge*, Fitzwilliam Museum and Cambridge University Press, 1980, 21, p13.)

28b

Mrs William Morris
Study for the oil painting *Water Willow*
Drawing by D. G. Rossetti
Red chalk

Size:	31cm × 25cm (12¼in × 9¾in).
Date:	1871.
Inscription:	Monogram, top right: 'D.G.R.'
Provenance:	Mrs Morris; May Morris; The Society of Antiquaries.

It is shown in a photograph of 'Mrs Morris's room' at Kelmscott House, Hammersmith.

29

Astarte Syriaca (Venus Astarte)
Drawing by D. G. Rossetti

Size:	23cm × 18cm (9¼in × 7in).
Date:	c1875.
Reference:	S.2496 p146–7.
Loaned by:	Birmingham City Museum and Art Gallery.

A sketch from Rossetti's MS notebook; it shows Janey as a rather jaunty Venus, holding her loosened girdle in both hands. Behind her attendant spirits can be discerned. This image is in strong contrast with the brooding Syrian counterpart in the painting (1875–77), for which Mrs Morris was also the model. Her dark mystery is fully conveyed in Rossetti's lines:

'Mystery: Lo! betwixt the sun and moon
Astarte of the Syrians: Venus Queen
Ere Aphrodite was. In silver sheen
Her twofold girdle clasps the infinite boon
Of bliss where of the heaven and earth commune:
And from her neck's inclining flower-stem lean
Love freighted lips and absolute eyes that wean
The pulse of hearts to the spheres' dominant tune.'

30

William Morris presenting a ring to his future wife
Caricature drawing by D. G. Rossetti
Pen and ink

Size:	24cm × 33cm (9½in × 13in), (overall measurement of paper).
Date:	c1857.
Reference:	S.597 p209.
Loaned by:	Birmingham City Museum and Art Gallery.

Sketched at Oxford during the painting of the Union murals; Morris gazes at Jane Burden, on left, who looks down at the ring which she is trying on her finger.

31

The Ms at Ems
Humorous drawing by D. G. Rossetti
Pen and ink

Size:	11cm × 18cm (4½in × 7in).
Inscription:	Title inscribed by Rossetti, lower right, in a letter to Mrs Morris dated 'July 21st 1869'.
Acknowledgement:	Facsimile reproduction by permission of the Trustees of the British Museum.
Reference:	S.605 p211.

Mrs Morris's health 'was so disquieting that it was thought necessary for her to try the cure at Ems' (*Collected Works of William Morris*, ed. May Morris 1909, v, pp xj–xij). 'The accompanying cartoon will prepare you for the worse – whichever that may be, the 7 tumblers or the 7 volumes' (*Letters to Jane Morris from D. G. Rossetti*, British Museum). William Morris sits in the centre gesturing and reading from Volume 2 of *The Earthly Paradise* to Mrs Morris who is

seated in a bath in front of him, drinking from a goblet marked 'No.2'. The remaining goblets are lined up on the floor beside the bath, the remaining six volumes of *The Earthly Paradise* are arranged on the shelf behind.

32

Death of a Wombat
Humorous drawing by D. G. Rossetti
Pen and ink

Size:	18cm × 11cm (7in × 4½in).
Date:	Inscribed: '6 November 1869'.
Acknowledgement:	Facsimile reproduction by permission of the Trustees of The British Museum.
Reference:	S.606 p211, DGR Cat. RA 271 p64.

'I never reared a young Wombat
To glad me with his pin-hole eye,
But when he most was sweet & fat
And tail-less, he was sure to die!'

Rossetti kneels in the foreground and weeps into a large handkerchief which covers his face. On the ground before him lies a dead wombat on its back. In the background on the left is a weeping willow and on the right a pedestal supporting an urn inscribed with the date. A black ink border surrounds the drawing.

33

Morris in a Punt
Humorous drawing by D. G. Rossetti
Pen and ink

Size:	18cm × 11cm (7in × 4½in).
Date:	Inscribed lower left: 'Kelmscott 11 Sept. 1871'.
Inscription:	Below drawing: 'Enter Morris, moored in a punt and jacks and tenches exeunt'.
Reference:	S.608 p211.
Acknowledgement:	Facsimile reproduction by permission of the Trustees of The British Museum.

Against a background of trees, Morris in fishing attire sits at the right end of a punt. He holds a fishing rod in his left hand but is absorbed in reading *The Earthly Paradise*. In the river below, three fish are laughing.

Rossetti wrote to Bell Scott as follows: 'Kelmscott, 15 September 1871: One day he (Morris) was here he went for a day's fishing in our punt, the chief result of which was a sketch I made.' He described Morris as 'Skald' in this letter, an heroic title given to Morris in Iceland during his first visit earlier in the year.

34

Album of copies after the Old Masters

Drawn and assembled by E. Burne-Jones. The copies are in pencil and watercolour, pasted in 1859–62. Folios 3, 4, 5, 6, 10, 15 and 18.

Size:	25pp, page size 33cm × 27cm (13in × 10⅝in).
Loaned by:	The Syndics of the Fitzwilliam Museum, Cambridge.

Burne-Jones was assiduous in recording information, drawn from life and copies made from historical sources, which filled many sketchbooks. He also gathered into albums numerous drawings and tracings copied from such earlier sources.

The first album he made is one pasted c1856/7, which consists mainly of tracings of medieval costume made from Camille Bonnard's book, *Costume des XIIIe, XIVe, et XVe Siècles* (1829–30). Rossetti owned an early copy of this book and Millais also used it for reference. Burne-Jones could very well have made his tracings while working as a pupil in Rossetti's studio in 1856.

He was very conscious of his debt to earlier masters. He studied during his lifetime every important phase of Western art, from classical antiquity to the High Renaissance. He stated that he was desirous of making his paintings 'a reflection of a reflection of something purely imaginary'.

In spite of this eclectic study it is noteworthy that he evolved a style that was very individual.

He made four visits to Italy, in 1859, 1862, 1871 and 1873 (see Nos 35 and 38) and his assimilation of Italian art is perhaps the most richly documented of all in both drawings and sketchbooks.

Although his understanding is thoroughly Victorian and links with attitudes that are well known in the writings of Ruskin, Swinburne, Pater and Berenson, he very often showed an original attitude to individual artists. He was interested in Carpaccio before he was 'discovered' by Ruskin, he had great respect – only matched in this century – for Piero della Francesca, and was later to quarrel with Ruskin over his (Burne-Jones's) admiration for the work of Michaelangelo and Signorelli.

In the album on exhibition the copies date from Burne-Jones's first visit to Italy in the autumn of 1859. They were nearly all made in Florence, Pisa and Venice, and among the works recorded are pictures by Giotto, Uccello, Masaccio, Gozzoli, Ghirlandaio, Botticelli, Filippino Lippi, Simone Martini, Bellini, Carpaccio and Titian.

Especially interesting are the copies from frescoes in The Campo Santo, Pisa, including a group from *The Last Judgement*, then attributed to Orcagna.

At this early stage, he follows the taste of many connoisseurs and tourists of the time in preferring the straightforward narrative approach of such artists as Gozzoli and Ghirlandaio. The sketches after Botticelli are particularly interesting in view of his later debt to this artist.

35

Signs of the Zodiac

Eleven charcoal drawings by Edward Burne-Jones

Size:	43cm × 21cm (17in × 8¼in).
Collection:	The Society of Antiquaries (Kelmscott Manor).

These are close in design with the small painted figures on the panelling lining the Green Drawing Room in the Victoria and Albert Museum and may well be the original sketches.

Morris and Co were commissioned in 1866 by the Department of Science and Art to carry out the complete decoration of this 'Morris Room', as it is now called; it was one of their first important secular works.

The drawings show Burne-Jones's increasing interest in classical art during the mid-1860s, to achieve more plastic rendering of the human form even when draped, and a fondness for the nude. His sketchbooks of the period are full of studies from the antique, drawn mostly in the British Museum.

During his second visit to Italy in 1862 Burne-Jones made copies of sixteenth-century Venetian painters for Ruskin, and after a third visit in 1871 he wrote that his favourite artists were now Michaelangelo, Signorelli, Mantegna, Giotto, Botticelli, Andrea del Sarto, Uccello and Piero della Francesca (See Nos 34, 38).

The Zodiac drawings anticipate the influence which the work of these masters and of Rossetti had upon that of Burne-Jones. The comparison, however, draws attention to a lack of strength and assurance in Burne-Jones's draughtmanship, in spite of his assiduous practice.

36

Cupid delivering Psyche

Watercolour on canvas by Burne-Jones

Size:	34cm × 91cm (13½in × 36in).
Inscription:	Signed and dated 'E.B.J. 1867'.
Collection:	Cecil French Bequest, Fulham.
Loaned by:	The London Borough of Hammersmith and Fulham.

The subject from 'The Story of Cupid and Psyche' in Morris's *The Earthly Paradise*. Around 1865 Burne-Jones by his own account designed 70 subjects for *Cupid and Psyche* alone.

Cupid is shown restoring Psyche to life after she has opened the forbidden casket in Hades (See Catalogue of Books, No 35).

'And kneeling down he whispered in her ear,
Rise, Psyche, and be mine for evermore,
For evil is long tarrying in this shore.'

According to Malcolm Bell, Burne-Jones's first biographer, this was the first picture to be painted in Burne-Jones's new home at North End, Fulham – The Grange, which he acquired in 1867. He and his family were to live in this house until his death in 1898.

37

Flying Figure
Oil on canvas by E. Burne-Jones

Size:	51cm × 34cm (20in × 13½in).
Date:	c1870.
Collection:	Cecil French Bequest, Fulham.
Loaned by:	The London Borough of Hammersmith and Fulham.

The blue monochrome and spontaneous handling of the drawing in this work link it with a number of other allegorical figure subjects of the same period: *Night* (watercolour, 1870), *Evening* (two watercolour versions, 1870 and 1872–3), and *Luna* (oil, 1872–5). See drawing of *Luna* from Kelmscott Manor (No 35).

38

The Wheel of Fortune
Watercolour (gouache) on canvas by Burne-Jones

Size:	114cm × 53cm (45in × 21in).
Date:	1871–85.
Inscription:	Signed 'E.B.J.'
Collection:	Cecil French Bequest, Fulham.
Loaned by:	The London Borough of Hammersmith and Fulham.

The figure, with three others, *Fame*, *Love* and *Oblivion*, was originally designed as part of a predella for an elaborate triptych, illustrating the Story of Troy, conceived about 1870, but never completed except in fragments. This figure would have stood at the extreme left.

This picture was begun in 1872 and finished in 1886, after a larger and better known version in oils of 1877–83, now in Paris (Coll: Vicomtesse de Noailles).

There is often difficulty in deciphering Burne-Jones's technique and Bell mistakenly calls it an oil painting. The design was a favourite one of the artist. For the naked male figures he used in defiance of Ruskin the studies he had made of Michaelangelo's *Captives*. His admiration for Michaelangelo is especially strong at this time and the picture reflects his increasing maturity.

In 1871 Burne-Jones had visited Italy for the third time, but made his first journey to Rome rushing to see the Sistine Chapel. He found Michaelangelo's *Sleeping Adam*, *The Last Judgement* and the two Signorelli's (*Publication of the Law* and *Death of Moses*) 'as beautiful as anything in the world' (See Nos 34, 35).

He claimed to have on hand in his London studios 60 pictures in the charge of his faithful assistant Rooke, and in his new confidence derived from Italy no longer cared what the public would think of them.

39

Series of drawings by Edward Burne-Jones
(i) **Female Figure**
Study of draped female figure
Chalk watercolour and gold paint on brown paper

Size:	29cm × 17cm (11½in × 6½in).
Inscription:	Signed and dated: 'E.B.J. 1862'.

(ii) **Study of Figures**
White chalk on brown paper

Size:	21cm × 24cm (8¼in × 9½in).
Inscription:	Signed and dated: 'E.B.J. 1865'.

A number of similar drawings were made by Burne-Jones at this time, in technique and character reminiscent of Leighton, Albert Moore and of Whistler, who was briefly attracted to ideal figure studies in the late 1860s.

(iii) **Lovers**
White chalk on brown paper

Size:	36cm × 25cm (14in × 10in).
Date:	c1866.

(iv) **Nude Study**
Red chalk

Size:	47cm × 24cm (18½in × 9¼in).
Date:	c1870.
Inscription:	Not in Burne-Jones's hand, 'S.N. from E.B.J.'

(v) **The Graiae**
Pencil and white chalk on green paper
Series of three drawings

Size:	Two 15cm × 22cm (6in × 8½in).
	One 15cm × 19cm (6in × 7½in).
Inscription:	Signed and dated: 'E.B.J. 1877'.

The drawings were studies for *Perseus and the Graiae*, No 3 in the final Perseus series.

A cartoon in gouache (Southampton) for this work was painted also in 1877 and an oil version (New York) in 1883–93.

(vi) **A Girl's Head**
Profile study in pencil

Size:	20cm × 15cm (8in × 6in).
Inscription:	Signed and dated: 'E.B.J. 1878'.

All are from the collection of the Cecil French Bequest, Fulham, and loaned by the London Borough of Hammersmith and Fulham.

40

D. G. Rossetti (photograph)
Death-bed portrait by F. J. Shields
Pencil

Size:	29cm × 24cm (11½in × 9½in).
Inscription:	'Done in anguish of heart, Dante Gabriel Rossetti, Easter Monday 1882, F. J. Shields'.
Loaned by:	A. R. Dufty.

41

William Morris
Portrait drawing on death-bed by C. Fairfax Murray
Pencil

Size:	27cm × 20cm (10¾in × 7¾in).
Inscription:	Top right: 'Oct 3 96 C.F.M.'
Collection:	The Society of Antiquaries (Kelmscott Manor).

42

Jenny and May Morris
Oil painting, conversation piece by George Howard (Earl of Carlisle)

Size:	48cm × 31cm (18¾in × 12in).
Date:	Undated.
Collection:	The Society of Antiquaries (Kelmscott Manor).

43

Naworth Castle
Watercolour by May Morris

Size:	25cm × 34cm (10in × 13½in).
Date:	Undated.
Collection:	The Society of Antiquaries (Kelmscott Manor).

Naworth Castle was the home of the Howard Family. Morris and his wife were very friendly with George Howard, the Liberal MP, and his wife (later Earl and Countess of Carlisle), and the Morris family, sometimes accompanied by Burne-Jones, often stayed as guests. The Firm decorated the Howards' house in Kensington Palace Green, and Morris also designed stained glass for Naworth.

44

Philip Webb's Study at Caxtons, Worth, Sussex
Watercolour by T. M. Rooke

Size:	38cm × 33cm (15in × 13in).
Date:	Undated.
Collection:	The Society of Antiquaries (Kelmscott Manor).

T. M. Rooke joined the Firm as an employee in 1869. He also acted as assistant and general factotum in Burne-Jones's studios at North End, Fulham. Philip Webb rented the cottage from Wilfrid Scawen Blunt and lived there in his retirement from 1901 until his death in 1915.

45

Italian town, possibly Mantua
Oil painting by unknown artist

Size:	64cm × 85cm (25in × 33½in).
Date:	16th century.
Collection:	The Society of Antiquaries (Kelmscott Manor).

One of two oil paintings from the collection of D. G. Rossetti, left at Kelmscott Manor by him. They are in early composition frames.

46

Bacchanal, with a Wine Press (Bacchanalean Group with a Vat)
Engraving by Andrea Mantegna, 1431–1506

Size:	33cm × 46cm (13in × 18¼in).
Collection:	The Society of Antiquaries (Kelmscott Manor).

The original copper plate is the second of a pair of engravings of Bacchanals (Hind V.6) which belong together now in the British Museum. According to E. Tietze-Conrat in her monograph *Mantegna*, London, 1955, pp241–4, Pl. 102, 103, the subject includes the following figures, reading left to right: a male figure on the shoulders of another; a standing figure leaning on a cornucopia, who may be Revelry or Comus 'flushed with wine and though erect, he is asleep' says Philostratus, or he may be Dionysus; two Pan or Satyr figures, one supporting a drunken boy; two drunken putti; another putto climbing into the wine vat; a Triton sitting on the vat and blowing a horn, while another quaffing wine and dancing turns away the other's horn. The huge vat spouting wine may illustrate the mouth of the river (Andros in Philostratus's account). Tietze-Conrat dates them 1465–70, Hind V.6 dates them c1490.

Mantegna was pupil and adopted son of the archaeologist-painter, one-time tailor in Padua, Squarcione. As well as a painter, Mantegna was a designer of architecture, of stage decor, of monuments, carvings, tapestries and vases. He reflected the humanist attitudes prevalent in Padua during the second half of the fifteenth century and his work is characterised by a strong interest in classical antiquity. He studied the sketchbooks of Jacopo Bellini during his stay in Venice which demonstrated the Florentine interests in perspective, the human figure and in architectural composition. He married Jacopo's daughter, Nicolosia.

In 1459 he was appointed court painter to Ludovico Gonzaga at Mantua. His most noteworthy work was the decoration of the Camera Degli Sposi in the Palazzo Ducale completed in 1474. He made visits to Florence in 1466, and to Rome in the 1480s.

Mantegna was also a pioneer engraver. He was not prolific – there are only seven engravings identified as by his own hand, and these were made in his studio under close supervision. He did not allow his designs to be reversed.

During his stay in Rome, Mantegna would have been able to see some of the most famous classical sculptures recently excavated. These included the sculptures that decorated the Arches of Titus and Constantine. From sketchbooks it is likely he knew also the Census frieze from the so-called Altar of Domitius Ahenobarbus. The latter works were in the Palazzo Santacroce in Rome in the seventeenth century, but it is probable that Mantegna knew them and exploited details from them in his Bacchanals and also in his paintings of the *Triumph of Caesar*, completed before 1492, now at Hampton Court.

It is possible that Morris gained inspiration for his *Vine* tapestry designs from the background to this engraving.

47

An Allegory of the Power of Love
Engraving by Cristofano Robetta, 1462–1522

Size:	28cm × 30cm (11in × 11¾in).
Inscription:	Signed 'Robeta' on tablet hanging from branch of tree on right.
Collection:	The Society of Antiquaries (Kelmscott Manor).

The original copper plate is in the British Museum. It was acquired from the Vallardi Collection in 1888 and has the *Adoration of the Magi* engraved on the reverse side. The *Adoration* is a free adaptation of Filippino Lippi's *Adoration* of 1496 (Uffizi). Impressions from both sides are among the commonest of Robetta's works, see A. M. Hind in *Early Italian Engraving*, London, 1938, vol. I.

Allegory:	Cat No 29, Pl. 292, p205.
Adoration:	Cat No 10, Pl. 276.

Cristofano di Michele, called Robetta, the son of a hosier, Michele di Cristofano Martini, was born in Florence in 1462. He worked in his father's shop in 1480 and became a practising goldsmith in 1498.

Cristofano was mentioned by Vasari in *Life of G. F. Rustici* as a goldsmith and a member of a dining society of 12 called 'Compagnia del Paiuolo' (the 'Kettle'), who met in Rustici's rooms. He was working until 1522.

Hind remarks on Robetta's lack of 'severe artistic training', which is reflected in his drawing. He assimilated something of Dürer's manner, but without the 'precision and subtlety' of Dürer. His work is typically Florentine, its grace and charm inspired by Filippino Lippi and Perugino's work in Florence between 1472 and 1505.

48

Apocalypse (Apocalipsis cum figuris, die Heimlich Offenbarung Johannis)
Series of 16 woodcuts by Albrecht Dürer, 1471–1528
(Latin and German editions 1498, Latin edition 1511)

Size:	Each 39cm × 29cm (15½in × 11½in).
Collection:	The Society of Antiquaries (Kelmscott Manor).

(i)   Title page *The Virgin Mary Appearing to St John in Patmos*, 1497–8
(ii) *The Vision of the Seven Candlesticks*, 1497–8
(iii) *St John before God and the Elders*, 1497–8
(iv) *The Four Horsemen*, 1497–8
(v)   *The Opening of the Fifth and Sixth Seals*, 1497–8

The prints are the first five in the edition, with the second,

The Martyrdom of St John the Evangelist, omitted. This represents the apocryphal story of John in Rome, thrown into a cauldron of boiling oil, from which he emerges unharmed, and possibly the print of this incident, which shows a rather distraught-looking saint squatting nude in a cauldron under which flames are being forced with bellows, was regarded as too sadistic for display when the album was broken up.

By 1505, when Dürer left his native Nuremberg to visit Venice and met there the illustrious Giovanni Bellini, and saw the works also of Giorgione and the young Titian, he was acknowledged through Europe as a great painter. However, as early as the 1470s, he was already known as a successful book illustrator whose work was sold all over Europe. Dürer and his wife gave prints to friends, his mother even presided over a sale of his prints at the Nuremberg 'Relics Fair'. During the last decade of the fifteenth century his graphic work embraced the whole range of print techniques, from relief prints of woodcuts, developed from the earlier unsophisticated woodcuts used to illustrate late Gothic broadsheets and books, to intaglio prints on copper, extending the pioneer works of metal engraving which had appeared earlier in Germany and in the Netherlands.

The *Apocalypse* woodcut series which the artist published in 1498, in both German and Latin editions, represent the height of his achievement as a print maker during his first Nuremberg period.

The somewhat harsh forms in his figure drawing for these, and the angular display, derived from the graphic work of a predecessor in Nuremberg, the painter Michael Wolgemut, to whom Dürer was apprenticed by his goldsmith father in 1486. However, Dürer's concept of the Virgin is chaste and lovely, reflecting the influence of humanist friends such as Pirckheimer, and it was to have considerable effect on both German and Italian painters. Vasari was to write of Dürer's later engravings, 'Albert did some copper engravings which amazed the world'.

Dürer also introduced into his prints some of the fear and distress of the age. There was no greater consciousness of the impending end of the world than that which prevailed at the end of the fifteenth century. Dürer's work at this time is full of storms and conflagrations, presented in rhythmic and vigorous relationships which symbolise the unrest and spiritual doubts of his time. Publication of the *Apocalypse* in 1498 coincided exactly with the burning at the stake of Savonarola in Florence.

In the *Apocalypse* woodcuts, thunder and lightning attending the supernatural events crack over the steep-roofed timber houses, topped by towers and spires, of medieval Nuremberg

represented in these prints. The city too was famous for its many great craft guilds. It is not surprising, therefore, that the young Morris and Burne-Jones, with their Gothic Revival sympathies, both Christian and architectural, should be drawn to these and other powerful images of Dürer, as early as their undergraduate days at Oxford.

In this interest they were encouraged by Ruskin, who wrote 'no scratching of the pen, nor any fortunate chance, nor anything by downright skill and thought will imitate so much as one leaf of Dürer's'. When Morris saw Dürer's engraving of *St Hubert* in 1855, he wrote: 'What a splendid engraving that S. Hubert is! O my word! so very, very gorgeous.' In 1857 Rossetti, who had just met Morris and Burne-Jones, wrote to Bell Scott: 'Both are men of real genius. Jones's designs are models of finish and imaginative detail, unequalled by anything unless, perhaps, Albert Dürer's finest works; and Morris, though without practice as yet, has no less power, I fancy.'

In 1863 Burne-Jones was commissioned by Dalziel to make designs for illustration of a projected *Illustrated Bible*. He made several designs in which it is evident that Dürer is the inspiration.

Burne-Jones also made several copies of German prints in his sketchbooks, including details from Dürer's *St Eustace* (c1501). This engraving was probably lent to him by Ruskin who, in 1865, gave him an impression of it, together with a number of other prints by Dürer. These can be seen hanging on the wall in Burne-Jones's house, The Grange, Fulham, in a painting by T. M. Rooke.

49

Melencolia I

Engraving by Albrecht Dürer, 1471–1528

Size:	24cm × 19cm (9½in × 7½in).
Collection:	The Society of Antiquaries (Kelmscott Manor).

This print is recorded by Hind, 73 State II, and Bartsch, 74 State II.

It is the last of three great works engraved on copper by Dürer between 1513 and 1514, the others being *Knight, Death and Devil* ('The Christian Knight'), 1513, and *St Jerome in His Study*, 1514. The *Knight* print had great significance for both Morris and Burne-Jones. They knew it in a woodcut version, as the frontispiece of an admired book, *Sintram and his Companions*, by H. de la Motte Fouqué. Morris and Burne-Jones, as so many others before and since, mused on this mysterious engraving and its allegory of the noble soul and the Christian Knight. Friedrich Nietzsche was to go further:

'Dürer's picture of the *Knight, Death and Devil* is a symbol of our existence.'

It has been conjectured that these three 'master engravings' together constitute a cycle of virtues – moral, theological and intellectual. It is known that Dürer sometimes sold the *St Jerome* and *Melencolia* together, and that they may have been conceived as companion pieces.

Melencolia I is the most hermetic of all Dürer's prints, and one that has caused great speculation as to its meaning. A massive winged female is seated on a low step in the midst of an apparently accidental accumulation of tools and geometric solids. 'Melancholy' leans in marked absorption one elbow on her knee, her face in shadow, eyes turned upward but focused on nothing. In spite of the many objects and living beings surrounding her, she seems alone. Behind her are visible the sharp-edged planes of a polyhedron and an open seascape empty of ships or human figures. Above it flutters a little dragon carrying the inscription 'Melencolia I'.

The feeling of melancholy of the whole scene is immediately conveyed. The massive winged woman appears oppressive and anguished; the inscription conceals rather than reveals the meaning. The print's 'dark melancholy' has always been recognised. The French Symbolist writer Gérard de Nerval, obsessed by this image and the 'mysterious language of the imagination', wrote in a sonnet of 'the Angel black sun of melancholy'; William Blake always kept a reproduction of it by him. Its mystery and symbolism have been the subject of extensive and detailed study by contemporary scholars of Dürer. See: *Dürer* by Karl-Adolf Knappe, London, 1965.

50

The Tulip Garden
Painting in oil on panel by Pieter Brueghel the Younger (1564–c1637)

Size:	43cm × 58cm (17in × 22⅞in).
Collection:	The Society of Antiquaries (Kelmscott Manor).

The painting is based on a drawing by Peter Brueghel the Elder, signed and dated 1565, as engraved by Peter van der Heyden, 1570, and published by Jerome Cook.

The elder Brueghel's drawing, now in the Albertina Museum, Vienna, is one of a series of the four seasons of which only this and *Summer* were executed by that artist, *Autumn* and *Winter* being completed after his death by Hans Bol. Inscribed along its lower margin are the words, 'De lenten Mert April Meij'. The engraving is faithful to the drawing but is reversed and had an inflated Latin inscription. A painting on canvas, possibly by Abel Grimmer (24cm × 38cm; 9½in × 14½in),

from the collection of the late Capt. E. G. Spencer-Churchill, closely follows the engraving. There appear to be four larger paintings, including the one reproduced, all attributed to the younger Brueghel and all on panels of approximately the same size; two are signed. But these larger paintings omit a boat on the canal, ships on the sea and birds in flight, all of which figure in the drawing, the engraving and the smaller painting. Their greatest deviation from the original composition, which diminishes the social contrast between foreground and background, is the substitution for the richly costumed *dîner sur l'herbe* in front of a pleasure-house in the left background of a peasant dance in front of cottages. The tulips in flower appear only in the larger paintings. The differences between these larger paintings are minor and may be seen especially in the position and spacing of the bulbs lying on the path in the left foreground.

The usual title of the composition is *Spring*, but in the Kelmscott Manor inventory this painting is listed as *The Tulip Garden*. William Morris had little taste for easel paintings in general, but it is not difficult to see why this one appealed to him. The elder Brueghel found inspiration in the miniature paintings of medieval manuscript books, such as the *Heures de Hennessey*, which Morris greatly admired, and something of their quality is transmitted to this painting. And in *Making the Best of It*, 1880, Morris advocated a garden quite like this, 'both orderly and rich'.

51

Morris in the Home Mead (photograph)
Carving by George Jack from a sketch by Philip Webb, on the 'Memorial Cottage' built in Kelmscott village in 1902
(i)   photograph
(ii) sketch by Philip Webb
(iii) photograph of preliminary clay model by George Jack from Webb's sketch

The sketch was given to George Jack by Philip Webb and is now in the possession of John Brandon-Jones.

52

The Morris Tomb in Kelmscott Churchyard
(i) photograph
(ii) preliminary sketches by Philip Webb, 1897

The preliminary sketches were preserved by George Jack and are now in the possession of John Brandon-Jones.

J.A.

'Morris in the Home Mead' carving by George Jack (P51) ▶

138

Catalogue of Textiles

Explanation of Terms

Repeats:	Where the repeat size is indicated, the measurements refer to the *whole* repeat, for instance, if a motif is arranged in a half-drop, the two half-drops are included in the dimensions. Height is expressed before width.
epi:	Ends (warp threads) per inch (metric equivalent = ep 25mm).
ppi:	Picks (weft threads) per inch (metric equivalent = pp 25mm).
Tapestry:	The term here indicates a weft-faced plain weave, into which each colour is inserted by hand. Morris and Company catalogues, on the other hand, call this 'Arras' tapestry.

1

'If I Can', embroidered hanging

Repeat size:	72cm × 29cm (28in × 11in).
Overall size:	169cm × 191cm (66in × 75in).
Date:	c1857, designed and embroidered by William Morris himself.
Fibre:	Embroidery wools on linen.
Embroidery:	The embroidery completely covers the canvas, using 'brick' stitch, with the addition of three-dimensional balls of wool to represent fruit.
Dyes:	The severe fading is a puzzle. Extremely poor light fastness is a characteristic of the family of Basic dyes; it is unlikely, however, that they were used here, because the first synthetic dye of this kind, Perkin's mauve, had only been discovered in 1856. The soft tones of the original colours on the reverse of the hanging would suggest that the fading is due to poor dyeing methods and probably exposure to strong sunlight.

The hanging is described by J. W. Mackail as of 'green trees with gaily-coloured birds among them, and a running scroll emblazoned with his motto in English: "If I Can"'.

◀ *Far left: 'Iseult with the White Hands', left: 'Penelope', two unfinished early 1860s embroideries in brick stitch, probably designed by William Morris.*

A. R. Dufty explains that: 'Morris adopted Van Eyck's motto "als ich kan", which doubtless he saw, possibly written in Greek letters . . . as Van Eyck usually wrote it, on his visit to the Low Countries in 1856, though he could have seen it on the *Portrait of a Man in a Red Turban* bought for the National Gallery in 1851. Thereafter he used it decoratively in German, French and English.'

It is significant that Morris used a bird image in this early hanging. The drawing is stiff and awkward here but was to improve after conscious efforts – resulting in the 'Bird' woven textile of 1878.

2

Embroidered serge curtains

Four similar plants are repeated regularly, each plant with five flower heads on stiff stalks rising from a leaf; warm dull red, pink, pale dull green and yellow on a blue ground.

Repeat size:	56cm × 38cm (22in × 15in), including four apparently similar but different motifs.
Overall size:	167.5cm × 206cm (66in × 81in), including fringe. The curtains are made of pieces of varying width weave which average about 68.5cm (27in). The widths were sewn together before being embroidered, with the weave facing one way and then the other as if this had not been noticed.
Date:	c1859, designed by William Morris; embroidered by Janey Morris, her sister Bessie and Jane Faulkner to hang round the walls of the principal bedroom at Red House.
Fibre:	Ground fabric warp and weft of singles worsted spun.
Weave:	2 × 2 twill; the cloth was mill woven, and commonly known as serge.
Dyes:	Indigo piece dyed (ie: dyed after weaving).
Embroidery:	Couched yarns of wool.

The design derives from an illumination in a Froissart MS in the British Museum (Hart. MSS. 4379/80); it was also the inspiration for the 'Daisy' wallpaper, the first Morris wallpaper to go into commercial production in 1864.

Similar embroidered blue serge can be seen in William Morris's only surviving oil painting, *Queen Guenevere*, or *La Belle Iseult* (1858), in the Tate Gallery, London.

3

'Vine and Acanthus' tapestry (called 'Cabbage and Vine' by Morris)

Tapestry of scrolls of foliage set in mirror-image fashion with three birds among the leaves on each side; mainly blues and buffs with touches of red.

Overall size:	Height varies from 188.5cm to 179cm (74¾in to 70in). Width: 236cm (113in).
Date:	Designed in 1879; the cartoon is in the Victoria and Albert Museum. Woven entirely by Morris himself on a vertical loom set up in his bedroom at Kelmscott House, it was begun on 10 May and finished on 17 September 1879 after 516 working hours; his diary recording progress is in the Victoria and Albert Museum.
Fibre:	Warp, heavy cotton 3-ply; weft, 2-ply soft worsted plus some touches of silk.
Weave:	Tapestry, with warp set at 10 epi, the tension slacking to 7 epi at the centre.
Dyes:	Mainly indigo with other plant dyes.

This was the first and only tapestry woven by Morris and represents a great achievement. Around 1877 he had begun to discuss with Wardle the possibilities of making tapestry; Wardle then encouraged him to start. Morris disliked the current Gobelins and Aubusson tapestries and did not know where to search for a skilled man to begin tapestry weaving. In November 1877 he wrote to Wardle: 'Therefore I feel that what ever I do I must do chiefly with my own hands . . . it is just like wood-engraving: it is a difficult art, but there is nothing to *teach* that a man cannot learn in half a day, though it would take a man long practice to do it well.' He analysed old tapestries thoroughly: in March 1878 he wrote to Wardle: 'I enclose a warp from a sixteenth-century piece of tapestry, which as you see is worsted: the pitch is 12 to the inch: nothing in tapestry need be finer than this.'

Morris wove in the traditional manner so that the weft is vertical when the tapestry is hung. He started at the left-hand side (as the viewer sees the finished piece) and, like all inexperienced tapestry weavers, found his warps were gradually pulled in, making the further end (viewed as the right-hand side) 9cm (3½in) narrower. His use of colour and technique changed as he wove; the overall effect is one of aged muted tones, similar to the verdure in an old tapestry whose yellows have faded, leaving bluish (indigo) leaves where there was once green. The reverse of the 'Cabbage and Vine' tapestry, however, indicates that a minimal degree of fading has taken place on the right side, thereby proving that Morris copied directly the colours of old tapestries he studied.

4

Mille Fleurs tapestry

Formal rows of many-coloured small flowering plants rising as if growing from the ground.

Repeat size:	100cm × 62cm (39in × 24in). The plants are similar but different, so build up to a large repeaa as in the serge curtains.
Overall size:	236cm × 148cm (92in × 58in).
Date:	Woven at Merton Abbey between 1912 and 1920, probably c1918, by four weavers (note the initials PS SM WS AW); probably designed by John Henry Dearle.
Provenance:	Bought from Morris and Company, 17 George St, Hanover Square, c1920 by Mrs M. C. G. Hinman.
Fibre:	Warp, cotton 4-ply; weft, mainly fine-quality worsted 2-ply, except for the brown which is like a woollen knitting yarn, plus some silk.
Weave:	Tapestry, 14 epi, c44 ppi.
Dyes:	Three tones of indigo, alum madder and associated plant dyes for yellows, greens and browns.

The attribution to J. H. Dearle has been made by A. R. Dufty, and is based on the colour and compact character of the design. Dearle, who started with the firm as a boy in 1878, was trained by Morris and, according to Lewis F. Day writing in 1899, 'learnt to work so like him that the designs of the pupil may well be mistaken, even by the experienced in design, for that of the master. As a matter of fact great part of the floral and other detail in the tapestries woven at Merton is entirely his.'

The tapestries bore no distinguishing mark according to H. C. Marillier (*History of Merton Abbey Tapestry Works*, 1927) until about 1912, when the name Merton Abbey (or MA), with occasionally the weavers' names or initials, were woven in. Here, the initials PS and WS probably relate to the weavers Percy Sheldrick and William Sleath.

5

Tapestry fragment

A bramble against a fence with a carnation and a thistle; mainly greys.

Overall size:	92cm × 40cm (36¼in × 15¾in).

Date:	c1890, probably a sample piece for one of the tapestries of the Holy Grail series produced for Stanmore Hall.
Fibre:	Weft of wool, incorporating a tremendous variety of 2-ply yarns, some softer and some hard.
Weave:	Tapestry, approximately 14 epi, 44 ppi.

The design is difficult to weave because of the subtle colour changes. It is much more skilled work than the 'Mille Fleurs'. Aymer Vallance wrote in 1897: 'For the Stanmore series . . . a moderately fine web was decided upon, of a uniform texture, i.e. the warp threads sixteen to the inch throughout.'

6

'Bullerswood' type pile carpet

Birds set among intertwined stems and foliage; blue ground in the field, red in the border. The design repeats once lengthways and in mirror fashion once in the width; it is close to the 'Bullerswood' carpet in the Victoria and Albert Museum.

Overall size:	747cm × 381cm (24ft 6in × 12ft 6in) including fringe.
Date:	c1889.
Fibre:	Warp, heavy 3-ply cotton; binding weft, jute or hemp; tufts, firm worsted yarn.
Weave:	10 epi, with 25 symmetrical knots per square inch.
Selvedge:	2-cord, overcast with blue wool; the outer warp thread is not bound by the ordinary weft.
Dyes:	Indigo dyed ground in centre, madder ground in border; other colours obtained from associated plant dyes.

The technical details correspond exactly to those given for the 'Bullerswood' carpet in *A History of British Carpets* by C. E. C. Tattersall, published 1934. It is hand knotted probably by women (see illustration in Lewis F. Day's article in the *Easter Annual* of the *Art Journal*, 1899).

This carpet belongs to the group of 'Hammersmith' rugs, which were hand knotted (as opposed to machine woven) and so named because they were originally made (from 1879) at Kelmscott House, Hammersmith. Their production was later transferred to Merton Abbey. With regard to its provenance, A. R. Dufty gives the following information: 'Acting upon advice by Mr R. Henshaw of 6 Lansdown Crescent, Bath, this carpet was found rolled up in the cellar of the Bath Art Gallery where it had been for a number of years. Since no

place in the Gallery was proposed for it, on representation made it was given on permanent loan to Kelmscott Manor by Bath City Council in 1976. The size is closely comparable with that of the "Bullerswood" Morris carpet in the Victoria and Albert Museum . . . Generally speaking the two designs are much alike. The V. and A. carpet was made for the Sanderson family of "Bullerswood", Chislehurst, in Kent in 1889. In view of the similarities, the Kelmscott carpet is doubtless of like date. Unfortunately the Gallery had no record of provenance.'

The design of this carpet owes much to Morris's study of Persian ones, which are the source for the Chinese-type birds. Is the inclusion of birds in Morris's carpet design peculiar to this and the 'Bullerswood' carpet?

This one epitomises much that was innate to Morris's view of textiles: his love of 'frank red and blue', the presence of birds within a context of flowers and foliage, the sense of repeat and impression of infinite growth emphasised by the birds best seen from one direction, an honest use of materials and the time-consuming technique. The boldness and flatness of images with the merest suggestion of planes were, Morris observed, especially appropriate to carpet design, remembering that a carpet was intended to be seen lying horizontally on the floor; its pattern should therefore be treated differently from textiles hung against a wall.

7

Pile 'Hammersmith' rug

The central field includes curves of buds and foliage in buff on a red ground; the border has flowers and stems on a blue ground.

Repeat of central field:	73cm × 30cm (29in × 12in) repeated in a mirror image.
Overall size:	193cm × 120cm (76in × 47in) with two 7.5cm (3in) fringes.
Date:	Probably around the turn of the century.
Provenance:	The rug was found by A. R. Dufty at Kelmscott Manor.
Fibre:	Warp, cotton; weft, jute or hemp; tufts, wool worsted.
Weave:	Ground set at 12 epi, 6 ppi; hand-knotted with symmetrical knots at 36 knots to the square inch (depth of pile, ¼in).
Dyes:	Madder, indigo and associated plant dyes.

8a and 8b

'Bird' woven furnishing

Pairs of birds facing each other, one pair perched, one pair

143

flying, set in a dense thicket of foliage. Made in the two colourways exhibited: 8a in two tones of blue with touches of fawn and red, 8b in two tones of red with fawn and green.

Repeat size:	157cm × 43cm (22½in × 17in).
Overall size:	a: 206cm × 133cm (81in × 52in).
	b: 44cm × 130cm (18in × 51in).
Date:	Designed in 1878; manufactured originally at Queen Square and then at Merton Abbey.
Fibre:	Warp, 2-ply worsted spun; weft, singles woollen spun.
Weave:	Treble cloth, hand woven on jacquard loom; 72 epi, 60 ppi.
Dyes:	Indigo, madder and associated plant dyes.

The three-layered construction of this cloth gives a fine surface appearance but the overall structure is heavy and fairly inflexible. It was sometimes used for upholstery (see the sofa in the Green Room at Kelmscott Manor) but was primarily designed for and used as hangings. The Morris and Company brochure for the Boston Foreign Fair in 1883 described how Morris himself had the 'Bird' pattern hung in his drawing room at Kelmscott House 'from the skirting to within two feet of the ceiling. The cloth is hooked to the top rail, and is but slightly plaited – only just enough modulation of the surface being allowed to just break the pattern here and there. The beautiful effect of a long wall hung in this way is quite inconceivable . . .' The same brochure refers to 'the heavy curtain stuffs sometimes called Tapestries, though that is a misuse of the word'. Later in the history of the Company 'tapestry' became the accepted term for the furnishings such as 'Bird', 'Peacock' and 'Tulip and Net' woven in wool, and those such as 'Dove and Rose' woven in silk and wool. The mirror image of the design constitutes a 'turnover' pattern; in woven textiles, this arrangement assisted the pointing of the design and threading up of the warp on the loom. However, the exact mirror image is broken where birds' wings overlap, thus disguising the structure of the repeat and creating greater flow from one area of the pattern to the next.

9a and 9b

'Peacock' woven furnishing ('Peacock and Dragon')
Pairs of peacocks and pairs of phoenixes similarly confronted are set among foliage; 9a: mainly blues, 9b: mainly reds.

Repeat size:	110cm × 85cm (43½in × 33½in).
Overall size:	a: 392cm × 285cm (154¼in × 112¼in), made up of widths pieced together.
	b: 50cm × 66cm (20in × 27½in).
Date:	Designed in 1878–9; woven first at Queen Square, then at Merton Abbey.
Fibre:	Warp, 2-ply worsted yarn, z-spun, s-plied; weft, singles woollen yarn, z-spun.
Weave:	Composite twill, hand woven on a jacquard loom.
Dyes:	Indigo, madder and associated plant dyes.

The Morris catalogue c1910 advertised this design in five colourways: 72in wide at 25 shillings per yard, 54in wide at 17s 6d per yard.

Aymer Vallance in 1897 wrote that this was a 'large pattern for which the artist himself had a special liking'.

The design has often been referred to as 'Peacock and Dragon'. In fact, the 'dragons' are phoenixes which represent what Morris considered to look like Chinese birds. They are not taken directly from Chinese sources, but from the exotic versions of those creatures featured in Persian carpets.

Here there is subtle disguising of the mirrored repeat in the device of crossing stems, an effect comparable with the overlapping wings in 'Bird'. In all Morris's woven textiles, the degree of expertise in the drawing of the pattern on the loom and the type and quality of the weave structure depended on the producer, whether that be Morris and Company's own workshop or a contracted outside firm.

10

'Vine' woven furnishing
Trailing vine stems, leaves and grapes overlaid by a formal meandering band with tulips inserted in it; blue ground with green, ivory, pale blue, warm red and pale pink.

Repeat size:	89cm × 40.5cm (35in × 16in).
Overall size:	196cm × 129.5cm (87in × 51in).
Date:	Designed c1890.
Fibre:	Warp, 2-ply worsted, very fine; weft, 2-ply worsted, very fine and softly spun.
Weave:	A composite twill as in 'Peacock', but of a different weight.
Dyes:	Indigo, madder and associated plant dyes.
Loaned by:	Society of Antiquaries.

11

'Tulip and Net' woven furnishing
Alternating rows of tulips and other flowers set among foliage; two tones of blue with pink, yellow and ivory.

Repeat size:	71cm × 41cm (28in × 16¼in).
Overall size:	236cm × 152cm (93in × 60in).
Date:	Designed c1890.
Fibre:	Warp, 2-ply worsted wool, z-spun, s-plied; wefts, singles woollen yarn z-spun, and 2-ply worsted z-spun, both s-plied.
Weave:	Complex structure, hand-woven on a jacquard loom; 44 epi, 84 ppi.
Dyes:	Tones of indigo and associated plant dyes.

In Morris and Company's catalogue of 1910 this design is offered in 72in width in all wool at 20 shillings per yard; in silk and wool at 28s 6d per yard, in this colouring only.

The design is one of several in which some of the flowers are difficult to identify; one wonders whether the associations conjured up by a name were not sometimes more important than the images actually depicted.

12

'Violet and Columbine' woven furnishing

Many different flowers and leaves among which violets and columbines are given emphasis through colour.

Repeat size:	96.5cm × 86cm (38in × 34in).
Overall size:	192cm × 165cm (6ft 4in × 5ft 5in).
Date:	Designed 1882–3.
Fibre:	Warp, 2-ply worsted spun; weft, 2-ply worsted spun.
Weave:	Double cloth with weave variations: 38 epi arranged with one on face, two on back; c166 ppi, with 25 double ppi appearing on the top layer.
Dyes:	Indigo, madder and associated plant dyes.

The design was first exhibited in the United States in 1883. The Morris and Company brochure for the Boston Foreign Fair states that 'certain designs like the "Violet and Columbine" are quite new, and have not been shown anywhere before the opening of this exhibition'.

It is offered in Morris and Company's catalogue of c1910 at 20 shillings per yard in three colourings.

Compared with the other wool furnishings exhibited, this cloth is less well constructed. The loose setting of the threads is probably indicative of the type of loom and place of manufacture; it may also be a characteristic of a later weaving and cheapened version of the design.

13

'Acanthus' woven furnishing

Acanthus leaves in equally balanced green and white.

Repeat size:	46cm × 34cm (18in × 13¾in).
Overall size:	172cm × 135cm (68in × 53in).
Date:	Designed circa early 1880s by Morris.
Fibres:	Warp, 2-ply worsted spun, highly twisted; weft, singles worsted spun.
Weave:	Damask; 90 epi, 56 ppi.
Dyes:	Indigo on yellow (weld or quercitron).

The splendid rich green is skilfully achieved by dyeing the cloth twice over, yellow first, followed by indigo. Here there is an unusual vibrance of colour due to the lustre of the fibre (possibly Wensleydale or Lincoln fleece) and careful dyeing.

14a and 14b

'Crown Imperial' woven furnishing

Crown imperials and other flowers and foliage set among formal curves of entwining lines in two tones of the same colour, 14a in red and 14b in blue.

Repeat size:	45cm × 23cm (17¾in × 9in).
Overall size:	a: 8.19m × 139cm (9yd × 55in).
	b: 12.74m × 139cm (14yd × 55in).
Date:	Designed in 1876.
Fibre:	Warp and weft of 2-ply worsted, z-spun, s-plied.
Weave:	Damask; 70 epi, 56 ppi.
Dyes:	a: two tones of madder.
	b: two tones of indigo.

The design is taken from a fifteenth-century Rhenish printed linen (no T.7022–1860 in the Victoria and Albert Museum), the pairs of birds from which have been replaced by the crown imperial flower.

15

'Tulip and Willow' block printed cotton

No obvious tulip image, but bunches of anemones (?) among willow foliage; blue and white, much faded.

Repeat size:	42cm × 45cm (16½in × 17½in).
Overall size:	195cm × 128cm (87in × 50in) two pieces being joined together.
Date:	Designed in 1873, Morris's second design for printed textiles. The design was originally printed by Clarksons. This discharge version was printed at Merton Abbey; a companion piece is

marked 449 Oxford Street on the selvedge and is therefore datable to 1882–1917; this piece must also have been printed between those years.

Weave:	Plain, but heavier than most printed cottons.
Dyes:	Indigo discharge. This piece was originally overprinted with yellow to give green and yellow on two intensities of discharge.

'Tulip and Willow' was the first design used at Merton for the overprinting of weld yellow on indigo (see Stanford 19, entry no 50).

16
'Marigold' block printed cotton
Vertical meandering foliated stripes set against a background of small-scale foliage and flowers; red on off-white ground; this piece is much faded.

Repeat size:	22cm × 23.5cm (8¾in × 9¼in).
Overall size:	Fragment approximately 68.5cm × 71cm (27in × 26in).
Date:	Registered as a chintz design in 1875, although used earlier as a wallpaper. It was the first design to be printed by Wardle. 'Morris & Company, 26 Queen Square, Bloomsbury' is printed on the selvedge, making this piece datable to 1875–7, the latter year marking the opening of the Oxford Street showrooms. It would have been printed by Wardle at Leek at this date.
Dyes:	Madder on alum mordant.

17a and 17b
'Brother Rabbit' block-printed cotton
A horizontal band of rabbits, face to face and back to back, alternating with bands of birds among oak and other foliage; 17a: blue and white, 17b: red and white.

Repeat size:	48cm × 51cm (12¾in × 8¾in).
Overall size:	a: 196cm × 87cm (6ft 5in × 2ft 10in). b: 48cm × 51cm (19in × 20in).
Date:	Designed in 1882, it was one of the first to be printed after the move to Merton Abbey.
Dyes:	a: indigo discharged. b: probably alizarin.

18a and 18b
'Bird and Anemone' block-printed cotton
Two birds with wings spread perched among foliage and flowers; 18a in blue and white, 18b in reds.

Repeat size:	52cm × 22cm (20½in × 8¾in).
Overall size:	a: 3.5m × 96cm (11ft 6in × 38in). b: 40cm × 48cm (16in × 18½in).
Date:	Designed in 1882; it was also used as a wallpaper. Both pieces were printed at Merton Abbey; 18a is labelled 31.10.37 and has a selvedge marked 'Regd. Morris & Company'; the red fragment 18b bears the inscription 'Regd. Morris and Company, 449 Oxford Street, London' and was therefore printed before 1917.
Dyes:	a: indigo discharge. b: madder on alum mordant, the cloth being first dyed red all over and then printed in red.

19a and 19b
'Strawberry Thief' block-printed cotton
Pairs of perched birds with tails almost touching set among foliage and flowers; multicoloured, 19a faded, 19b unfaded.

Repeat size:	52cm × 44cm (20½in × 17½in).
Overall size:	a: 184cm × 158cm (72½in × 62in). b: 31cm × 2.31m (12in × 9ft), made of three pieces sewn together.
Date:	Design registered in 1883. Printed at Merton Abbey.
Dyes:	Indigo, madder, weld and cutch; the recipe, photographed from the Merton Abbey Dyebook, is given in Stanford 19, entry no 50.

These pieces, which come from the dining room at Kelmscott Manor, were commented on by Elfrida Manning who wrote in her diary after a visit in March 1925: 'The little dining-room is hung with very faded "Strawberry Thief" pattern.' (Journal of the William Morris Society, Summer 1980.)

20
'Kennet' block-printed cotton
A large-scale meander of peony/anemone-type flowers set against a background of small-scale vine leaves and grapes; blue ground with green and yellow, faded.

Repeat size:	63cm × 23cm (25in × 9in).
Overall size:	195cm × 195cm (77in × 77in).
Date:	Design registered in 1883. Printed at Merton Abbey.
Dyes:	Mid-tone indigo, discharged at two different strengths to give pale blue and white, and overprinted with yellow which has preserved the indigo from fading, as in 'Strawberry Thief'.

This piece comes from the Green Room at Kelmscott Manor, where all the walls are hung with 'Kennet'.

21

'Flowerpot' block-printed cotton

A small-scale design of two motifs of vases of flowers set within a formal arrangement of stems; blue ground with white, red and yellow.

Repeat size:	10cm × 10cm (4in × 4in).
Overall size:	175cm × 51cm (69in × 20in).
Date:	Designed in 1883. Printed at Merton Abbey.
Dyes:	Indigo discharged and overprinted.

Designed for linings and possibly dress fabrics.

22

'Wandle' block-printed cotton

A very large-scale design with diagonals of red and white meandering stripes with peony-type flowers at intervals set against a complex interlacing of flowers, stems and foliage.

Repeat size:	91cm × 44cm (36in × 17½in).
Overall size:	95cm × 96.5cm (37½in × 38in).
Date:	Design registered July 1884. Printed at Merton Abbey.
Dyes:	Indigo discharged and overprinted with madder and weld on alum mordants.
Loaned by:	William Morris Gallery, Walthamstow.

23a and 23b

'Lea' block-printed cotton

Swirling acanthus leaves interlaced with a secondary smaller scale pattern of stems and flowers; 23a in reds, 23b in blue and white.

Repeat size:	42cm × 24cm (16½in × 9½in).
Overall size:	a: approx 5.46m × 98cm (6yd × 38in).
	b: 1.8m × 98cm (5ft 11in × 36in).

Date:	Design registered in 1885. Printed at Merton Abbey. These pieces are both later than 1917; the blue piece (b) is labelled '17 George Street, Hanover Square', and cost 4s 11d per yard.
Dyes:	a: two tones of alum mordant, subsequently dyed in madder or alizarin.
	b: mid-tone indigo dye resisted.

This is a very skilled design, lending itself very well to both positive and resist printing. It is interesting that 23b, though giving the impression of a discharged pattern, is in fact resist-dyed; the reverse of the cloth displays an almost solid medium blue, unlike a discharged pattern in which the voided areas of the design are apparent on both sides of the textile. The attached label bears the number 3015; this refers to a recipe in the Merton dyebook, Berger Collection (Morris and Co archives). The label of the Kelmscott length corresponds exactly to entry no 54, Stanford 19; the two samples must therefore have been printed by the same technique.

24

'Acanthus' block-printed cotton velveteen

Acanthus leaves in different shades of red.

Overall size:	Uneven fragment approx 88cm × 72cm (35in × 28in).
Date:	Designed 1888–9, probably by J. H. Dearle. Printed at Merton Abbey.
Dyes:	Madder or alizarin on three tones of alum mordant; although the ground appears to have been dyed, it has been printed with a pale tone of alum mordant.

25

'Little Scroll' block-printed cotton

Scrolls of small pointed leaves densely covering the ground with the addition of dots resembling berries.

Repeat size:	29cm × 30cm (11½in × 11¾in).
Overall size:	96.5cm × 69cm (38in × 27¼in).
Date:	This is a late design, one of several produced by the Company but not designed by Morris himself. The piece is labelled '3/6d. per yard by Morris and Company, 17 George Street, Hanover Square'; thus it postdates 1917.
Dyes:	Dark indigo discharged to white.

J.H. and D. O'C.

Catalogue of Ceramics

1

Daisy tile
Earthenware; overglaze painted in blue, green and yellow on white engobe; rows of alternate open and closed daisy heads in clumps.

Size:	15cm² (6in²).
Date:	Early 1860s.
Designer:	William Morris.
Loaned by:	Private Collector.

The design similar to the motif employed in the 'Daisy' wallpaper has been linked with the embroidered blue serge drape, displayed elsewhere in the exhibition (Textiles No 2). The simple pattern was also used for the glass quarries produced by Morris, Marshall, Faulkner & Co.

During this early period the tiles themselves were imported from Holland with the patterns being applied in the company's workshop and fired in the glass kiln in the basement.

'The same kiln that was used for firing stained glass was made to serve for the tiles also. An iron muffle with iron shelves carried the glass in the middle part, while the tiles were so placed as to be exposed to the greatest heat, at the top and bottom. A small wind-furnace was employed for slips and for colour-testing experiments.' (Vallance, *William Morris; his art, his writings and his public life*, London, 1897, pp79–80.)

2

Tiles
Two sets of two tiles set vertically, earthenware; overglaze painted in green, blue and yellow on white engobe; each set has a single figure design of a woman standing against a blue background, representing Philomena of Athens, and Cleopatra of Egypt.

Size:	13cm² (5$\frac{1}{10}$in²).
Thickness:	2.5cm ($\frac{4}{5}$in).
Date:	Early 1860s.
Designer:	Attributed to Burne-Jones.
Loaned by:	Private Collector.

In a pencilled draft for a prospectus of Morris, Marshall, Faulkner & Co, Morris wrote:

'. . . we have been peculiarly successful in the revival (as we think we may call it) of the art of painting on China tiles for walls similar in manner to the ancient majolica. Of these we keep in stock several sets of figures (painted each on two tiles) [these five words are scored out] with appropriate diapers . . .

suitable for decoration of fire places etc. in private houses . . .' (British Museum Add. MS. 45.336 fol. 26v.)

Several examples of the figured tile sets and the working drawings have survived, including Burne-Jones's designs of 'Beauty and the Beast', 'Cinderella' and 'Sleeping Beauty'. The arrangement of these two-tile sets within a fireplace may be seen at Queen's College Hall, Cambridge.

3

Tiles
Fireplace in the Green Room, Kelmscott Manor (photograph)
Earthenware; underglaze painted in cobalt blue on white engobe. Three designs are employed: leaf scroll with pendant grape or blossom form; division of surface area into 16 squares filled alternately with a long-necked swan and water-willow branches; and sunflower surrounded by leaves.

Size:	13cm² (5$\frac{1}{10}$in²).
Date:	Early 1860s.
Manufacturer:	Morris, Marshall, Faulkner & Co.

4

Tiles
Panel of 16 earthenware tiles arranged within a square wooden frame; overglaze painting in green, blue, yellow, black, portraying Paris, Venus, Minerva and Juno, among trees and vegetation. Above these figures, the legend in black on blue ground reads:
'Paris of Troy you may see in company of ladies three
Venus, Minerva and Juno – all naked for that he may know
the Fashion of their bodies Fair – alas the deed th[a]t he did there
that day the gold apple he gave to Venus so tha[t] might have',
continuing underneath the central composition:
'Helen the Fair for his leman – which was the death of many amo
For thereby as the stories tell – Full many a woe to Troy beFell
thereby of Troy the case is this
no stone upon another is'.

Size:	13cm² (5$\frac{1}{10}$in²).
Date:	Early 1860s.
Designer:	Attributed to Burne-Jones.
Loaned by:	Private Collector.

5

Tiles

Earthenware with an impressed back-stamp of a rose containing the words 'Sands End Pottery, Fulham, Wm. De Morgan & Co.' on two of the three tiles; underglaze painted in cobalt and turquoise blue, green, yellow and aubergine on white engobe; each tile contains a section of undulating vegetal scroll with 'artichoke' blossoms, and leaf motifs.

Size:	23cm² (9⅛in²).
Thickness:	1.3cm (½in).
Date:	c1888–97.
Loaned by:	Private Collector.

The surface decoration and its colouring are greatly influenced by the so-called 'Rhodian' wares of Turkish Iznik production, datable to the second half of the sixteenth century, a large number of which were purchased by the South Kensington Museum in 1876. Shortly after, De Morgan became involved in organising into panels and repairing the various Islamic tiles for Leighton's Arab Hall. A similar design for a vertical tile series is to be seen among the De Morgan watercolours held by the Victoria and Albert Museum, London (Prints & Drawings Dept, E 526–1917).

6

Charger

Earthenware; lustre painted in metallic oxides giving colours of copper red, gold and silver, on opaque white glaze; central composition shows a woman seated on steps, playing a harp, and by her side a cupid figure with pan-pipes; around the rim a series of three putti playing wind instruments; the base decoration consists of a series of leaf sprays and a diaper pattern enclosing stylised heart or circle motif.

Diameter:	46cm (16½in).
Height:	5cm (2in).
Date:	c1883.
Designer:	William De Morgan.
Loaned by:	Society of Antiquaries.

De Morgan became interested in the technique of lustre painting and firing, as shown in the wares of Persia, Spain and Italy. During the Merton period he experimented successfully with the traditional rather than the contemporary industrial techniques, and this work was the subject of his lecture to the Royal Society of Arts in 1892.

The two designs, for the rim and the cavetto of this charger, exist in the Victoria and Albert Museum holdings, London (Prints & Drawings Dept, E 1282-1917 and E 1257-1917), and are said to date before 1883. The putti figures playing

instruments continued to be used as ceramic designs by De Morgan on later wares, for instance the 1901 two-handled vase made at the Cantagalli factory (Gaunt & Clayton-Stamm, *William De Morgan*, London, 1971, pl.137).

7

Dish

Earthenware; underglaze painted in cobalt and turquoise blue, green, aubergine, black on white; central design of carnation from which radiate panels holding thistle motifs; on the base concentric circles in black and the two shades of blue on white, with painted mark in black 'Wm. De Morgan and Co.' and the initials 'CP'.

Diameter:	20.2cm (7⁹⁄₁₀in).
Height:	2.8cm (1¹⁄₁₀in).
Date:	c1885.
Painted by:	Charles Passenger.
Loaned by:	Private Collector.

The palette and carnation motif owe much to sixteenth-century Turkish Iznik ware, while the radiating bands scheme can be seen on the underglaze painted wares of Iran, Seljuq and Ilkhanid periods (thirteenth-fourteenth centuries).

The Passenger brothers, Charles and Fred, worked with De Morgan from 1879 to 1907 at Cheyne Row, Chelsea, Merton Abbey and at Sands End. Their initials are found on De Morgan pieces from the mid-1880s.

8

Plate

Staffordshire body of Bodley & Son; lustre painted in metallic oxides giving colours of copper red and silver on opaque white glaze; the figure of a peacock dominates the central composition, while the reverse is decorated with circles and squiggles.

Diameter:	23cm (9⅛in).
Date:	c1875.
Designer:	William De Morgan.
Loaned by:	Birmingham City Museum and Art Gallery.

9

Vase with two handles

Earthenware with pronounced glaze crackle; underglazed painting in cobalt and turquoise blue, green and aubergine; among the stylised leaf forms, five lizards; impressed stamp on base, ovoid shape and legend 'De Morgan Merton Abbey', and the initials 'FP'.

Diameter:	21.5cm (8½in).
Height:	15.8cm (6¼in).
Date:	1882–8.
Painted by:	Fred Passenger.
Loaned by:	Birmingham City Museum and Art Gallery.

10

Tile

Frit body; underglaze painted in cobalt and turquoise blue on white engobe; stylised floral motifs including tulips and serrated leaf forms; 'Kutahya' ware of the type associated with Iznik production, Turkey.

Size:	25cm² (9⅞in²).
Thickness:	1.2cm (⅜in).
Date:	Circa first half of 16th century.
Loaned by:	Private Collector.

11

Plate (riveted)

Frit body; underglaze painted in cobalt and turquoise blue, green, red on white engobe; the lobed rim is decorated with a wave pattern represented by a series of spirals, while in the central medallion there is a stylised arrangement including hyacinth sprays flanking a lobed ovoid shape; the reverse decoration consists of isolated rosettes alternating with twin tulip and leaf motifs; so-called 'Rhodian' wares of Iznik production, Turkey.

Diameter:	28.8cm (11³⁄₁₀in).
Height:	5.6cm (2¼in).
Date:	Circa second half of 16th century.
Loaned by:	Private Collector.

These wares, thought in the late-nineteenth century to have been manufactured on the island of Rhodes, were very popular in Britain and the rest of Europe, inspiring among others Cantagalli of Italy, Deck of France, as well as Morris and De Morgan. Archaeological excavations have since shown that production centred in the north-west Anatolian town of Iznik. The earliest use of the red pigment is recorded in the tiles of the Sulaimaniya mosque complex, Istanbul, built by Sinan for the Ottoman Sultan in 1550.

12

Jug with handle (chipped)

Porcelain; underglaze painting in cobalt blue; the decoration is contained in three panels separated by a vertical scroll band, common on Chinese wares of the period, infilled with stylised landscape scenes; two concentric rings painted on the high foot; Japanese production.

Rim diameter:	9.2cm (3⅝in).
Height:	19.5cm (7⅝in).
Date:	Late 17th century.
Loaned by:	Society of Antiquaries.

Such shapes were made in the Far East for the European markets with prototypes and even moulds being sent out for copying.

13

Plate

Porcelain; underglaze painting in cobalt blue; the rim decoration is divided with two alternating panel designs of floral and foliage arrangements, while a vase of flowers and sprays forms the central composition; Chinese 'Kraak' ware.

Diameter:	21.5cm (8½in).
Date:	Second half of 17th century.
Loaned by:	Society of Antiquaries.

After capturing a Portuguese carrack galleon with a cargo of Chinese porcelain of this type, the Dutch referred to the ware as *'Kraak' porselein*.

14

Plate

Porcelain; underglaze painting in cobalt blue; the rim decoration consists of a series of linked circles containing rosettes; the stylised landscape placed centrally is framed in a faceted octagon; Chinese or possibly Japanese production. Painted seal-mark on the back is meaningless.

Diameter:	27.5cm (10⅞in).
Date:	Second half of 17th century.
Loaned by:	Society of Antiquaries.

An octagon of similar shape was originally incorporated by Morris in the 'Orchard' carpet, but his letter dated 24 August 1880 states that this '4 × 4 form is out and much improved by the alterations the 3 yellow bordered pots are not so flat as they should be . . .' (British Museum Add. MS. 45338 fol. 133v).

P.L.B.

15

The Ignis Charger

Large round earthenware dish with a wide rim and depressed centre, painted in ruby lustre. The central panel is decorated with an allegorical figure surrounded by fish and putti holding flaming torches. The reverse side is painted with a scale pattern.

Diameter:	50.8cm (20in).
Height:	10cm (4in).
Rim:	9.1cm (3½in).
Date:	Late Fulham period.
Inscription:	'DM'.
Provenance:	Presented by William De Morgan to the Chelsea Public Library.
Loaned by:	Chelsea Public Library.

16

An angel holding a dove

A mosaic by William De Morgan, one of his experiments in glazed coloured slip, detached from the biscuit backing after firing, cut to shape and mounted. Probably executed in the early 1870s, when he and William Morris were interested in this technique. De Morgan, however, did not persevere with the medium.

Size:	61cm × 45.5cm (24in × 17¾in).
Date:	Chelsea period, early 1870.
Loaned by:	Chelsea Public Library.

17

Tiles

Two boldly designed tiles with animal motifs, 'Ostrich' and 'Sea Horse', two-tone colour variations, in green and blue and bronze lustre. The background is painted with a pale green leaf design. Probably part of a composite panel of nine tiles arranged in three rows.

Size:	15cm² (6in²).
Date:	Fulham period.
Loaned by:	Fulham Public Library.

18

Tiles in wooden frame

Panel of six tiles painted in enamel colours with conventionalised roses on a long-necked vase, itself patterned with bronze and white flowers on a yellow background. The vase is surrounded by turquoise blue flowers and green leaves on a black background.

Size:	Tiles: 20.3cm² (8in²).
	Panel: 61cm × 40.6cm (24in × 16in).
Date:	Fulham period.
Loaned by:	Chelsea Public Library.

The making of tile panels played an important part throughout De Morgan's career. He started to make tiles in his Turkish pastiche style (then referred to as Persian) from the 1870s on, with enamels that were new at the time and characterised by richness and depth of colour.

19

Tiles

Panel composed of four tiles with small patterned border, at top and bottom of panel.

Two conventionalised peacocks, shown facing left and right but with heads turned towards each other. Decorated in colours of the Iznik palette, blue and green.

Size:	20.3cm² (8in²).
Date:	Early Fulham period, 1890.
Loaned by:	Chelsea Public Library.

20

Vase

Small red lustre vase with carnations in silver lustre contained in an all-over tear-drop pattern.

Size:	29.5cm × 15.2cm (11½in × 6in).
Inscription:	Inscribed on base: 'De Morgan. Sands End Pottery. 1890'.
Loaned by:	Fulham Public Library.

V.A.

'Kutahya' tile from Turkey (C10) ▶

Catalogue of the Firm's Furniture

1

Round table

Designed by Philip Webb in 1860, and described by May Morris as the 'first made' and used in Red House.

Height: 74cm (29in).

Diameter: 140cm (55in).

Underframe: 70cm² (27½in²).

Webb was probably paid 15 shillings for the paper design.[1] If the Sussex range represents the most famous contribution of the Firm – the kind of furniture that 'you can pull about with one hand' – this piece (and Janey's work table, No 2) represents the other significant side of the Firm's early activity: the production of heavy furniture that looks 'medieval', and which, as Morris put it, should 'not be so very light as to be nearly imponderable; it should be made of timber rather than walking sticks'.[2]

By 1860, the emphasis on the kind of 'revealed construction' which Pugin associated with the Middle Ages – in the form of wedge and halving joints which got away from the 'glue pot' – was already something of a design cliché; but, despite the claims made by members of the Firm on behalf of 'revealed construction', much of it served a purely aesthetic purpose, and was not so well made as the 'glue pot' dovetail and tenon joints hidden in Regency and Victorian furniture. When the Firm showed painted pieces in this style at the 'medieval court' of the 1862 Exhibition, it was noted by the press that Morris's furniture was not as well constructed as the 'medieval' work of rival designers.

This round table, in keeping with the interiors of Red House, is very 'medieval' in style: chamfered, splayed-out legs end in crenellated bases which look rather like mailed boots;[3] the boarded sides are punched with plate tracery, and edged with a wavy chamfer; the dowels are 'revealed' and protrude 0.6cm (¼in). But its solid joinery construction is far from simple and 'workaday'. The round table is *not* simply a board resting on a trestle table; the decorative detail, cut-out design on the panels, and construction of the thick turned oak legs – which change in section three times – must have required the most sophisticated of carpenter's skills. The heavy square underframe allows the sitter's legs to be set well under the table, giving greater comfort. So, of the two main design criteria outlined by the 1912 catalogue, this piece scores highly on 'convenience'; but the other criterion – 'economy of space' – is not much in evidence. Warington Taylor was later to criticise Webb's 'medieval' work for being rather out of place 'now there are no more castles'.[4]

◀ *The main staircase at Kelmscott Manor*

2

Janey's work table

Probably designed by Webb for use in Red House, at the same time as the round table (No 1).

Height: 76cm (29⅞in).

Diameter: 58cm (22⅞in).

An interesting feature is the round tray, with bentwood edges, which is dowelled into the main frame underneath the oak table-top. For a small work table, this has a very cumbersome ('massive') design, typical of the style of work against which Taylor was later to react: there are *five* legs and *five* stretchers with chamfered edges. For 'medieval' seamstresses only . . .

3

Green bedroom suite

Designed in 1861–2 by Ford Madox Brown, this suite seems to be of the 'severe feudal' type. The connotations of 'feudal' certainly apply to most of the techniques – boarded construction, mortise, tenon and halving joints, use of pegs and dowels, chamfering and heavy section wood. The fact that *three* of these washstands are kept at Kelmscott seems to cast doubt on the assertion that these pieces were produced solely for Madox Brown's 'own use':[5] 'What was good enough for an artisan was good enough for him.'[6] Madox Brown did, in fact, design similar pieces for an 'ideal artisan's dwelling' at the Jubilee Exhibition in Manchester, 1887; but the widespread use of washstands in artisan bedrooms (apart from the 'ideal' ones) during the mid-nineteenth century has yet to be proven, as has the assumption that this 'simple' and 'honest' furniture would find favour with artisans, even if they could afford it. We also lack evidence about Madox Brown's washing habits, so the question must remain open.

The painting of furniture was a common medieval practice, as a way of protecting pieces from the smoke and grime of open hearth fires, but the use of paint or stain in the nineteenth century (these were originally *stained* green) was more a matter of style, often disguising the use of different woods, such as deal, or of woods with a dull grain such as ash. A few years after these pieces were made, however, Warington Taylor drew the Firm's attention to the practical disadvantages of this fashionable practice:

'Memo on furniture – A glass of hot brandy and water, if slightly upset, produces an ugly ring on an ordinary French polished mahogany *table . . . On our stained black and green furniture, these marks become much more offensive – the stain comes off, re-polish or not, the mark remains.*

'Summa – I do not think stained furniture is practical, we ought to be content with natural wood.'[7]

155

Taylor was referring to dining tables – but the point applied with even more force to the washstands, and with considerable irony to Madox Brown (whose views, recorded by E. M. Tait, have been quoted above).

(i) Washstand

Height:	90cm (35½in).
Width:	92cm (36¼in).
Depth:	49cm (19in).

Consists of a board top, with a hole for the basin, surrounded by a 'splashback'. The cupboard below has holes for ventilation in the side panels. All the edges are chamfered, and there are outsized hinges on the door.

(ii) Towel rail

Height:	91.5cm (36in).
Width:	71cm (28in).

Three round-section horizontal rails pierce the triangular end pieces, which are each mounted on a pair of uprights.

(iii) Dressing table

Height:	85.5cm (33⅜in).
Width:	122cm (48¾in).
Depth:	62cm (24½in).

Consists of a boarded top and back board with chamfered edges. Heavy-section legs are bolted on to the underframe, which has a decorative neo-Gothic shape. The drawer is suspended on side-runners, and does not require a handle: this may have been a design innovation.

(iv) Bed

Length:	200cm (78in).
Width:	117cm (45½in).

A heavy board construction with chamfered edges. The octagonal legs, which are 16cm (6⅜in) in diameter, taper towards the top.

4

Egyptian armchair

Designed by Rossetti, probably towards the end of his association with the Firm, and based on the mid-Victorian notion of Egyptian furniture.

Height:	43.5cm (17in).
Width:	50cm (19½in).
Depth:	51cm (20in).

Although this piece is arguably the most sophisticated and self-conscious from the point of view of design, it relies heavily on simple 'stick' methods of construction – notice how the rails are 'dowelled' through the legs and protrude a prominent centimetre. The most obvious 'design' feature, perhaps, is the extension of the arm to form a continuous band round the back of the chair; however, unlike the bent bow back of the Windsor chair, this is constructed out of three separate pieces which are joined underneath by means of a metal plate. The seat frame extends beyond the back to produce a brace support for the back of the chair – a device commonly found in early Windsor chairs, but in this case serving a more aesthetic purpose. The back rails, too, are self-consciously decorative, with their cut-out semi-circular motif and painted gilt bands on the spindles.

5

The Sussex Range

Probably the most commercially successful product of the Firm, the 'Sussex' range was in continuous production from 1866 onwards. The different designs were developed and refined by Ford Madox Brown and Dante Gabriel Rossetti from a prototype found by Warington Taylor (the Firm's young business manager) while he was 'with an old carpenter' in Sussex. This prototype may well have been a 'Sheraton fancy chair' – a country version of a sophisticated Regency design. Since Taylor's famous account of the discovery (see no 6, entry on adjustable chair) gives the impression that the chair was found *in* a Sussex carpenter's workshop – very provincial, very vernacular – the myth of 'good citizens' furniture' has gained support from the manuscript letter to Webb. In fact, it is likely that Taylor discovered an unsold Sheraton chair, perhaps being repaired, in a Sussex furniture shop. Other remarks dating from the time show that Taylor was becoming increasingly excited by neo-Georgian designs.

In the exhibition there are four distinct designs that share certain common characteristics – they all combine an ebonised wood structure with rush seats, and are made from a combination of simple turned parts (front legs, rails, spindles and stretchers) with more complex carved and shaped pieces (arms and back uprights).

Warington Taylor wanted the Firm to produce 'chairs you can pull about with one hand'; this lightness, combined with the delicacy of their design, must go a long way towards explaining their popularity – in the context of the more ponderous designs that dominated the market in the mid-1860s. That the lightness, and delicacy of construction, owe a great deal to the knowledge and skill of eighteenth-century cabinet-makers can be seen in the shaping of the back uprights which curve at the 'waist', and subtly alter in section with the change from a rounded 'back' to a tapering rectangular leg; or again, in the elegantly shaped arm of the armchair which terminates in a turned detail. The use of a mortise and tenon joint at the junction of the back with the seat frame gives the chair more strength than would otherwise be provided by the more simple dowel joint in the front leg (reminiscent of Windsor chairs), and gives the opportunity to lighten the chair by tapering away superfluous wood. The use of finely turned parts is, of course, a very old chairmaking practice, but it is perhaps the small scale of the section that distinguishes the Sussex chair from pre-eighteenth-century models.

The many different processes involved in the making of each individual piece provide evidence of the specialised division of labour that must have been practised in the Firm's first workshops; a skilled turner would have produced the spindles and stretchers on a lathe, while experienced carpenters would have been responsible for the carved arm pieces; the assembly and painting of all the components would have been done by workmen, while the rush seating may well have been handed on to outworkers. This division of labour must have helped to keep the price down, but whether the figures quoted in the 1910/12 catalogues were low enough for the 'artisan' market is debatable. All the evidence suggests that this market would not have been attracted to the special features of the Sussex range.

(i) **Chair**

Height:	84.5cm (33in).
Width:	44cm (17½in).
Depth:	42cm (16½in).
Price:	7 shillings (1912).

With rectangular rush seat. The back rails are connected by turned spindle.

(ii) **Armchair**

Height:	86cm (33½in).
Width:	49cm (19in).
Depth:	42cm (16½in).
Price:	9s 9d (1912).

This piece also has a curved and shaped arm, which terminates in a shaped finial. The arm support is noteworthy for its curious insertion through the seat from a specially provided stretcher beneath the seat. This may have been devised as a way of avoiding the weak joint that would have occurred if the arms had been inserted into the seat frame directly above the front leg.

(iii) **Chair**

Height:	44cm (17¼in).
Width:	43cm (16¾in).
Depth:	42cm (16½in).
Price:	10s 6d (1912).

With cruciform back and oval rush seat. Design attributed to Ford Madox Brown. The back rails pass through a wooden 'sphere', the front of which has been flattened for the sitter's comfort.

(iv) **Rossetti armchair**

Height:	89cm (35in).
Width:	52cm (20¼in).
Depth:	46cm (18¼in).
Price:	16s 6d (1912).

With rounded rush seat. Although most commentators suggest that this was first designed in 1865, there is some evidence that a version of the armchair – perhaps even the original 'vernacular' piece from which it may have been derived – was in Rossetti's possession in 1864. It is more elaborate than the rest of the Sussex range, in design and detail: the curved and shaped arms, which terminate in a simple version of the traditional eighteenth-century cabinet-makers' scroll over-arm; and the back, which resembles the shape of an eighteenth-century 'wheatsheaf', but which instead of being a solid splat back simply consists of nine sticks which are slotted through a wooden 'tie' – similar to the construction of the 'comb piece' in a Windsor chair. Unlike the rest of the Sussex range, this chair has a curved back rail.

6

Adjustable chair

Known, particularly in America, as the 'Morris chair', although William Morris appears to have had very little to do with it.

Height:	100cm (39¼in).
Width:	63cm (24¾in).
Depth:	86cm (33¾in).

This design was adapted by Philip Webb from a prototype found in Sussex in the mid-1860s. It is constructed of black ebonised wood, with a curved back which has slats of the 'ladder back' type to hold the loose buttoned cushions in place, and acorn finials. The padded arms, side rails and stretchers are simple 'bobbin-turned' spindles.

Warington Taylor, who was convalescing from an attack of consumption at Beach Cottage, Hastings – he later died of the disease, at the age of 34 – came across the prototype 'with an old carpenter'. He wrote to Webb about the design, the back and seat of which were 'made with bars across to put cushions on . . . moving on a hinge . . . a chair model of which I saw with an old carpenter at Hurst Monceau, Sussex, by name Ephraim Coleman'.[8] Webb's version took the original idea of a neo-Georgian easy chair, with inclined seats, and simply added bobbin-turned stretchers; in other words, the Firm simply added a new – and unnecessary – piece of styling. Adjustable chairs of one kind or another – easy chairs, lounging chairs, club chairs – had been on the market for over 30 years.[9] One example was on show at the 1862 Exhibition, the same exhibition as housed the Firm's 'medieval' painted furniture. It is strange that so many commentators – and so much of the Firm's publicity – credited Morris & Co with this major breakthrough in 'design for use', for the distinctive features of the 'Morris chair' had very little to do with Morris, his Firm *or* considerations of 'use'.

7

Daybed
Designed by Philip Webb and made by the Firm.

Length: 160cm (62½in).
Depth: 71cm (27¾in).

A long seat, with loose cushions covered in 'wine' chintz. This piece has a frame of ebonised wood, with bobbin-turned rails in a fixed end, supported on six legs with connecting stretchers (also bobbin-turned). A decorative, carved bracket strengthens the join of the headboard to the main frame; the same ornamental motif appears on the front apron. Looking back on the period of his association with the Firm, Webb wrote that 'in trying to combine art with the crafts there seem to me only two ways of making it – in the Devil's slang of these times – "pay"; one, is to make comparatively few articles of a costly kind and do them all by skilled designs in a small way . . .'[10] We do not know how many of these daybeds were produced or how much they cost, but we have evidence that Webb was under constant pressure at this time from Warington Taylor to charge a realistic figure for his services, in particular for the time he spent on paper designs. Like Morris, he thought that five per cent was a reasonable profit margin – until Taylor persuaded him to 'vigorous, stern action if the firm is to be saved. If you do not act no one else will. Everyone treats it as a joke . . .'[11]

8

Upholstered furniture
'. . . If you want to be jack of all trades you must have separate staffs – Peter Robinson does not do his mourning business in his bedding warehouse . . . With 12 men being made to do one day one thing one another, we can only have disorder and less . . . You cannot manage more than one class of work with one establishment. If you make that pay it is as much as you can do . . .'[12]

'In the same building as the cabinet and joinery works [at Holland and Sons, after 1890] is an upholstery shop where all kinds of stuffed furniture are finished and covered. This in itself, with the making up or cleaning of curtains, blinds, carpets, cushions etc is a large and by no means unimportant business, comprising an entire department of the Firm. In the early days, the boards which Morris and Co used to affix to houses they were decorating bore the word "upholders": this archaic form has been dropped, but the work covered by it continues and has multiplied . . .'[13]

The upholstered furniture produced by the Firm, from 1875 onwards, was not particularly original in design: it relied on ideas which the trade had been marketing, with some success, for over half a century. The Oxford Street showroom, which opened in 1877, would have provided an important retail outlet for these stuffed and padded products. What makes them interesting is the use of Morris & Co's fabrics. Unfortunately, none of the items in the Exhibition has its original coverings – which wore out long ago – but they are covered with original William Morris prints.

Morris & Co offered a wide variety of pieces for covering – sofas, daybeds, club chairs, divan chairs, and the Saville chair – as well as a choice of fabrics (chintzes, woven wools, velvet and so on). The introduction of upholstered furniture probably coincides with the reorganisation of the Firm, the opening of the showroom, and the expansion of the textile side of the business; this furniture may have gone into production *after* the textiles had been produced, and after the Firm's premises had expanded.

9

Couch

Length: 170cm (66⅛in).
Depth: 70cm (27⅛in).
Height of seat: 38cm (14⅞in).

A long upholstered seat, which has one end inclined to provide a back and head rest: a characteristic nineteenth-century type of couch, with the arm extending half the length of the piece. Although the design was commonplace (Holland and Son would probably have had it in stock), the covering – a blue 'Bird' fabric produced by the Firm in about 1878 – is not.

10

Divan easy chair

Height: 84cm (32¾in).
Width: 75cm (29¼in).
Depth: 61cm (24¼in).

Apart from the legs, no woodwork is visible; comfort depends on deeply sprung upholstery. A very typical late-nineteenth-century design, with buttoned back and arms, covered in 'Peacock and Dragon' wool produced by the Firm. Mrs Morris was photographed sitting in a similar chair, at Rossetti's home in Cheyne Walk. In 1912 the same design, covered in chintz, sold for £7 10s 0d.

11

Mahogany occasional table

Designer: George Jack.

This piece, which has cabinet-makers' marks on the joints under the table, represents a neo-Georgian design which was increasingly characteristic of the Firm's output from the 1890s onwards. It is an elegant example of the cabinet-maker's skill 'equal to the best productions of Chippendale and Sheraton'.[14] George Jack, who trained as an architect under Philip Webb, had become the chief furniture designer for Morris & Co in 1890, at the same time as the move to Holland and Son's workshops. Since then he had been responsible for many elaborate neo-Georgian designs, often using precious woods and veneering and inlay techniques. The fine detail work on this table includes the fluted and beaded edge of the six-sided top; the shaped underframe which is mortised and tenoned into hexagonal tapering legs; and the stretchers which end in a circular centre-piece.

A carved mahogany table, very similar to this, was shown at the Arts and Crafts Exhibition of 1889; it was designed by George Jack in the previous year. The table may pre-date his promotion to chief designer. By 1912 (when it was still selling well) two versions of the occasional table were featured in the catalogue: one, with carved and curved stretchers and legs, cost £9 15s 0d; the other cost £4 10s 0d. At this stage, the Firm was Morris's in name only . . .

H.S.

1 William Morris, quoted in Paul Thompson, *Work of William Morris*, p70.
2 *Ibid.*
3 *Ibid*, p73.
4 E. M. Tait, 'Madox Brown, Pioneer of Art Furniture', in *The Furniture*, III, 1900–1, pp61–2.
5 See 'Ford Madox Brown's Furniture', in *The Artist*, 22, 1898, especially pp48–50, and E. M. Tait, *op cit*, pp61–3.
6 Quoted in W. R. Lethaby, *Philip Webb and his Work*, p49.
7 *Ibid*, pp48–9.
8 The original source of this often-quoted – and misinterpreted – letter is a manuscript, in Taylor's handwriting, bound among the 'Letters from Warington Taylor to Philip Webb', Victoria and Albert Library, Reserve Case JJ 35. This manuscript also includes a pencil and ink drawing of the 'Chair Model'. In the article 'Ford Madox Brown's Furniture' (see Ref 5) it is erroneously implied that Madox Brown sought inspiration from things to be seen in old country inns. He persuaded the Firm to manufacture the Sussex chairs (p49). While Madox Brown *may* have spotted the commercial potential of the range, he certainly did not 'see' the chair model in an old country inn.
9 See, among many other references, John Gloag's *Short Dictionary of Furniture*, London, 1977, p240, and Edgar Kaufmann's article in the *Architectural Review*, 108, August 1950. One possible 'inspiration' for the Sussex chair with rush seat is illustrated in Gloag, *op cit*, p721.
10 Quoted in W. R. Lethaby, *op cit*, pp61–2.
11 Quoted in W. R. Lethaby, *op cit*, p57. Taylor made other attempts to persuade Webb during the same period (pp53–5).
12 One of Warington Taylor's memos, quoted in W. R. Lethaby, *op cit*, pp56–7.
13 *Ibid.*
14 *A Brief Sketch of the Morris Movement*, 1911, pp55–6.

Catalogue of Traditional Furniture and Personal Items from Kelmscott Manor

1

Boarded standard

Oak, banded and studded with iron; iron lock and carrying handles; detachable oak base.

Height:	58.4cm (23in).
Width:	57cm (22¼in).
Depth:	40.6cm (16in).
Date:	c1600–50.

A standard was a type of travelling chest, designed to be carried between two men, and normally slung on a pole by its handles. Of coffers, standards and trunks, standards were the more heavily built of the three. As a type of furniture, they were prevalent from the first half of the fifteenth until the early eighteenth centuries. This example, normally on show in the Old Hall of Kelmscott Manor, is quite elaborate, with its rosette headed studs, and the turned handles, with their decorative abutted knobs and intervening rings in the centre of each handle. Most standards of this type had domed or gabled lids. A comparable example is illustrated in Victor Chinnery, 'Oak Furniture, The English Tradition', *A History of Early Furniture in the British Isles and New England* (Antique Collectors Club Ltd, London, 1969), p353.

2

Glass roundel

Stained and painted, leaded glass.

Diameter:	30cm (12in).
Date:	c1600.

The iconography of this roundel represents the Court of Heaven; five figures sit on a recessed dais; Christ is seen crowning the Virgin Mary on the right. Around the lower edge of the roundel, with their backs to the viewer, are seven more figures. A number more lean over the back parapet wall, which divides the dais from its background. The central panel is treated as one unit, in which all the imagery is painted on to it. With the exception of the crowns, whose yellow stain would have been painted on the reverse side of the roundel, the rest of the central panel is painted in grisaille, a monochromatic technique using finely graduated amounts of black enamel, composed of iron or copper oxide mixed with a flux of powdered white glass; the effects of shading in the figures would be achieved by stippling with a brush of short, stiff bristles. The imagery of the roundel seems ironically appropriate, as a counterbalance to William Morris's identification of Kelmscott Manor with an 'earthly paradise'. The combination of the different stained glass techniques used, together with the figure treatment and handling of the

arches above the central figures, would suggest a date of c1600, and a possible Flemish provenance.

3

Chinese chair

Red lacquered wood, with a silver-gilt medallion set in the splat, a scalloped top rail, and four plain stretchers; central section of seat caned.

Height:	106.6cm (42in).
Width:	50.8cm (20in).
Depth:	45.7cm (18in).
Date:	Mid-19th century (?).
Provenance:	D. G. Rossetti.

This chair is one of a pair, both in the collection of the Society of Antiquaries at Kelmscott Manor. The roundel set in the back splat represents two birds on branches. The attribution of ownership to D. G. Rossetti, made by A. R. Dufty, is on the basis of Rossetti's known taste for exoticism. Rossetti brought with him a number of items of furniture when he came to live at Kelmscott Manor in 1871. The only direct evidence of his furniture is contained in a letter of Jane Morris (British Museum Add. MS. 52333B, ff. 137–41). This chair does not, however, figure among that list.

4

Chinese chair

Huang Hua Li (Chinese rosewood); box frame, the back splat which curves slightly contains incised and carved decoration. The front skirt has a stepped frame, with foliate and geometric scrolls. The inset panel is of woven bamboo; the stretchers are plain.

Height:	72.3cm (28½in).
Width:	58.4cm (23in).
Depth:	48.2cm (19in).
Date:	16th century (?).
Provenance:	William Morris, 26 Queen Square, Bloomsbury, London.
Identification:	May Morris, Memorandum referred to in her Will, specifying furniture and effects given to the University of Oxford. See A. R. Dufty, 'William Morris and the Kelmscott Estate', in *The Antiquaries Journal*, 1963, vol XLIII, part I, p110.

A comparable chair is illustrated in *World Furniture*, ed. Helena Hayward (Paul Hamlyn, London, 1965), ill. 1066.

5

Indian chest

Ebonised and gilded wood; iron carrying handles at sides. Detachable base, which may have been made for another piece of furniture.

Height:	68.5cm (27in).
Width:	111.7cm (44in).
Depth:	58.4cm (23in).
Date:	18th century.

This may have been a bridal chest; the elaborate decoration, which covers the sides, contains on the front the image of a prince and princess emerging from a temple on a litter. The front of the chest shows signs of repair. The central lock opening is recent. On the left and right, ovoids indicate the previous location of hasps which are now removed.

6

Corner cupboard and stand

Japanned wood; lacquered and gilded; stand with fretwork brackets.

Height:	219cm (86¼in).
Width:	60.9cm (24in).
Depth:	35.5cm (14in).
Date:	18th century; stand 19th century (?).
Provenance:	D. G. Rossetti.
Identification:	BM Add. MS. 52333B, fol. 141.

This corner cupboard and stand is one of a pair, in the white panelled room at Kelmscott Manor, left behind by D. G. Rossetti following his departure from the house in 1874. He attempted unsuccessfully to retrieve it, along with a number of other items, in 1878. Evidence of Rossetti's taste for this type of furniture is contained in A. H. Treffy Dunn's painting *Dante Gabriel Rossetti in his Sitting Room at 16 Cheyne Walk* (W/C, 1882, National Portrait Gallery, London). In the corner of the sitting room at 16 Cheyne Walk, behind Rossetti's chair, is shown a wall-hung japanned corner cabinet.

7

Cassone

Italian cypress wood, with poker work decoration.

Height:	67.3cm (26½in).
Width:	104cm (41in).
Depth:	55.8cm (22in).
Date:	c1600.
Provenance:	Drawing room, Kelmscott House.

A cassone is an Italian marriage chest. This example, with its use of stylised flat pattern, would have appealed to Morris. It is one of a number of items transferred to Kelmscott Manor from Kelmscott House after William Morris's death in 1896. Jane Morris gave up Kelmscott House and spent part of her time with May Morris at Kelmscott Manor.

8

Box chair

Oak; English joined armchair; open frame arms, but otherwise solid panels. Seat lid is hinged and lifts up to reveal internal cavity in base.

Height:	105.4cm (41½in).
Width:	55.2cm (21¾in).
Depth:	49.5cm (19½in).
Date:	2nd quarter of 16th century (?); possibly a 19th-century remake.

Box chairs are fairly standard items of oak furniture. Like other examples (see Harold Osborne, *The Oxford Companion to the Decorative Arts*, Clarendon Press, Oxford, 1975, p362), this contains a cavity in its base for storage, probably for books. The Kelmscott Manor example, known as 'Janey's chair', is a slight variant on the standard form, as it has curving, sloping arms with pillar supports. The front of the chair back has quite elaborate incised decoration of an interlacing scroll with a palmette rosette in the centre of each whorl of the scroll. The rear of this panel is plain; its condition would indicate that it is not a reproduction piece, but its authenticity has nevertheless been questioned. Clive Wainwright of the Department of Furniture and Woodwork, Victoria & Albert Museum, has suggested that it may be a remake, assembled from different pieces.

9

Jewel casket

Painted by Dante Gabriel Rossetti and Elizabeth Siddal. Painted wood; iron frame, hinges and clasp.

Height:	17.7cm (7in).
Width:	29.2cm (11½in).
Depth:	17.7cm (7in).
Date:	pre-1862.
Provenance:	Jane Morris.
Identification:	May Morris Memorandum; see A. R. Dufty, 'William Morris and the Kelmscott Estate', in *The Antiquaries Journal*, 1963, vol XLIII, part I, p111.

The casket, constructed in the form of a hinged, gable-lidded box, has 14 panels, seven of which still have painted decoration. Five out of the six panels on the front elevation have figurative decoration which is Arthurian in character. The corresponding decoration of the panels on the rear has been almost completely obliterated by an unsuccessful previous restoration. The lid pivots on a hinge at the junction of the side and roof, to reveal six internal compartments with drawers below. Elizabeth Siddal's suicide in 1862 provides a terminal date for the design and manufacture of this piece. It is tempting to speculate that it may have been given to Jane Morris as a wedding present in 1859. Certainly its design and decoration are in keeping with the character of the painted furniture from the early phase of the Firm's activities.

10

Four-poster bed

Oak; bedposts with turned balusters.

Height:	213.3cm (84in).
Width:	157.4cm (62in).
Depth:	205.7cm (81in).
Date:	Possible 19th-century remake of 17th-century original.

Clive Wainwright of the Department of Furniture and Woodwork, Victoria & Albert Museum, has suggested that the bed, like the oak box chair, may be a later remake, assembled from earlier pieces. In addition, the base shows evidence of the restoration carried out between 1964 and 1967 by Archer Cowley & Co Ltd of Oxford. There appears to be a discrepancy in the details of decoration between the bed end and the bed head, which has lattice inlay. The bed hangings are embroidered in silks and wools on white cloth. The valance displays Morris's poem 'For the bed at Kelmscott' (1891). It was embroidered by May Morris, assisted, reputedly, by Lily, sister of W. B. Yeats. The curtains may also be embroidered by May, who took over the embroidery section of Morris & Co in 1885. Their pattern derives from Morris's first design for wallpaper, 'Trellis', of 1864, with the birds designed by Philip Webb. The bedcover was embroidered by Jane Morris, who signed it: 'Si je puis. Jane Morris, Kelmscott'. Its delicate, naturalistic decoration includes a quotation from Morris's poem 'A Garden by the Sea', from the *Life and Death of Jason* (1867).

11

Chest of drawers

Oak, with ebony and bone inlay.

Height:	114.3cm (45in).
Width:	104.1cm (41in).
Depth:	55.8cm (22in).
Date:	Early 18th century.
Provenance:	William Morris's study, Kelmscott House, Hammersmith.
Identification:	May Morris's Memorandum, published by A. R. Dufty, *op cit*, p110.

The panels of inlay, with their design of a bird on a branch, remind us of Morris's love of flat pattern. The upper-right-hand corner of the chest appears in D. G. Rossetti's painting, *Marigolds*, of 1874, now in the collection of Nottingham Castle Museum and Art Gallery. See Virginia Surtees, *The Paintings and Drawings of Dante Gabriel Rossetti (1828–1882): A Catalogue Raisonné*, Clarendon Press, Oxford, 1971, vol 1, pl34; vol 2, p335. From this painting it is evident that the chest of drawers was then housed in the Green Room at Kelmscott Manor, whose mantelpiece appears in the painting.

12

Paint box

Metal box, one section in front for brushes; lid used as a palette. Oil paints in tubes.

Height:	21.6cm (8½in).
Width:	45.7cm (18in).
Depth:	5.7cm (2¼in).
Provenance:	D. G. Rossetti.
Identification:	Label on outer lid (worn and tattered) 'D. G. Rossetti's paint box'.

Three manufacturers of oil paints may be identified: Winsor & Newton, Reeves and Gunther Wagner, Vienna. The paint box is now normally displayed in the Tapestry Room at Kelmscott Manor, which particular room Rossetti took over as his studio, when he came to live there in July 1871.

13

Vargueno

Rosewood, with ivory inlay.

Height:	138.4cm (54½in).
Width:	98.4cm (38¾in).
Depth:	46.9cm (18½in).
Date:	Late 16th/early 17th century.
Provenance:	William Morris's study, Kelmscott House, Hammersmith.
Identification:	A. R. Dufty, *Kelmscott* (The Society of Antiquaries, London, 1969), pp22–4.

A vargueno is a sixteenth/seventeenth-century Spanish type of drop-front desk, resting on either a chest or a trestle stand. As in this case, the interior is often elaborately decorated with ebony, tortoiseshell, ivory or other inlays in intricate, geometrical patterns. The term is nineteenth-century in date. Some varguenos have pedestal bases, but the Kelmscott Manor example rests on a matching cupboard, with one shelf in its interior. The use of the inlay would suggest a sixteenth-century date, but this is contradicted by the twin cabinet structure, more common in seventeenth-century examples. See Grace Hardenorff Burr, *Hispanic Furniture from the Fifteenth through the Eighteenth Century*, 2nd edition, revised and enlarged, The Archive Press, New York, 1964, cat no S 74, fig 129, p138, which illustrates a comparable example.

14

Two peacocks

Persian. Brass, pierced and chased; inlaid with turquoises.

Height:	84cm (33in).
Date:	19th century (?).
Provenance:	Kelmscott House, Hammersmith.
Identification:	A. R. Dufty, *Kelmscott, op cit*, p24.
Exhibition:	Burlington Fine Arts Club, London, *Exhibition of Persian and Arab Art*, 1885.

May Morris describes these in her nostalgic recollection of Kelmscott House, quoted by A. R. Dufty: 'Opposite the fireplace stood the great Italian cypress-wood chest and thereon, with several pieces of oriental work, a pair of lordly peacocks of carven brass with jewelled necks, the guardians of a secret treasure. That side of the room had more than a touch of the Thousand and One Nights, for above this table of Eastern riches rose up a carpet spread like a canopy across the ceiling.'

15

Tapestry, representing Samson and the Lion

Wool, Brussels or Antwerp.

Height:	260cm (102in).
Width:	258cm (101½in).
Date:	Mid-17th century.
Identification:	A. R. Dufty, *Kelmscott, op cit*, p13.

This tapestry, together with its four companions representing scenes from the life of Samson, which decorate the Tapestry Room at Kelmscott Manor, are the only furnishings known to have been in the house when William Morris took over the lease of the Manor in May 1871 from the Turner family, who had owned the house since 1666. Nothing more is known, however, about when the Turners may have acquired the tapestries. Morris and Rossetti were at odds with one another in their opinion of the tapestries. Morris felt that they gave an air of romance, and liked their faded colours. (See J. W. Mackail, *The Life of William Morris*, Longmans, Green & Co, London, 1922, p237.) Rossetti apparently hated them and wanted to make a bonfire of them, taunting Morris about the resemblance between Samson and him, each with their unkempt, shaggy locks. (See Roderick Marshall, *William Morris and his Earthly Paradises*, The Compton Press Ltd, Tisbury, 1979, pp208–9.)

16

Lock of William Morris's hair in a silver frame

Hair; repoussé frame with glass mount.

Height:	9.5cm (3¾in).
Width:	5cm (2in).
Date:	Post 1896.
Inscription:	'William Morris 1834–1896'.
Designer:	Philip Webb.
Made by:	R. S. Catterson-Smith.
Provenance:	Mrs Virginia Surtees, by whom it was given to the Society of Antiquaries, London, on 17 December 1967.

A second version of this, but framed and mounted in gold, was bequeathed by May Morris to the Department of Metalwork, Victoria & Albert Museum. R. S. Catterson-Smith collaborated with Morris and Burne-Jones in the preparation of the Kelmscott Press *Chaucer* for publication. The signature R. Catterson-Smith and the address 11 Blenheim Road, Bedford Park, W. appear in the Kelmscott Manor Visitors' Book (British Museum Add. MS. 45412, fol. 4v) in the year 1894, after 27 October.

17

Cartoon for stained-glass window
St Ellyw, Llanelly, Carmarthenshire

Height:	59cm (23in).
Width:	46cm (18in).
Scale:	1:12.
Inscription:	Centre bottom: 'Llanelly'; bottom right-hand corner: 'Return to Morris & Co., Merton Abbey, Surrey'. Stamped bottom left-hand corner: 'Morris & Company (Art Workers Ltd.) Merton Abbey S.W.10'.
Identification:	A. C. Sewter, *The Stained Glass of William Morris and his Circle*, Yale University Press, 1974.
Collection:	A. R. Dufty.
Documentation:	The entry in the *Catalogue of Designs*, dated 9 January 1911, cited by Sewter, names the glass-painters as follows: Stokes, Glasby, Titcomb and Burrows.

The window was bequeathed by Jane Emma Bythway, wife of William Bythway, in memory of her husband (d1909). This design shows a different system of leading from the Oakley design, with stronger use of colour also. The mannered treatment of the figures and drapery is in keeping with its late date.

18

Cartoon for stained-glass window
Oakley Church, Essex, East Window.

Height:	42cm (16½in).
Width:	33cm (13in).
Scale:	1:24.
Inscription:	Bottom right-hand corner: 'The property of Morris & Company 26 Queen Square Bloomsbury W.C.'
Identification:	A. C. Sewter, *op cit*.
Collection:	A. R. Dufty.

This three-light window represents in its lower panels, from left to right: the Infant Christ and the Four Marys, the Nativity and the Flight into Egypt. Sewter dates the window to 1882, on the basis of an entry in the *Catalogue of Designs* for that year of Morris & Company. This names the glass-painters as follows: Adoration and Nativity by Bowman; Flight into Egypt and Choir of Angels by Dearle; Angels in tracery by Pozzi; quarries by Singleton; scrolls and other

tracery by Campfield. However, no window of this design exists at either Great Oakley or Little Oakley, Essex.

19

The Kelmscott Manor Visitors' Address Book
Bound in maroon leather, gold tooled.

Size:	Quarto.
Collection:	British Museum Add. MS. 45412, William Morris Papers, vol XXII (ff 12).
Provenance:	Presented by Robert Steele, Literary Executor to May Morris.

The entries run from 24 August 1889 to 27 July 1904. It is interesting to note that they span the time of Morris's death, after which May Morris was the Manor's main occupant, with her mother a frequent member of the household.

D.D.B.

Catalogue of Books at Kelmscott Manor

The following are the principal texts that have been consulted for information on the publications of the Kelmscott Press and related works, and I acknowledge the assistance given to me therein.

A Note by William Morris on his Aims in Founding the Kelmscott Press together with a Short Description of the Press: and an Annotated List of the Books Printed Thereat, S. C. Cockerell, Kelmscott Press, 1898.
The Kelmscott Press and William Morris, Master Craftsman, H. Halliday Sparling, London, 1924.
The Private Presses, Colin Franklin, London, 1969.
The Story of Cupid and Psyche, A. R. Dufty, Clover Hill Editions, London and Cambridge, 1974.
William Morris and the Art of the Book, with essays on William Morris as: Book Collector by Paul Needham, Calligrapher by Joseph Dunlap, Typographer by John Dreyfus; Pierpont Morgan Library, Oxford University Press, London, 1976.
The Typographical Adventure of William Morris, R. C. H. Briggs, Exhibition Catalogue, William Morris Society, 1958.
In Fine Print: William Morris as Book Designer, Exhibition Catalogue December 1976–March 1977, William Morris Gallery, Walthamstow, 1976.
Morris and Company in Cambridge, Exhibition Catalogue, September–November 1980, Fitzwilliam Museum and Cambridge University Press, 1980.

All books and other publications are from the collection of The Society of Antiquaries at Kelmscott Manor, except where otherwise stated. They are in chronological order. They include books which influenced Morris and books which were influenced by him. (References to Fine Art entries relate to the Catalogue of Paintings, Prints and Drawings, pp125–138. Abbreviations used when referring to source books are explained on p37.)

1

Writing books
(Four books bound together in old crimson calf)
Ludovico Vicentino (Arrighi), Giovanniantonio (Giovanni Antonio) and Sigismundo Fanto

Specification:	Quarto. 192 pages.
Publication:	130 copies printed from woodblocks.
(i) recto:	La Operina di Ludovico Vicentino da imparare di scrivere littera Cancellarischa.
verso:	Il Modo & Regola de scrivere littera.

Rome 1522–25
(ii) recto: Il modo de temperare le Penne Con le

varie Sorti de littere ordinato per Ludovico Vicentino.
verso: Ludovico Vicentino al Candido littore felicita.

Rome 1523
(iii) recto: La Vera arte di scrivere, (Lo presente libro Insegna La Vera arte delo Excellente scrivere de diverse varie sorti de litere, Giovanniantonio Tagliente).

Venice 1525
(iv) recto: Thesauro de Scrittori (Opera artificiosa laquale insegna a scrivere diverse sorte littore, Sigismundo, fanto nobile ferrarese).

Venice 1525

Morris may have owned these books by the late 1860s when his style of calligraphy began to take on Italian characteristics instead of the earlier favoured medieval gothic forms.

2

De historia stirpium commentarii insignes, maximis impensis et vigilius elaborati, adiectis tarvndam vivis plusquam
Leonarto Fvchsio (L. Fuchs).

Size:	Folio.
Publication:	Basileae, in officina Isingriniana (Basil), 1542.

One of the major sources of reference for Morris's drawing and designing of plant forms.

3

The Herball or Generall Historie of Plantes
(gathered by John Gerarde of London, Master in Chirvrgerie Very much Enlarged and Amended by Thomas Johnson Citizen and Apothecarye of London)

Publication:	Printed by Adam Islip Joice Norton and Richard Whitakers, London, 1633.
Inscription:	The book is inscribed: 'with her father's love March 25th 1882'. Another page has the sum £3 entered on it and is signed: 'Mary Morris'.

It is the chief source (with the *Stirpium*) for Morris's drawing and designing from plant forms. See Sow Thistle, p293; Double white and blacke Poppie, p369; The great Daisie, p634; Eyebright, p663; Wilde Artichoke, p1153; and The common Willow, p1389. Not only did Morris use these illustrations for botanical information but also for designing adaptations from their beautiful patterned linear arrangements, which in turn derive from earlier medieval examples.

4

Vita Nova

Secondo la lezione di un Codice inedito del Secola XV
Colle Varianti dell'Edizioni piu accreditate

Size:	Octavo.
Publication:	Pesaro della Typographia Nobile, 1829.
Inscription:	On fly-leaf: 'Jane Morris from D. G. Rossetti, 1878'.

The *Vita Nova* was a major inspirational work for both the poetry and painting of Rossetti (see Ref 13, p39).

5

Gothic furniture in the style of the fifteenth century, designed and etched by A. W. N. Pugin

A. W. N. Pugin

Illustrations:	24 plates.
Published by:	Ackermann, London, 1835.

Pugin believed that the Gothic and Christianity were synonymous, and therefore comprised all that was true. In contrast classical forms were associated with Paganism.

The illustrations in this work provided the required detailing for architects and designers of the Gothic Revival, especially during the 1840s. Pugin's writings, from his first architectural pamphlet, *Contrasts*, 1836, and later works such as *True Principles*, 1841, to the *Glossary of Ecclesiastical Ornament* of 1844 and *Floriated Ornament* of 1849, 'revolutionised the taste of England. My cause as an architect has run out'. So he wrote in 1851. They were to influence considerably Ruskin, the PRB, and Morris, first when an undergraduate.

6

The Anatomy of Melancholy

Democritus Junior

Size:	Folio.
Publication:	Printed for Henry Cripps in 1676, 6th edition, Oxford 1851.

On the fly-leaf of this book is the pen and ink (and crayon?) drawing of Janey Morris by D. G. Rossetti. (See No 26 Fine Art.)

7

The Germ, Nos 1–4

Size:	Octavo.
Publication:	Published January 1850 (Price One Shilling) by Aylott & Jones, 8 Paternoster Row, London.

Inscription:	'May Morris a legacy from H.T. Nov. 1920'.

The magazine was the invention of D. G. Rossetti, who was eager to 'distinguish himself in literature, no less than in painting', as recounted by his brother William, who became the magazine's first editor. In William's words his brother 'wanted to have some safe vehicle both for ushering his writings before the public, and for diffusing the Praeraphaelite (sic) principles in art'.

The aims of the magazine, however, are more clearly stated in the sub-title 'Thoughts towards Nature in Poetry, Literature and Art'. William Rossetti again enlarges on this, 'that an artist, whether painter or writer, ought to be bent upon defining and expressing his own personal thoughts, and that these ought to be based upon a direct study of Nature, and harmonized with her manifestations'.

The appearance of the magazine had a strong Puseyite flavour, with its black and heavy Gothic type for the cover, which emphasises the Pre-Raphaelites' ambiguous use of religion and their conviction about the morality of art. They believed that the artist had a duty to communicate, and that the substance of his message would have social, therefore moral, significance.

The original title went through several changes; initially in the Summer of 1849 it was to be called *Monthly Thoughts in Literature, Poetry, and Art*. By September this was shortened to *Thoughts towards Nature* and finally in December 1849 Cave Thomas's suggestion that it be called *The Germ* was accepted. For publication No 3 in March the title was again changed to *Art and Poetry*.

The first edition included Gabriel Rossetti's prose-tale *Hand and Soul*, and his debt to Dante and the catholic flavour of his language are already evident. In the setting devised for his hero Chiaro living in thirteenth-century Tuscany and described in this verse we see the same devotional furnishings as in his study for *The First Anniversary of the Death of Beatrice* of 1849 (No 14 Fine Art). Other contents of No 1 included:

The Love of Beauty, F. Madox Brown
Dream Land, Ellen Alleyn (Christina Rossetti)
Songs of one Household: (My Sister's Sleep), Dante G. Rossetti
Her First Season, Wm. M. Rossetti.

No 2 contained the celebrated poem 'The Blessed Damozel' by Rossetti.

The first instalment included also two etchings by Holman Hunt; later editions included etchings by James Collinson, Ford Madox Brown, and Walter Deverell. A portrait of Shakespeare's Viola by Deverell was drawn from Elizabeth

Siddal. Brown, in addition to an illustration to William Rossetti's poem 'Cordelia', also contributed a pragmatic article 'On the Mechanism of a Historical Picture' (February) in which he advocates painting only from friends and intimates, as paid models are always found to be 'stiff and feelingless'.

In spite of some favourable opinion the magazine commercially was a failure, and never sold more than two hundred copies of any one edition. It folded after a run of four months only.

A letter from Thomas Carlyle, probably to the Editors, dated Chelsea 31 March 1850, contains the following encouraging comments: 'A decidedly good and promising No. 1. Genius of various Kinds looks through it: – intellectual genius and what you will think stranger, *pictorial* genius; for there is symmetry, clearness, a glance here and there of noble veracity in various kinds. In great haste.'

Although it was a period when periodicals were likely to be successful, the editors were too narrow in their selection of material, maintaining that their journal 'was not open to the conflicting opinions of all who handle brush and palette'.

The first reprinting did not come until 1898, but the brief history of *The Germ* is best told by William Michael Rossetti in his Preface to an edition printed by Elliot Stock in 1901.

A recent reprinting of *The Germ* has been made with a Preface by Andrea Rose and was published by the Ashmolean Museum, Oxford, and Birmingham Museum and Art Gallery in 1979.

8

The Poetical works of Edgar Allan Poe with a notice of his life and genius by James Hannay, Esq
Edgar Allan Poe

Size: Octavo.
Published: London, 1853.
Inscription: 'William Morris. Exeter Coll: Oxon'.

In his early days Rossetti was attracted to dramatic and sometimes grotesque imagery. His first drawings, from c1844 to 1848, show both French influence (the lithographs of Garvarni and Delacroix's paintings of *Faust*), and that of the American Edgar Allan Poe. A drawing Rossetti made in 1847 illustrates Poe's poem 'The Raven'. Entitled *Angel Footfalls*, it depicts the raven perched on a helmeted bust; the man who has been reading by lamplight gazes at a troop of female spirits as they pass before him.

9

Oxford and Cambridge Magazine, conducted by members of the two Universities for 1856
Edited William Morris

Size: Octavo.
Published: London, 1856.
Inscription: 'Jane Morris Kelmscott'.

After Morris had passed his final schools at Oxford in the autumn of 1855, he and friends had banded themselves into an exclusive Brotherhood, seven in number. Dixon, one of the seven, proposed that a magazine should be launched and the idea was taken up enthusiastically by the others. Morris was to be the 'proprietor' and to assume financial responsibility for the venture which Burne-Jones estimated would be not less than £500 per annum.

Morris and Burne-Jones went to Cambridge to enlist the support of their friend Wilfred Heeley and others in the 'Trinity set'. This was offered with enthusiasm. However, in spite of the title they agreed, the *Oxford and Cambridge Magazine*, the contributions were to come mostly from the Oxford group.

The first number of the magazine, with Morris as Editor, appeared on 1 January 1856. It contained 72 pages set in double columns and was printed by Messrs Bell and Daldy. It cost one shilling. Nearly 1000 copies of the first edition were printed in all, but most were given away as presentation copies so little profit ensued. For the second and subsequent editions Morris persuaded Fulford to be the editor for £100 per annum. The number of copies sold continued to decline steadily, however, in spite of warm praise of the magazine from both Ruskin and Tennyson. Morris and Burne-Jones by August were turning their attention to painting. Burne-Jones wrote 'the Mag is going to smash – let it go! The world is not converted and never will be.' It was decided to close the magazine therefore at the end of the year after 12 editions had been printed.

The best contributions had come from Rossetti and Morris, and the influence of *The Germ* and *Frasers Magazine* was evident. Rossetti's poems 'The Burden of Nineveh', 'The Blessed Damozel' and 'The Staff and Scrip' were published in different editions, as were Morris's 'Guendolen' and 'Rapunzel'. This involvement had given both poets valuable experience.

Ruskin's wry comment on the adventure was that he had 'never known an honest journal get on yet'.

10

The Heimskringla
Snorri Sturluson
Illuminated manuscript of *The Story of the Ynglings*
Translated from the Icelandic by William Morris
Calligraphy and decoration also by Morris

Date: c1873.

This manuscript is one of two in the Collection at Kelmscott Manor. The title of the other is *The Story of Egil, the son of Scaldrim*, again translated from the Icelandic by Morris.

Morris's interest in calligraphy began early: 'I remember as a boy going into Canterbury Cathedral and thinking that the gates of heaven had been opened to me, also when I saw my first illuminated manuscript. These first pleasures which I discovered for myself were stronger than anything else I have had in life!'

He followed up his interest as a student at Oxford studying the medieval manuscripts in the Bodleian Library, and later having settled in London, in the British Museum. As early as 1856 he tried his hand at writing and decorating manuscript pages and soon gained the admiration of Rossetti and Ruskin. 'Do-it-yourself' illumination became especially popular in the 1850s and 1860s following encouragement given in books by men such as Owen Jones and Noel Humphries in the 1840s. These were filled with gothic lettering and with chromolithographed coloured borders of medieval inspiration.

In 1856 Morris contributed his poem 'Guendolen' under the title 'Hands' to the July issue of the *Oxford and Cambridge Magazine* and in August he presented Georgiana Macdonald, who was to marry Burne-Jones, with the poem included in manuscript form in his longer work 'Rapunzel'. The manuscript included decorative initials, borders and figures, deriving, it is said, from English fourteenth-century illumination.

Joseph Dunlap (in *William Morris and the Art of the Book*) describes his decoration of this period as combining 'the animal and vegetable in forms unknown to biology', although his later decoration will most certainly 'spring from the Soil'.

After 1865 he and Burne-Jones were spending their Sundays attempting to emulate the great printers of the fifteenth century and planning *The Earthly Paradise* (see No 28). However, at the end of the 1860s we see Morris beginning to experiment with written letters, as in the Prologue to *The Earthly Paradise*.

At this point it would appear that Morris was beginning to be influenced by the writing books of Arrighi (1522, 23, 25) and Tagliente (1525), (see No 1), which he may have owned by then, bringing a new freedom and flourish to his letter forms. In the *Story of Rhodope* (c1868) Morris introduces capital letters of good proportions, with a leafy background, which point to the decorated initial he would soon be painting and the increasing organic emphasis he would give to his calligraphic pages. These changes are again described in some detail by Joseph Dunlap in his essay. Between 1869 and 1875 Morris turned out a very large amount of calligraphic and illuminated work, astonishing in view of his other heavy design and administrative commitments.

He preferred to work on vellum, but in spite of Fairfax Murray's efforts on his behalf to obtain suitable vellum through the Vatican in Rome, he was obliged to work on paper. Only a few of his many ventures were ever completed (Alfred Fairbank has estimated Morris produced 'more than 1500 pages of writing in several styles'). He took most of his texts from Icelandic sagas but his output included three copies of Fitzgerald's *Rubaiyat* of Omar Khayyam and a book of his own verse.

Icelandic texts included *The Story of the Dwellers at Eyr* and the *Story of the Volsungs and Niblungs*. The latter Morris saw as a Northern work to set against Homer's *Iliad*. The work exhibited c1873 belongs to this period.

Between February and August 1870 he had turned his attention to the writing and decorating of a *Book of Verse* – 25 of his own poems – to give to Georgiana Burne-Jones, in which Burne-Jones, Fairfax Murray and George Wardle all became involved. It was the first of four illuminated manuscripts. Morris found consolation in his friendship with 'Georgie', who at this time had problems with her own marriage.

In 1874 Morris wrote that he had 'taken rather to the Italian work of about 1450'. However Morris's letter forms remain his own even though they hint at uncial, Lombardic and other precedents.

Vines began to embrace the initials and to creep into the margins. In 1875 Morris was obliged to give up calligraphy, for his experiments with dyes for the Firm's textiles were taking up more and more of his time.

In 1888 he showed several of his manuscripts at the first exhibition of the Arts and Crafts Exhibition Society, but his heart remained with the written rather than the printed letter.

In 1891 when the Kelmscott Press was in operation, Morris wrote that 'pleased as I am with my printing . . . I couldn't help lamenting the simplicity of the scribe and his desk and his black ink and blue and red ink, and, I almost felt ashamed of my press after all'.

It is significant that he makes Dick say in *News from Nowhere* that in the twenty-first century 'many people will write their books out'.

11

Grettir, Grettis Saga

The Story of Grettir the Strong
Translated from the Icelandic by Eiríkr Magnússon and William Morris

Size: Octavo.

Publication: London, 1869.

Morris's deep attraction to literature became evident very early in his life. Childhood frailty and consequent isolation probably laid the seeds of his introspective nature and personal sensitivity. His parents' well stocked library of popular romantic works of the period enabled him to read most of Walter Scott's works by the age of seven.

In his early undergraduate days he formed friendships with members of his own sex, rather than with women, and these friendships were to prove the most lasting and rewarding of his life. He was attracted most of all to the image of the romantic hero, protagonist against injustice and misfortune, who was prepared to risk all in heroic and individual action.

As his knowledge of literature increased – especially after 1868, when he met and became friendly with Frederick Startridge Ellis, the antiquarian book dealer and publisher – he found his archetypal heroes in such works as the great classical stories of Homer and Virgil, the northern medieval romances of Chaucer and the classics of the Middle East.

As Morris gradually extended his study of Northern literature through Celtic, Anglo-Saxon and Norse sources, he became aware of the epic literature of Iceland. He was fortunate to meet (through Ellis) the Icelandic translator, Eiríkr Magnússon, and together they began a systematic study of Icelandic works.

The first book read was *The Eyrbyggja Saga*. In a beautiful manuscript form of this work completed in 1870, Morris set forth very fully what the meaning of such poetry was to him – 'a help in the darkness until the new days should come not for one person or another, but for all the world' says Mackail (Life WM, vol I, p263).

Within a few months they had gone through the bulk of the heroic literature. In January 1869 their translation of *Gunnlaug Wormtongue* was published in the *Fortnightly Review*. The *Grettis Saga* was published in April 1869. It includes a brief but critical analysis of the literature, showing how they had mastered the essence of the subject.

In 1871, immediately after acquiring the tenancy of Kelmscott Manor, he made his first trip to Iceland. His letters home tell of his pleasure in the new awareness of 'one's animal life', of exhilaration in the fresh air, in riding and in the rough life, sleeping in a tent, and spending nearly every day of his six weeks in the saddle. A sense of wonder is also revealed at the austere grandeur of the landscape, as when he caught his first glimpse of the 'Great Rift', the 'most storied place of Iceland'. A feeling of terror of this harsh land overwhelms him too on occasions and illuminates his writing of mountain journeys in *The Glittering Plain* and *The Well at the Worlds End*.

12

The Roots of the Mountains

The roots of the mountains wherein is told somewhat of the lives of the men of Burg-dale, their friends, their neighbours, their yeomen and their fellows in arms
William Morris

Specification: Quarto. Superior edition printed in Howard's Basle type at the Chiswick Press.

Publication: Published by Reeves and Turner. 250 paper copies.

Inscription: 'To Janey with Will's best Love December 4th 1889'.

The Roots of the Mountains was finished in 1889 and first published in November 1890. It is the second of the two books produced for Morris by the Chiswick Press. *A Tale of the House of the Wolfings* was the first. Both were experiments towards the raising of the standard of English book design from the deplorable condition into which it had then sunk. He was encouraged and advised by his great friend and fellow socialist, Emery Walker. Walker gave a famous lecture to the Arts and Crafts Exhibition Society in November 1888 after which the two men were closer than ever. 'Type and paper may be said to be to a printed book what stone or bricks and mortar are to architecture, without which there can be no book, in the one case, and no architecture in the other!' Walker said in his lecture, typical advice to which Morris was to give his full attention during the next few years.

In the planning of these two books Morris also worked closely with C. T. Jacobi, then head of the Chiswick Press. In consequence great care was taken in arranging the text on the page, in relating it to the headlines and page numbering, and in balancing two opposite pages so that the double opening formed a single unit, emphasised by the narrowness of the inner margins in comparison with the outer margins.

The title pages of both are remarkable for their simplicity at a time when the aim of the average printer was to crowd title pages with a display of as many type varieties and sizes as the compositor could devise.

The Roots of the Mountains included a few improving modifications, including the replacing of a lower case 'e' with a more legible form after criticism of this letter in the printed text of the *Wolfings*; Morris declared it to be 'the best looking book issued since the seventeenth century'.

Morris had a quantity left over of the Whatman paper specially ordered for the job, and this was used to print 75 copies of the *Gunnlaug Saga*, with initials left blank to be rubricated by hand (1890/91). Two of Morris's textile designs printed at his Merton Abbey works were used for the cloth of the binding.

13

The Story of the Glittering Plain, which has also been called the Land of Living Men or the Acre of the Undying
William Morris

Specification:	Small quarto. Golden type, border designed by Morris. Bound in stiff vellum with wash leather ties.
Publication:	200 paper copies at two guineas, and six on vellum dated 4 April, issued 8 May 1891. Sold by Reeves and Turner.
Reference:	Cockerell No 1.

This book appeared first in the *English Illustrated Magazine* Nos 81–4, (June–September 1890). A trial page set in Golden type was struck off on 31 January 1891 and printed about a month later.

The 1891 version was the first book issued by the Kelmscott Press in the small quarto format adopted for all the first six books. The border, designed by Morris in 1891, was engraved by W. H. Hooper. The initials which appear in the text and were engraved by George Campfield had originally been designed by Morris for *The Golden Legend* (No 19).

14

In 1894 (17 February) Morris as publisher issued the reprinted edition of *The Story of the Glittering Plain*

Specification:	Large quarto. Troy type with a list of chapters in Chaucer type, and illustrations by Walter Crane. Bound in limp vellum.
Publication:	250 copies in black and red on paper at five guineas, seven on vellum at twenty pounds.

Inscription:	This copy is inscribed 'to May from William Morris, March 15th 1894'.
Reference:	Cockerell No 22.

The second edition in 1894 was a much more elaborate volume, printed as a large quarto on Perch paper. It contained 23 woodcuts after designs by Walter Crane, making it second only to the *Chaucer* in amount of illustration.

These illustrations were not a great success. They were engraved by A. Leverett, another experienced craftsman engraver, but his rather ragged and fussy lines accurately following the pen lines of Crane's drawings do not balance in weight and quality of line the sharp clear typography.

15

The Love Lyrics and Songs of Proteus . . . with the Love Sonnets of Proteus by the same Author now reprinted in their Full Text with Many Sonnets Omitted from the Earlier Editions
Wilfrid Scawen Blunt

Specification:	Small quarto. Golden type, printed in black and red, with the initials printed in red by the author's wish. Border designed by Morris. Bound in stiff vellum.
Publication:	300 paper copies at two guineas, none on vellum. Dated 26 January, issued 27 February 1892. Sold by Reeves and Turner.
Reference:	Cockerell No 3.

Morris wrote to his daughter Jenny: 'It looks very gay with its red letters, but I think I prefer my own style of printing'. This is the only book in which initials this size were printed in red, which gives it a different appearance from other books printed at the Kelmscott Press.

Wilfrid Scawen Blunt, diplomat, traveller, poet, 'man-about-town', an inveterate pursuer of women, moving in the highest social circles at home and abroad, became a great friend of both Morris and his wife Janey, whom he met in 1883 at Naworth Castle, the home of Mrs Howard, friend of Janey and the wife of George Howard the Liberal MP, later Earl of Carlisle. Gabriel Rossetti having died in 1882, Wilfrid became Janey's lover in 1883; they were both in their early 40s and remained lovers until 1913. Blunt continued his friendship with Morris until the latter's death in 1896, participating with him in protests for socialist and other political causes.

16

The Nature of Gothic
A chapter of *The Stones of Venice*
John Ruskin

Specification:	Small quarto. Golden type, full border and decorated initials by Morris. Bound in stiff vellum.
Publication:	500 paper copies at thirty shillings, none in vellum. Dated in the preface 15 February and published by George Allen, 22 March 1892.
Inscription:	Inscribed: 'to May with William Morris' best love April 2nd 1892'.
Reference:	Cockerell No 4.

Ruskin's *Stones of Venice* (1851–3), and in particular this chapter, profoundly influenced Morris first during his student days at Oxford and continued to shape his thinking about art and craftsmanship and their role in society. Its importance he reveals in the preface when he states this chapter to be 'one of the very few necessary and inevitable utterances of the century'.

He acknowledged his debt to it again in a lecture, 'The Prospects of Architecture in Civilisation', published in *Hopes and Fears for Art*, Ellis and White 1892, which he delivered at the London Institution on 3 October 1881.

The chapter 'The Nature of Gothic' was first issued separately in 1854, in a sixpenny pamphlet. Sydney Cockerell is said to have suggested the printing again of this chapter by the Kelmscott Press.

17

The Defence of Guenevere
William Morris

Specification:	Small quarto. Golden type, printed in black and red. Bound in limp vellum.
Publication:	300 paper copies at two guineas, ten on vellum at about twelve guineas. Dated 2 April, issued 19 May 1892. Sold by Reeves and Turner.
Inscription:	Copy inscribed: 'to May from William Morris May 26th 1892'.
Reference:	Cockerell No 5.

This book was set up from a copy of the edition published by Reeves and Turner in 1889, the only alteration, except for a few corrections, being in the eleventh line of 'Summer Dawn'.

It is divided into three parts: the poems suggested by Malory's *Morte d'Arthur*; the poems inspired by *Froissart's Chronicles*; and poems on various subjects.

It was the first book bound in limp vellum, and the only one of which the title was inscribed by hand on the back.

18

A Dream of John Ball and A King's Lesson
William Morris

Specification:	Small quarto. Golden type, printed in black and red. Frontispiece (woodcut) designed by Burne-Jones. Bound in limp vellum.
Publication:	300 paper copies at thirty shillings, 11 on vellum at ten guineas. Dated 13 May, issued 24 September 1892. Sold by Reeves and Turner.
Inscription:	Inscribed: 'with WM's best love Oct. 5th 1892'.
Reference:	Cockerell No 6.

A Dream of John Ball and *A King's Lesson* (originally called *An Old Story Retold* were first published in *The Commonweal*, 1887–88. They first appeared in book form in this edition with an illustration by Burne-Jones, the couplet below ('When Adam delved and Eve span who was then the gentleman'), in lettering designed by Morris.

This was the first Kelmscott Press book to have an illustration by Burne-Jones. The design was re-drawn from the frontispiece to this first edition, and engraved on wood by W. H. Hooper, who engraved all Burne-Jones's designs for the Press, except those for *The Wood beyond the World* and *The Life and Death of Jason*. The inscription below the figures and the narrow border were designed by Morris.

The design shows both Burne-Jones's decorative abilities and his deficiency as a draughtsman, compared to the great draughtsmen of the same period in France. In spite of the unified rich decoration of the whole page, weak drawing such as Adam's awkward and inefficient handling of his digging tool, detract from the assurance of the whole design.

However, the skill of the craftsman, W. H. Hooper, is clear. Hooper had been brought out of retirement to work for the Kelmscott Press. He had gained his skills as a wood-engraver translating drawings into engraved illustrations for *Punch* and *The Illustrated London News*. This design proved popular and was used again for other publications including reproduction in the *Daily Chronicle* on 11 February 1895.

19

The Golden Legend
Jacobus de Voragine
Translated by William Caxton

Specification:	3 volumes. Large quarto. Golden type in black with borders by Morris. Woodcut title and two woodcuts designed by Burne-Jones. Half-holland binding, with paper labels in Troy type.
Publication:	500 paper copies at 5 guineas, none on vellum. Dated 12 September, issued 3 November 1892. Published by Bernard Quaritch.
Inscription:	Inscribed 'to May with WM's best love 1892'.
Reference:	Cockerell No 7.

This was intended to be the first of the Kelmscott Press books and from it the Golden type designed by Morris derived its name, but lacking the required size of paper and letting impatience gain the upper hand he published a much shorter work first, *The Glittering Plain* (No 13).

In July 1890 Morris bought a copy of *The Golden Legend* translated by William Caxton and printed with woodcut illustrations by Wynkyn de Worde in 1527. In September he decided to print an edition of this work himself, to be published by Bernard Quaritch. Morris had already begun to design his first type based on the Roman faces of fifteenth-century printers in Venice. Emery Walker, Morris's partner in all but name, supplied photographic enlargements of lines from Morris's copy of Aretino's *Historia Fiorentina*, printed in Venice in 1476 by Jacobus Rubeus in a type that closely resembled Jenson's. Drawing over the enlargements Morris absorbed their characteristics and drew the design for his own type on the same large scale.

The Syndics of the Cambridge University Library lent a transcript of Caxton's first edition; F. S. Ellis edited the text.

By May 1891, 50 pages were ready for printing, and Volume I was finished in October, with the exception of the illustrations. These designs by Burne-Jones, and the title page, the first designed by Morris, were not engraved until June and August 1892 respectively, by which time Volume III was nearly through the Press.

20

The Recuyell of the Historyes of Troye
Raoul Lefevre
Translated by William Caxton

Specification:	2 volumes. Large quarto. Troy type, with table of chapters and glossary in Chaucer type, in black and red. Borders and woodcut title designed by Morris. Limp vellum binding with silk ties.
Publication:	300 paper copies at nine guineas; 5 on vellum at £80. Dated 14 October and issued 24 November 1892. Published by Bernard Quaritch.
Inscription:	Copy inscribed: 'To May William Morris' best love November 28th 1892'.
Reference:	Cockerell No 8.

A reprint of the first book printed in English and a tribute to William Caxton. Morris described it in a note for Quaritch's catalogue as: 'a thoroughly amusing story, instinct with medieval thought and manners. For though written at the end of the Middle Ages and dealing with classical mythology, it has in it no token of the coming Renaissance, but is purely medieval'.

In 1892, 2000 copies of an advertisement of the book with specimen pages were printed for Quaritch at the Press. It was the first book to be printed in the second typeface that Morris designed, the large gothic type, 'Troy'. He had designed it hoping 'to redeem the gothic character from the charge of unreadableness which is commonly brought against it'. Morris's models were gothic founts used by early printers in Germany, such as Zainer of Augsburg, Koburger of Nuremberg and Peter Schoeffer, the printer of the Mainz Bible of 1462. Morris had examples of all three. He preferred his Troy type to the Golden, and thought it just as readable.

Morris also designed a large number of new initials and ornaments for this book. At the same time he was designing a smaller variant of his gothic type, the 'Chaucer', named after the edition of Chaucer's works he was then designing.

Morris was to design in 1893 a fourth type, a gothicised Roman, based on that used in 1467 at Subiaco by Sweynheim and Pannartz, who were the first to introduce printing to Italy. Only the lower-case letters were designed and cut, but the fount was later developed by Walker and Sydney Cockerell for St John Hornby's Ashendene Press and called 'Subiaco'. Later Morris declared that the punches for all his types had been cut with great intelligence and skill by a printing trade craftsman found for him by Walker, named Edward Prince. Prince cut Morris's designs most satisfactorily in steel, and later cut punches for many other English and Continental private presses.

Type casting was carried out in London by the firm of Sir Charles Reed and Son. The firm's manager was Talbot Baines Reed, the author of a scholarly *History of Old English Letter Foundries*. In 1890 he gave a lecture at the Royal Society of Arts on 'Old and New Fashions in Typography'. He gave careful supervision to the casting of the Kelmscott types.

21

News from Nowhere: or an Epoch of Rest, Being some Chapters from a Utopian Romance
William Morris

Specification:	Octavo. Golden type, in black and red. Woodcut frontispiece engraved by W. H. Hooper from a design by C. M Gere. Bound in limp vellum.
Publication:	300 paper copies at two guineas, ten on vellum at ten guineas. Dated 22 November 1892 and issued 24 March 1893. Sold by Reeves and Turner.
Inscription:	Copy inscribed 'To May with WM's best love March 25th 1893'.
Reference:	Cockerell No 12.

News from Nowhere was first published in serial form in *The Commonweal*, the official organ of the new Socialist League (Morris was its editor), from January to October 1890 and was reprinted in book form by Reeves and Turner in 1891. From the latter edition, with a few corrections, the text for this Kelmscott Press edition was set up. There was a delay between the printing of the text and the issue of the book which was caused by the production of the frontispiece.

The illustration 'View of the Manor House from the Garden Gate' was designed by C. M. Gere (1869–1957), one of the three illustrators from the Birmingham School to work for the Press, the other two being E. H. New and A. V. Gaskin. It is perhaps the best known image published by the Press in spite of the greater involvement and fame of its two principal illustrators, Morris's old friend E. Burne-Jones and his new friend and fellow socialist, Walter Crane. The drawing was cut on wood by another fine craftsman in the Press team, the engraver W. H. Hooper. The great period of co-operation between draughtsman and engraver in England was ending when this image was made.

Gere's illustration shows the main entrance to Kelmscott Manor, the beautiful sixteenth/seventeenth-century Oxfordshire farmhouse on the Upper Thames which became the country home for Morris and his family from 1871, when he and D. G. Rossetti, the painter/poet, first entered into a joint tenancy of the house. Morris named his home in Hammersmith and the Press after this manor. It continued to symbolise, as the text of this book reveals, the ideal social and artistic environment he would have wished for all men in place of the ugliness and corruption of life in Victorian industrialised Britain.

Morris published an essay about his greatly loved Kelmscott Manor 'Gossip about an old House' in the *Quest*, November 1895. His biographer Mackail also makes frequent reference to this love, and to the happy days spent there by his family, although always a love tinged with melancholy, because of its beauty, as Morris puts it, but possibly also because of Rossetti's usurping of both the house and Janey's love during the three years he shared the tenancy, from 1871 to 1874.

22

The History of Godefrey of Boloyne and of the Conquest of Iherusalem
Edited by H. Halliday Sparling

Specification:	Large quarto. Troy type, with list of chapter headings and glossary in Chaucer type, in black and red. Borders and woodcut title designed by Morris. Limp vellum binding with silk ties.
Publication:	300 paper copies at six guineas, six on vellum at twenty guineas. Dated 27 April and published 24 May 1893 by William Morris at the Kelmscott Press.
Inscription:	Copy inscribed: 'to May with William Morris' best love July 4th 1893'.
Reference:	Cockerell No 15.

Reprinted from Caxton's edition of 1481, this was the first book Morris published himself at the Kelmscott Press; hitherto editions printed at the Press had been sold through other publishers.

23

Utopia
Sir Thomas More, edited by F. S. Ellis
Reprinted from the 2nd edition of Ralph Robinson's translation, with a foreword by William Morris

Specification:	Octavo. Chaucer type, with reprinted title in Troy type, in black and red; borders designed by Morris. Limp vellum binding with silk ties.

Publication:	300 copies printed on paper at thirty shillings, eight on vellum at ten guineas. Dated 4 August 1893, issued 8 September 1893. Sold by Reeves and Turner.
Inscription:	Copy inscribed: 'to May from WM Oct. 8th 1893'.
Reference:	Cockerell No 16.

The *Utopia* was one of several visions of ideal society which helped to shape Morris's own thinking, culminating in his acceptance of Socialism in the 1880s and the inspiration for his writing of *News from Nowhere*, published in the early 1890s.

24

The Tale of Beowulf, out of the Old English tongue by William Morris and A. J. Wyatt
William Morris

Specification:	Large quarto. Troy type, with argument, side notes, list of persons and places, and glossary in Chaucer type. Printed in black and red; borders and woodcut title by Morris. The borders in this book were used only once again in the *Jason*. Bound in limp vellum.
Publication:	300 paper copies at two guineas, eight on vellum at ten pounds. Dated 10 January, issued 2 February 1895. Published by William Morris.
Inscription:	Copy inscribed: 'to May with WM's best love Feb 7th 1895'.
Reference:	Cockerell No 32.

The verse translation was begun by Morris with the aid of Wyatt's careful paraphrase of the text on 21 February 1893, and finished on 10 April 1894. Morris wrote the argument by 10 December 1894.

As he had been so involved in Icelandic literature, it was natural for Morris when he turned to Old English to choose *Beowulf*. He undertook his verse form of the tale in close collaboration with the Cambridge Anglo-Saxon scholar, A. J. Wyatt, who was then editing *Beowulf* for the Cambridge University Press. Wyatt was paid £100 for the literal translation he supplied to Morris.

25

The Well at the World's End
William Morris

Specification:	Large quarto: double columns. Chaucer type, printed in black and red. Borders by Morris and four woodcut illustrations designed by Burne-Jones. Bound in limp vellum.
Publication:	350 paper copies at five guineas; eight on vellum at twenty guineas. Dated 2 March, issued 4 June 1896. Sold by William Morris.
Inscription:	Inscribed: 'to May with WM's best love May 23rd 1896'.
Reference:	Cockerell No 39.

This book was delayed in the press for various reasons and was longer 'on hand' awaiting completion than any other. It appears in 12 lists from December 1892 to November 1895, described as 'in the press'. Trial pages were printed in September 1892.

The publishers Longmans also issued an edition from Morris's manuscript at the Chiswick Press, and the Kelmscott Press version was set up from sheets of that edition. It was finished in 1894, although not issued until 1896. Most of the borders and ornaments were used again in the unillustrated work *The Water of the Wondrous Isles*, issued in 1897. (Cockerell No 45.)

26

Geoffrey Chaucer, Works
Edited by F. S. Ellis

Specification:	Folio. Chaucer type with headings to longer poems in Troy type, in black and red. Borders by William Morris. Woodcut title and 87 woodcut illustrations designed by E. Burne-Jones. Bound in half-holland.
Publication:	425 copies on paper at twenty pounds, 13 on vellum at 120 guineas. Dated 8 May and published 26 June 1896 by William Morris.
Inscription:	Copy inscribed: 'to May with William Morris' best love June 12th 1896'.
Reference:	Cockerell No 40.

The *Chaucer* is the most splendid of all the Kelmscott Press editions. It represents the height of Morris's achievement as printer, typographer, and book designer. It took him nearly four years to produce and was completed only three months before his death in October 1896.

Morris first talked of printing the *Chaucer* in 1891. In 1892 he had ordered the Chaucer type, a reduced pica version of Troy which proved too large when two trial pages were set up in the latter type in February 1892. The third trial, an extract from the *Knightes Tale*, was set up in double columns of 58 lines in Chaucer type and was approved by Morris.

The first public announcement made in December 1892 quoted about 60 designs by E. Burne-Jones, but by November 1894 Morris informed his subscribers that it had been found necessary to increase this number to upwards of 70. He also announced an increase in the print run, from 325 to 425 copies.

The final number of illustrations proved to be 87, completed by Burne-Jones just before Christmas 1895.

From 1893 Morris was designing borders and initials for the book, and a specimen page was shown at the Arts and Crafts Exhibition in 1893.

Walker's help again proved invaluable in the translating of Burne-Jones's designs into woodcuts. This previously slow process was speeded up by the use of a photographic process introduced by Walker, which he called a planotype. A print was made of the original drawing and was then reworked in pen and ink by Robert Catterson-Smith, who described his task as 'to get rid of everything but the essential lines'. The result was re-photographed on the woodblock and then cut by W. H. Hooper, the most reliable of all the craftsman wood engravers used by Morris.

Walker again persuaded Morris to accept the use of electrotypes to reproduce his designs for initials and recurrent ornaments, to speed production of the book.

By August 1894 the first sheet was printed at the premises of the Press at 14 Upper Mall, Hammersmith, and as printing progressed so slowly in January 1895, another press was set up at 21 Upper Mall. The two presses at No 14 were now used almost exclusively for printing the *Chaucer*. By September 1895 printing of the text was at last finished. Morris's health was now failing and Burne-Jones became anxious about the *Chaucer*. 'He has not done the title page yet, which will be such a rich page of ornament with all the large lettering, I wish he would not leave it any longer.'

Morris, however, designed the title page by February 1896 and the book was then complete. Two copies were delivered to Morris and Burne-Jones on 2 June 1896, a year and nine months after its first page had been printed.

Morris intended to design four bindings for the *Chaucer*, two of which were to be carried out at the Doves Bindery under the direction of T. J. Cobden-Sanderson, the remaining two by J. & J. Leighton, who had previously been responsible for binding the Press editions.

However, by the end of 1895 Morris was able to complete only one design (No 27), for a white pigskin binding with silver clasps, to be made by Douglas Cockerell at the Doves Bindery, Chiswick.

Forty-eight copies of the *Chaucer* were eventually bound to this design.

Eighty-five of Burne-Jones's finished pencil drawings for the *Chaucer* illustrations were purchased by the Rt. Hon. Stanley Baldwin MP (whose mother was Lady Burne-Jones's sister) and presented by him to the Fitzwilliam Museum, Cambridge.

27

Design for the special binding of the Kelmscott Chaucer, drawn in December 1895
William Morris
Pencil, pen and wash

28

The Earthly Paradise
William Morris
Volume 1 of 8 volumes: Prologue: The Wanderers.
March: Atlanta's Race. The Man born to be King

Specification:	Medium Quarto. Golden type in black and red. Borders and woodcut titles designed by Morris. Bound in limp vellum with silk ties.
Publication:	225 paper copies at thirty shillings, six on vellum at seven guineas. Dated 7 May 1896, issued 24 July 1896. Published by William Morris.
Reference:	Cockerell No 41.

This is the first of an eight-volume edition of Morris's work, the last volume of which appeared in September 1897 almost a year after his death.

None of the ten borders and four half-borders that were designed for this work appears in other books; three of the borders were designed by Robert Catterson-Smith under Morris's direction.

Morris from his earliest days had shown great facility in writing, first when he was a schoolboy at Marlborough and during his undergraduate days, and later, working in Street's architectural office at Oxford, prose and verse flowed easily from his pen. In 1856 he founded the *Oxford and Cambridge*

Magazine (No 9), became its editor and supported it financially. His contributions to the magazine were colourful but immature and later he would himself describe them as crude and very young.

However, in the same year Rossetti, both admiring and envious of Morris's facility, wrote to his friend and fellow poet, William Allingham: 'Morris' facility at poetising puts one in a rage. He has been writing at all for little more than a year, I believe, and has already poetry enough for a big book.'

Even before his first book of verse the *Defence of Guenevere* was published in 1858, Morris had begun a cycle of dramatic poems on the Fall of Troy. He followed this with an Arthurian verse cycle but was pre-empted by the publication of Tennyson's first volume of *Idylls* in 1859. With such works indicating the direction of his interests, Morris began *The Earthly Paradise*. Its subjects were to be drawn from romantic tales of heroism and beauty, both classical and medieval, European and Oriental. Morris wove them all together in a literary fabric, essentially fourteenth-century and Chaucerian. He set out the circumstances in the Prologue. There were to be 24 stories in verse, arranged as a series of tales exchanged two each month by a group of Norse exiles and their Greek hosts. In Morris's interpretation evoked by his vision of history and the language of Chaucer were combined elements of Norse legends, medieval English and French tales and traditional oriental stories, such as the 'Arabian Nights', latinised in Western translations.

Although Morris said: 'I by nature turn to Romance rather than classicism', some of his earliest compositions were drawn from Greek history and mythology. In fact, the great myth the 'Quest of the Golden Fleece' grew to such length in the telling (10,534 lines) that it had to be published separately in 1867 as the *Life and Death of Jason*.

The Troy cycle was begun in 1857 and Morris continued to write in a desultory way for *The Earthly Paradise* until his move to Red House at Upton in 1860. By then six of the 12 projected poems had been completed, but decoration of his new home, the foundation of the Firm in 1861, and its subsequent participation in the International Exhibition of Art and Industry in London in 1862 preoccupied Morris to such an extent that it was 1864 before he returned to the 'Big Book' project.

Together from 1864 to 1868, Morris and Burne-Jones now joined together in planning an elaborately illustrated edition of *The Earthly Paradise*. Georgiana, the wife of Burne-Jones, tells in her *Memorials* of their close involvement. 'The last visit we paid to Upton was in September 1865 . . . Indoors the talk of the men was much about the Earthly Paradise, which was to be illustrated by two or three hundred woodcuts', many of them designed and some even drawn on the block.

Technical difficulties over integration of contemporary type forms with the woodcut illustrations proved too great and the vast project could not be realised. Morris, who had now completed 42,000 lines of rhymed verse, sought the co-operation of his friend and publisher F. S. Ellis, and the poems were published in three volumes, in 1868, 1869 and 1870 respectively. These editions were decorated by a charming small woodcut of three musicians, designed by Burne-Jones and cut by Morris. They were printed by Strangeways and Walden of Leicester Square.

The books proved successful and Morris achieved much popular acclaim as a modern Chaucer. *The Saturday Review* of 30 May 1869 contains a recommendation to read Morris's latest verse 'for conveying to our wives and daughters a refined, although not diluted version of those wonderful creations of Greek fancy'.

29

Laudes Beatae Mariae Virginis
Edited by S. C. Cockerell
Latin poems taken from a Psalter written in England c1220 in the collection of William Morris

Specification:	Large quarto. Troy type in black and red and blue. Bound in half-holland.
Publication:	250 copies on paper, at ten shillings, 10 on vellum at two guineas. Dated 7 July 1896, issued 7 August 1896. Published by William Morris.
Reference:	Cockerell No 42.

This was the first book printed in three colours at the Kelmscott Press. The manuscript from which the poems were taken was one of the most beautiful of the English books in Morris's possession, regarding both writing and ornament, which he had acquired in 1893 and referred to as the Nottingham Psalter.

No author's name is given to the poems, but after this book was issued the Rev. E. S. Dewick pointed out that they had already been printed at Tegernsee in 1579, in a 16mo (sextodecimo) volume, in which they were ascribed to Stephen Langton, Archbishop of Canterbury. A note to this effect was printed in Chaucer type on 28 December 1896 and distributed to subscribers. The psalter has now been associated with Reading Abbey.

30

The Story of Sigurd and Volsung and the Fall of the Niblungs
William Morris

Specification:	Small folio. Chaucer type, with title and headings to the four books in Troy type, printed in black and red. Borders by Morris and two illustrations designed by Burne-Jones. Bound in limp vellum.
Publication:	160 paper copies at six guineas, six on vellum at twenty guineas. Dated 19 January, issued 25 February 1898.
Reference:	Cockerell No 50.

The two borders in the book were almost the last designed by Morris and were intended for an edition of *The Hill of Venus* to be written in prose by Morris and illustrated by Burne-Jones. Morris developed his borders from ornament in two late-thirteenth-century psalters in his library at Kelmscott House. One of these was almost certainly the *Windmill Psalter*, Morris's last acquisition, the folded leaves of which with strongly serrated edges are closely similar to those on Morris's border. Morris 'justly considered' *The Story of Sigurd* as 'his masterpiece' and an edition was projected early in the history of the Press. It is listed as 'in preparation in 1895' when the *Chaucer* was near completion, and as 'in the press' in June 1896. In 1895 the number of illustrations projected was about 25; by 1896 this had been increased to 40. In January 1897 only two pages were in type; 32 copies of these were then printed and given to friends.

31

Love is Enough or The Freeing of Pharamond: a morality
William Morris

Specification:	Large quarto. Troy type, with stage directions in Chaucer type; printed in black, red and blue. Two illustrations designed by Burne-Jones.
Publication:	300 paper copies at two guineas, eight on vellum at ten guineas. Dated 11 December 1897, issued 24 March 1898.
Note:	The vellum copy in the Kelmscott Manor collection contains a note in S. C. Cockerell's hand: 'Defective copy, not for sale'.
Reference:	Cockerell No 52.

This was the second book printed in three colours at the Kelmscott Press.

In the autumn of 1871 after returning from his first trip to Iceland Morris began a poetic romance, *Love is Enough*. He envisaged this poem as appearing in an illustrated and decorated edition.

Rossetti wrote in October 1871 that the book would have 'woodcuts by Ned Jones, and borders by (Morris) himself some of which he has done really beautifully'.

Burne-Jones wrote also that 'it will come out sometime next summer and I shall make little ornaments to it'.

Trial pages were printed in 1872, but like *The Earthly Paradise* the project in the form proposed was advanced no further. Twenty-three unillustrated and little-decorated copies were published in 1873. The final version was printed by the Press in 1898, its penultimate production.

Frontispiece and tailpiece were designed by Burne-Jones, the latter, 'Coronation of the Lovers', being one made for the projected edition of 25 years before, as frontispiece.

32

Volsunga Saga
The Story of the Volsungs and Niblungs with certain songs from the Elder Edda
Eiríkr Magnússon and William Morris
Translated from the Icelandic by E. Magnússon and W. Morris

Specification:	Large quarto. Printed in black and red. Bound in half-holland.
Publication:	Published by Longmans Green and Co. Dated 9 November 1901.
Inscription:	Copy inscribed: 'Jane Morris, Kelmscott 1901'.

The collection *The Three Northern Love Stories and Other Tales* was first printed in 1875. It was reprinted at the Chiswick Press with the Golden type designed by Morris for the Kelmscott Press, and finished on 9 November 1901.

33

The English Bible
Containing the Old Testament and the New translated out of the original tongues by special command of His Majesty King James the First and now reprinted with the text revised by a collation of its early and other principal editions and edited by the late Rev. F. H. Scrivener, M.A. LL.D., for the Syndics of the University Press Cambridge, Volume I

Binding:	Bound in stiff vellum.
Publication:	Five volumes were produced between 1903 and 1905. Volume I was finished in December 1902, issued 1903. Printed by T. J. Cobden-Sanderson and Emery

Walker at the Doves Press, 1 The Terrace, Hammersmith. Sold at the Doves Press, and by C. J. Clay & Sons, Cambridge University Press Warehouse, Ave Maria Lane, London. 500 paper copies at 15 guineas; two on vellum, not for sale.

The Doves Press books are the simplest and purest in style of all the private press productions, and are acknowledged as masterpieces of fine, plain printing.

They represent the highest achievement of Emery Walker as sole director of the Doves Press, assisted by his compositor, Mason, after the Kelmscott Press had closed down in 1898. They are printed for the most part in the same format, all with the same typeface and in only one size. The paper was hand made by Batchelor. The Doves watermark of 'two doves breasting a perch', with the initials 'C.S.' and 'E.W.' was designed by Cobden-Sanderson.

The type was adapted from that used in the fifteenth-century Jensen edition of *Pliny* and set close, evenly spaced, with minimum leading. As with the Kelmscott Press, the use of fine materials and a strong black print impression was mandatory. Doves books in consequence have great strength and assurance but are sometimes criticised for being too spare and controlled – the 'finest ceremonial type cut' says A. Pollard in 1921.

However, in compensation for the absence of decoration Edward Johnston, Britain's leading authority on lettering in the twentieth century and an outstanding calligrapher, was employed to add unconventional drawn initial letters to the Press's books. These are placed outside the text area, usually printed in bright red. There is no finer example of a page boldly and superbly 'flourished' by Johnston than the opening page of the Book of Genesis in the Doves Bible.

On the other hand, the role of T. J. Cobden-Sanderson was a subdued one. Although very inventive in his designs for binding, he appeared to influence very little design and decoration with the Press. The overall high quality of all that the Press produced is yet another tribute to the ability, integrity and modesty of its director, Emery Walker.

34

Works

'Tutte le opere di Dante Alighieri Fiorentino'
Dante Alighieri

Publication: 105 paper copies with oak boards at ten guineas, six on vellum at fifty guineas. Printed and issued by the Ashendene Press, Shelley House, Chelsea, 1909.

The Ashendene Press was one of the most famous presses to come into being as a result of the printing revival which followed the lead set by the Kelmscott Press.

It began in 1894 with the setting up of a small press by St John Hornby in the summer house in his parents' garden at Ashendene, Hertfordshire ('the little garden-house of happy memory'). Mostly for Hornby's own pleasure, and to give to his friends, ten small books of high quality were printed there before he moved the Press to his own home at Shelley House, Chelsea, where it remained until the Press's demise in 1935.

It maintained throughout the highest standards in production of printed works, which ranged from small children's books, such as Oscar Wilde's *The Young King and Other Tales*, to 'stately folios', such as the *Dante* now at Kelmscott. This folio *Dante* is said to stand beside the Kelmscott *Chaucer* and the Doves Bible as one of the monuments of the private presses.

The Press again owed much of its success to the variety and skill of its craftsmen and women. Walker and Cockerell joined forces to complete for Hornby the design of the fourth fount envisaged by Morris at the Kelmscott Press, the 'Subiaco'. The Ashendene Press is often identified with the use of Subiaco type, and from then on it replaced, except for minor works, the old traditional face, 'Fell', from the Clarendon Press, Oxford, which had been used previously.

Florence Kingford, Cockerell's wife, painted illustrations on vellum for such works as the *Songs of Solomon*. Douglas Cockerell with Katherine Adams prepared fine bindings for the Press (the former's work is often hidden under the trade name of W. H. Smith, as Cockerell, was in charge of their bindery for many years). Katherine's work, which was inclined to be elaborate, was sometimes referred to rather casually; Sydney Cockerell would ask if a book had been 'Katied'.

At the turn of the century Edward Johnston and his pupil, Graily Hewitt, were reviving interest in early calligraphy, and their graceful initials, in red, blue and green, add to the liveliness of both Doves and Ashendene productions. This accords with Hornby's taste for 'a certain gaiety of treatment in the use of coloured initials and chapter headings'.

Works of the Ashendene Press were often grand and sometimes absurd, for example a minute Queen's doll's house book of *Horace* which was printed in an edition of three copies, but always visually stimulating. Unlike Morris, Hornby printed for pleasure, not for reform.

35

The Story of Cupid and Psyche

William Morris

With illustrations designed by Edward Burne-Jones, mostly engraved on the wood by William Morris; the introduction by A. R. Dufty

Publication: Printed at the Rampant Lions Press, Cambridge and published for the Society of Antiquaries, London, by Clover Hill Editions, London and Cambridge, 1974. Number XVI of 130 copies, numbered I to CXXX, each with a portfolio containing a set of collotype prints of the 47 original 'Cupid and Psyche' drawings and a set of proofs of the 44 wood-engravings.

Work ceased on *The Earthly Paradise* in 1867 or 1868. Sydney Cockerell, who became Secretary of the Kelmscott Press in 1894, has recorded that Burne-Jones finished the designs for four of the tales, *Cupid and Psyche*, *Pygmalion*, *The Ring Given to Venus*, and *The Hall of Venus*. Various drawings and sketches by him for all these survive, the most advanced work being done for *Cupid and Psyche*. Burne-Jones stated that around 1865 he had designed 70 subjects for this subject alone. At least 44 woodblocks were cut from them, 38 by Morris personally.

After the death of Morris in 1896 an attempt was made by Burne-Jones and Cockerell to revive the project using Troy type with the woodcut illustrations, but this failed with Burne-Jones's death in 1898.

The Story

The tale of *Cupid and Psyche* has folk origins. In primitive form it is traditional, current in places as far apart as Hindustan and Scotland. However, Morris found inspiration in a version classical in origin and presented in sophisticated form in a bizarre and romantic novel by Lucius Apuleius written in the second century AD. It is likely he used the 1566 translation by William Adlington of the *Golden Ass*.

He introduces the story told in heroic couplets with the following argument: 'Psyche, a King's daughter, by her exceeding beauty caused the people to forget Venus; therefore the Goddess would fain have destroyed her; nevertheless she became the bride of Love, yet in an unhappy moment lost him by her own fault, and wandering through the world suffered many evils at the hand of Venus, for whom she must accomplish fearful tasks. But the gods and all nature helped her, and in process of time she was reunited to Love, forgiven by Venus and made immortal by the Father of gods and men.'

At first her anxious father, fearful of the consequences of her matchless beauty, sought the advice of the oracle of Apollo at Miletus who cruelly counselled that she should be left alone upon a bleak mountain top to be seized as wife by some monster.

Venus also would tolerate no rival for the eyes and hearts of man and sent her son Cupid to bemuse Psyche with doctored darts, which would cause her to marry the most unattractive of mortals. Cupid fell utterly in love with her at first sight. He tricked her into coming to his palace, 'a house made beautiful with beaten gold', where he visited her nightly. He did so in total darkness lest she find out he was a god. But Psyche, encouraged by her jealous sisters, lit a lamp and beheld Cupid who angrily fled from her.

While she bathed, Venus was told of Cupid's duplicity and – beside herself with anger – she swore to seek them out and punish them, especially mortal Psyche.

Distraught in her search for Cupid, Psyche entered the very Temple of Venus, who had her seized, and then set her a number of supernatural tasks. Psyche, with divine intervention, accomplished them all and so was forgiven by Venus and made immortal by Jupiter.

As Richard Dufty has pointed out in his scholarly and entertaining introduction to the Clover Hill edition, Morris's interpretation is far from the racy and often bawdy account of Apuleius. He eliminates much of Apuleius's subtlety and irony and, inhibited by Victorian taboos concerning the facts of human behaviour – especially those of a sexual nature – softened the characters of the gods and goddesses and created a narrative poem, a succession of pen pictures full of naturalistic detail which we now see to be thoroughly Pre-Raphaelite in character. He does away with the woodcut where the busybody seagull upbraids Venus and her son Cupid: 'He with his whore-hunting on the mountains and you with your splashing about at the seaside have deserted mankind.'

Psyche was pregnant and thus Venus was to be a grandmother, but this is ignored, as are Venus's sensual 'seventh kiss'; her violent, jealous attack on Psyche, pulling out her hair and tearing her clothes to shreds; and her solace at a party from which she returns tipsy, decked with roses, reeking of aphrodisiac ointments.

Morris even makes Venus forgive Psyche and kiss her, although there are precedents for a more sympathetic Venus in Spencer in the sixteenth century, and again in the seventeenth century, when both Venus and Cupid are occasionally introduced into the Christian fold.

Cupid and Psyche, like the whole of *The Earthly Paradise*, is escapist, although this may be excused as being therapeutic in view of Morris's abhorrence of the ugly manifestations of the industrial revolution. What is less excusable is the banality of some of Morris's writing, so that posterity's judgement of him has been that of a writer of 'tapestry verse', without depth. However, as Dufty concludes more charitably, it is a 'medieval tapestry world . . . suffused with Botticellian Spring!'

The Illustrations
It seems from the lists compiled by May Morris that the *Cupid and Psyche* story was the first in *The Earthly Paradise* to be written by her father. Georgiana Burne-Jones records that 70 designs for *Cupid and Psyche* were made by her husband in 1865, (although possibly in error for 1864). Philip Webb also seems to have been involved, possibly being consulted on the architectural scenes. A volume of 86 initial sketches in pencil for *Cupid and Psyche* were given to the Birmingham Museum and Art Gallery in 1922 by J. R. Holliday, and 47 tracings by the artist's hand are now on loan from the Ruskin School to the Ashmolean.

The intention was that the blocks should be engraved, or 'cut', commercially, but after the first sample, believed to be of 'Psyche and Pan' (No 36, 10) contracting out was abandoned. May Morris records her father at home at 26 Queen Square: 'In the evenings – what a delight! . . . he would work with bright cutting tools and a little block of wood, which sat on a plump leather cushion . . . these were the wood blocks for one of its [*The Earthly Paradise*] stories, the *Cupid and Psyche* illustrations.'

George Wardle, who later became manager of the Firm, also recalls how: 'a few of the blocks were given at first to "the trade" to be cut, but the result was so unsatisfactory that Morris tried to get the cutting done by un-professional hands. G. H. Campfield, the foreman of Painters to the Firm, and Miss Lucy Faulkner, sister of Charles Faulkner, each made a trial. I also was asked, and I began cutting the block of "Psyche passing by the shrieking tower". I then cut the "Despair" of Psyche at the flight of Cupid; after this I cut no more. Morris himself, seeing that wood engraving of this kind did not require an apprenticeship, took up the work and he liked it so much that he cut all the remaining blocks. The greater number are therefore by him.'

Burne-Jones's drawings and designs where the female form is involved have a charming and delicately erotic flavour and reveal a sensuality that is characteristic of the artist.

In all Burne-Jones's work his decorative ability is stronger than his analysis of form, a criticism that may be levelled also at Morris's translation of the designs into woodcut illustrations wherein, as can be seen in the great *Chaucer*, the

magnificence of the whole – type, image, border decoration, paper and binding – is not always matched by the quality of drawing or sensitivity of line in the main illustration, as in the first illustration to *The Frankeleyns Tale*.

It might be commented also that Charles Ricketts, Walter Crane and many others involved in the movement of Art Nouveau at the turn of the century were aware of such appeal and exploited it in their own illustrations.

36

Cupid and Psyche
Preparatory drawings
Designs by E. Burne-Jones

Loaned by

1 Drawings 'Venus' and 'Psyche'
   Preliminary sketches on one sheet for
   woodcuts 1 and 2, p3   BMAG

2 Drawing 'Cupid's first sight of 'Psyche'
   Finished drawing for woodcut 4, p16   AMO

3 Designs 'The Procession to the Hill' for
   woodcuts 6 and 7, pp10 and 11
   (i) Early sketch for whole scene on one
       block   BMAG
   (ii) Early sketch showing extension of scene
       from one to two blocks for woodcuts 6
       and 7, pp10 and 11   BMAG
   (iii) Sketch at intermediate stage   BMAG
   (iv) Sketch approximating to final design   BMAG

4 Drawing 'Psyche in Cupid's Palace'
   Preliminary sketches for woodcuts 9, 10, 11,
   12, pp21, 27, 29   BMAG

5 Drawings for 'Psyche at bath'
   (i) and (ii) Revised design for woodcut 12,
   p29   BMAG

6 'Psyche entering Palace'
   (i) 'Cupid and Psyche', detail of frieze from
       No 1 Palace Green, London
       Compare with woodcut 9 'Psyche
       entering the Court of Palace', p21   BMAG
   (ii) 'Psyche entering Palace'
       Final tracing for transfer to wood block;
       neither block nor pull is recorded   AMO

7 'The Song at her getting up'
   (i) Preliminary sketch   BMAG
   (ii) Final tracing of development of
       preliminary sketch for transfer to wood
       block; neither block nor pull is recorded.   AMO

180

8 'Psyche expecting Cupid'
Preliminaries to woodcuts 18 and 19, p31
- (i) Paired sketches on one sheet, of the Cupid and Psyche scenes   BMAG
- (ii) Early version of Psyche scene   BMAG
- (iii) Final tracing of Psyche scene for transfer to wood block, before revision   AMO
- (iv), (v), (vi), (vii) Sketch studies for Psyche   BMAG

9 Early sketch for 'Psyche spying'   BMAG

10 'Psyche and Pan'
- (i) Final tracing   AMO
- (ii) Pull from woodcut   WMG

11 Drawings for 'The Court of Venus'
- (i) Early sketch   BMAG
- (ii) Development of design for woodcut 34, p61   BMAG

12 'Psyche before Venus'
- (i) Preliminary sketch   BMAG
- (ii) Finished drawing on tracing paper   AMO
- (iii) Block prepared for engraving, but not cut   BMAG

13 'Proserpine Giving the Casket'
Final drawing on tracing paper; neither engraving nor pull is known   AMO

14 'Psyche and the opened Casket'
- (i) Preliminary sketch   BMAG
- (ii) Final drawing on tracing paper   AMO

15 'Cupid reviving Her' (Psyche)
- (i) Preliminary sketch for woodcut 49, p87   BMAG
- (ii) Pen and ink sketch (by D. G. Rossetti) 'The meeting of Beatrice and Dante in Paradise' c1859   BMAG

16 'Council of all Heavens' (dei conscripti) and Psyche's 'entry among the Gods'
Early sketches; only the latter scene was taken further   BMAG

17 'Psyche's Entry among the Gods'
Preliminary sketch for woodcuts 50 and 51, pp90 and 91   BMAG

BMAG: Birmingham Museum and Art Gallery
AMO: Ashmolean Museum, Oxford
WMG: William Morris Gallery, Walthamstow

37

Cupid and Psyche
Ten proofs from original blocks, related to drawings and designs described in No 36

38

Punches and Matrices of The Kelmscott Press Types, Golden, Troy and Chaucer

The punches of all the Kelmscott Press types were cut by a freelance trade craftsman, Edward P. Prince. The matrices were struck and cast by the firm of Sir Charles Reed and Sons (see No 20).

May Morris describes how, as the exacting task of cutting the Golden type progressed, her father would carry about the latest smoke proofs in a watch box to examine in his spare moments.

39

Pamphlets on art, design and socialism

- (i) An address to the Birmingham Society of Arts and School of Design by their President, William Morris, M.A, 19.2.1879

  Printed by: E. C. Osborne, 83 New Street, Birmingham.

  Loaned by: Ray Watkinson.

  This address was directed towards art students especially.

- (ii) Labour's Pleasure versus Labour's Sorrow
  William Morris

  An Address to the Birmingham Society of Arts and School of Design by William Morris, Esq., M.A. in the Town Hall, Birmingham, 19.2.1880

  Published by: Birmingham Society of Arts and School of Design.

  Printed by: Cund Bros at their works in Moor Street, London.

  Loaned by: Ray Watkinson.

- (iii) The Decorative Arts (Their Relation to Modern Life and Progress)
  William Morris
  An address delivered before the Trades' Guild of Learning by William Morris

  Published by: Ellis and White, 29 New Bond Street, London.

  Loaned by: Ray Watkinson.

- (iv) Democratic Federation
  Chants for Socialists
  No 1, The day is coming
  William Morris

  Specification: 8 pages, not dated.
  Publication: London, Reeves.

(v) The voice of toil
All for the cause
Two Chants for Socialists
Publication: Reprinted from *Justice*, London, not dated. Both copies have book plates of Edmund Gosse.

(vi) Stories from *The Earthly Paradise*
William Morris
The Earthly Paradise, Preface, Prologue: The Wanderers
The Penny Poets No XI
Publication: The Masterpiece Library, 'Review of Reviews' Office, London. This series was produced and edited by W. T. Stead.
Loaned by: Ray Watkinson.

(vii) Monopoly or How Labour is Robbed
William Morris
Specification: Cover, designed by Walter Crane, includes illustration with central group of figures depicting 'The Fruits of Labour', supported by 'Labour', menaced by 'Soldiers', 'Police', 'Capitalist' and 'Landlord'.
Publication: The Freedom Library. Price one penny. Published by Office of *Freedom*, 127 Ossulston Street, London NW. Printed by W. Reeves, 83 Charing Cross Road, London WC.
Loaned by: Ray Watkinson.

(viii) William Morris
J. W. Mackail
An Address delivered the XIth November MDCCCC at Kelmscott House, Hammersmith before the Hammersmith Socialist Society
Specification: Printed in black and red (title page) on hand-made paper. Bound in vellum at the Doves Bindery.
Publication: Published by the Doves Press, No 1 The Terrace, Hammersmith MDCCCCI.
Loaned by: Ray Watkinson.

It was the third book printed by Cobden Sanderson and Emery Walker at the Doves Press. This edition is in tribute to Morris, who died in 1896.

40
Cartoons for the Cause
(Souvenir of the International and Trade Union Congress of 1896)
Walter Crane

The publication contains twelve cartoons in the cause of Socialism by Walter Crane, dating from December 1884.

These include:
(i) The Party Fight and New Party
(ii) Capitalist Vampire
(iii) The Triumph of Labour 1891
(iv) A Garland for May Day 1895
Published by: Twentieth Century Press, 1896.
Acknowledgement: Reproduction by courtesy of the Victoria and Albert Museum.

These cartoons provided inspiration for much socialist imagery. Some trades union banner makers appear to have used the publication as a pattern book.

Notes
1
Kelmscott Press Type Founts

(i) Golden Type
The letter 'h' was the first letter cut in two forms. The first, rejected by Morris, is close to the Jensen 'h', preserving even the slight rightward swelling at the top of the stem. The second, modified to Morris's instruction, caps the stem with a slab serif and has a flatter curve in its shoulder. By mid-October 1890 all the lower-case letters were cut and Morris began simple proofing in 1891.

(ii) Troy Type
In the summer of 1891 Morris began designing a new type 'to redeem the gothic character from the charge of unreadableness which is commonly brought against it'.

The new Gothic type had no specific model. The final designs for the new alphabet were handed over to Prince in August and September 1891, the lower case being completed first. Though gothic letter forms still look strange to modern eyes, Morris's Troy type was a great achievement and is probably his most important contribution to letter design. It arose naturally from his instinctive taste: 'To say the truth', he wrote, 'I prefer it to the Roman.'

(iii) Chaucer Type
The Chaucer type was a smaller pica (12 point) version of Troy, which Prince began cutting in February 1892, within a few months after finishing off the larger version.

(iv) Subiaco Type

In June 1892 Morris wrote to Prince that in three months he hoped to 'be ready with a new set of sketches for a fount of type on English body', the same size as Golden.

On 5 November 1892 Cockerell, who had just begun to catalogue the Kelmscott House Library, recorded that Morris had taken a copy of the Subiaco *De civitate dei* 1467 and had begun to design a lower case after its model. Cockerell later stated that the project had been abandoned without the punches being cut, but there is evidence from a trial setting in the Paul Mellon Library, New York, that an entire lower case was cut, in 16 point size. Morris's design was a version rather than a copy of the Subiaco type, which included shorter descenders and many other variations.

The character of all four types is discussed in detail by John Dreyfus in his essay on 'William Morris as Typographer' (*William Morris and the Art of the Book*, The Pierpont Morgan Library, Oxford University Press, New York and London, 1976).

2

Kelmscott Press Paper

Morris regarded it as a matter of course that the paper to be used at the Kelmscott Press would be hand made and chose as his model a Bolognese paper made in 1473. Accompanied by Walker he visited Joseph Batchelor's paper mill near Ashford in Kent. Batchelor taught him the technique of paper making and Morris made two sheets with his own hands. Batchelor then produced for Morris three papers which were so satisfactory that no others were used for the books produced at the Press. Each paper had a watermark designed by Morris which was used to identify them thereafter. Their names, sizes and the dates of first delivery were as follows:

(i)   Flower (16in × 11in) 12 February 1891
      Flower (16in × 22in) 22 April 1891
(ii) Perch (16¾in × 22in) 17 February 1893
(iii) Apple (18¾in × 12¾in) 14 March 1895

See: John Dreyfus, 'William Morris as Typographer', in *William Morris and the Art of the Book*, The Pierpont Morgan Library, Oxford University Press, New York and London, 1976.

J.A.

Chronology

1828 Birth of Dante Gabriel Rossetti
1832 Reform Bill
1833 Birth of Edward Burne-Jones
1834 Birth of William Morris, 24 March, Elm House, Walthamstow
1837 Victoria comes to the throne
1839 Chartist riots
1840 Family moves to Woodford Hall, Walthamstow
Birth of Jane Burden
Birth of Wilfrid Scawen Blunt
1847 Death of Morris's father
1848 Goes to Marlborough
H. Holman Hunt, J. Millais and D. G. Rossetti found the Pre-Raphaelite Brotherhood
Revolutions abroad
Chartist Petition rejected by House of Commons
1851 Louis Napoleon's coup d'état. The Great Exhibition
1853 Goes up to Oxford, meets Edward Burne-Jones
1855 Tours French Cathedral cities
1856 Articled to G. E. Street, the architect. Forms friendship with Philip Webb. Founds *Oxford and Cambridge Magazine* and writes for it. Street moves office from Oxford to London. Meets Rossetti, takes rooms with Burne-Jones and gives up architecture for painting
1857 The painting of the Oxford Union frescoes. Meets Jane Burden
Indian Mutiny
1858 Publishes *The Defence of Guenevere and Other Poems*
1859 Marries Jane Burden. Commissions Philip Webb to design Red House, Upton
Charles Darwin publishes Origin of Species

1860 Lincoln President
Garibaldi proclaims Victor Emmanuel King of Italy
1861 Morris, Marshall, Faulkner and Company formed. Birth of Jenny Morris
Outbreak of American Civil War
Bismarck praises 'blood and iron'
1862 Birth of May Morris
1863 Battle of Gettysburg
1865 Moves from Red House to Queen Square, Bloomsbury
End of Civil War, Assassination of Lincoln
1866 Firm decorates Armoury and Tapestry Room, St James's Palace
Prussia defeats Austria
1867 Publishes *Life and Death of Jason*
Firm decorates Green Dining Room, South Kensington (now the Victoria and Albert) Museum
Marx publishes Das Kapital *Volume I*
Garibaldi marches on Rome
Fenian troubles in Ireland, 12 killed in Clerkenwell bombing
1868 Publishes Parts 1 and 2 of *The Earthly Paradise*, begins to learn Icelandic
1869 Publishes with Eiríkr Magnússon *The Saga of Gunnlaug Worm Tongue* and *The Story of Grettir the Strong*
Margarine invented
1870 Publishes Parts 3 and 4 of *The Earthly Paradise* and translations of *The Volsungs* and *The Niblungs*
Franco-Prussian War
1871 Leases Kelmscott Manor jointly with Rossetti, leaves him there with Janey, goes off to Iceland
The Commune in Paris. German Empire proclaimed at Versailles
1872 Publishes *Love is Enough*
Invention of the telegraph

1873 Travels to Italy with Burne-Jones. Second visit to Iceland

1874 First Impressionist exhibition in Paris

1875 Firm dissolves, Morris becomes sole proprietor of Morris and Company. Publishes *Three Northern Love Stories* and a verse translation of the *Aeneid*
London's main drainage completed
Trouble between Russia and Turkey

1876 Publishes *The Story of Sigurd the Volsung* and *The Fall of the Niblungs*. Becomes treasurer of the Eastern Question Association
Bell's telephone, Edison's phonograph

1877 Founds The Society for the Protection of Ancient Buildings ('Anti-Scrape'). First public lectures. Firm opens showroom in Oxford Street
Russia declares war on Turkey

1878 Buys (and christens) Kelmscott House, Hammersmith
Congress of Berlin, Peace between Russia and Turkey

1881 Morris and Co moves to Merton Abbey
Trouble in Ireland

1882 Century Guild founded
First petrol engine

1883 Made Honorary Fellow of Exeter College, Oxford, reads *Capital* in French, joins Democratic Federation
First New York skyscraper

1884 Writes for the Social Democratic Federation journal *Justice*, lectures for socialism on London street corners and in Scotland and North of England. Resigns from the Federation
Art Workers' Guild founded
Maxim machine gun invented

1885 Joins in the formation of the Socialist League. Edits and backs *Commonweal*. Arrested (and quickly discharged) at police court after demonstration. Publishes *The Pilgrims of Hope*

1886 Publishes *The Dream of John Ball* in *Commonweal*

1887 Publishes translation of *The Odyssey*. 'Bloody Sunday' (13 November) Trafalgar Square demonstration broken up by police. Morris sees crowd's defeat, goes to funeral of victim

1888 Publishes *Signs of Change* and *The House of the Wolfings*
Arts and Crafts Society founded
Invention of pneumatic tyres

1889 Publishes *The Roots of the Mountains*. Attends International Conference of Socialists in Paris
Eastman invents roll film

1890 Publishes *News from Nowhere* serially in *Commonweal*. Leaves Socialist League, founds Hammersmith Socialist Society.

1891 Founds Kelmscott Press
Publishes *The Story of the Glittering Plain, Poems by the Way* and (with Magnusson) Volume 1 of the *Saga Library*. Health deteriorates

1892 Refuses Poet Laureateship. Publishes Volume 2 of *Saga Library*

1893 Publishes (with Belfort Bax) *Socialism, its Growth and Outcome*

1894 Publishes *The Wood beyond the World*. Reconciled with the Social Democratic Federation
Dreyfus Case

1895 Translation of *The Tales of Beowulf*
Invention of wireless, telegraphy and cinematography

1896 Publishes *The Well at the World's End*. Kelmscott Press issues *The Works of Geoffrey Chaucer*. Dies 3 October and is buried at Kelmscott

Bibliography

The fullest Morris bibliography is still the one in *Pre-Raphaelitism: A Bibliocritical Study*, by William E. Fredeman, Harvard, 1965. Since 1965 several major books have appeared, all of which contain good bibliographies:

William Morris, His Life, Work and Friends, Philip Henderson, Thames and Hudson.
William Morris, F. Kirchhoff, Prior/Twayne.
William Morris, Jack Lindsay, Constable.
William Morris, Romantic to Revolutionary, E. P. Thompson, (revised edition) Merlin.
The Work of William Morris, Paul Thompson, Heinemann/Quartet.
William Morris and his World, Ian Bradley, Thames and Hudson.
William Morris as Designer, Ray Watkinson, Studio Vista.
William Morris Wallpaper and Chintzes, Fiona Clark, Academy.
William Morris and the Art of the Book, ed Paul Needham, Oxford.

Clark and Needham between them provide excellent introductory bibliographies to Morris in his roles as designer and printer.
William Morris: Designs for Printed Textiles, by Linda Parry (Victoria and Albert Museum leaflet) is obtainable from the Museum.

Morris's own writings are assembled in *The Collected Works of William Morris*, edited by May Morris, 24 vols, Longmans, 1910–15, reprinted by Russell and Russell, New York. His *Letters* were edited by Philip Henderson, London, 1950. The bulk of the occasional writings on art are collected in *William Morris: Artist, Writer, Socialist*, by May Morris, Basil Blackwell, Oxford, 1936.

The following works are currently in print:
Aims in Founding the Kelmscott Press, Irish University Press.

Beauty of Life, Brentham Press.
Choice of Verse, ed Geoffrey Grigson, Faber.
Clara's Lovers, ed Jack Lindsay, Inca Books.
The Defence of Guenevere, Scolar Press.
Dream of John Ball, Oriole Editions.
Early Romances in Prose and Verse, Everyman.
Icelandic Journals, Centaur Press.
News from Nowhere, ed James Redmond, Routledge.
Ornamentation and Illustrations from the Kelmscott Chaucer, ed Fridholf Johnson, Dover.
Political Writings, ed A. L. Morton, Lawrence and Wishart.
Selected Writings, ed G. D. H. Cole, Nonsuch.
Selected Writings, ed Asa Briggs, Penguin.

There are also a number of facsimile editions in print, or recently in print, of *The Well at the World's End, The Wood beyond the World* and of *News from Nowhere*, and of the complete Kelmscott *Chaucer*. The Clover Hill edition of *Cupid and Psyche* is still in print. *A Bibliography of Design in Britain 1851–1970*, by Anthony J. Coulson, The Design Council, 1979, is the standard bibliography on design; on literature the *Cambridge Bibliography* is the standard work.

Exhibition catalogues
Arts and Crafts Exhibition Society catalogues, 1888–1916.
William Morris Centenary Exhibition, Victoria and Albert Museum, 1934.
Victorian and Edwardian Decorative Arts, Victoria and Albert Museum, 1952.
Morris and Company 1861–1940, Arts Council, 1961.
Morris and Company in Cambridge, Fitzwilliam Museum, Cambridge, 1980.
Textiles by William Morris and Morris & Co 1861–1940, Oliver Fairclough and Emmeline Leary, Thames and Hudson, 1981.

Dante Gabriel Rossetti
The best bibliography is still that contained in
Pre-Raphaelitism: A Bibliocritical Study, by
William E. Fredeman; the standard biography is
still *A Victorian Romantic, Dante Gabriel
Rossetti*, by O. Doughty, Oxford, 1949. His
Letters are available in the *Letters of DGR*,
Oxford, 1965, and his subsequently released
correspondence with Morris's wife is in *DGR and
Janey Morris, their Correspondence*, edited by
John Bryson, Oxford, 1976.

Edward Burne-Jones
Edward Burne-Jones, a Biography, Penelope
Fitzgerald, Michael Joseph.

Philip Webb
Philip Webb and his Work, W. R. Lethaby,
Oxford University Press, 1935, reprinted by
Ravendale Press, London, 1979.

Wilfrid Scawen Blunt
*A Pilgrimage of Passion, The Life of Wilfrid
Scawen Blunt*, Elizabeth Longford, Weidenfeld
and Nicolson.

Arts and Crafts Movement
*The Arts and Crafts Movement, A study of its
sources, ideals and influence on design theory*,
Gillian Naylor, Studio Vista, 1971.

Museums and Houses

Museums

The following museums possess a complete or near-complete range of Morris patterns:

The Victoria and Albert Museum
The William Morris Gallery, Lloyd Park, Walthamstow
The Whitworth Art Gallery, University of Manchester

The following museums contain major Pre-Raphaelite collections:

The Ashmolean Museum, Oxford
The Birmingham City Museum and Art Gallery
The City Art Gallery, Manchester
The City Art Gallery, Southampton
The Fitzwilliam Museum, Cambridge
The Guildhall Art Gallery, London
The Lady Lever Art Gallery, Port Sunlight
The Tate Gallery
The Victoria and Albert Museum
The Walker Art Gallery, Liverpool
The Whitworth Art Gallery, University of Manchester

Houses

Red House, Bexleyheath, Kent (by written arrangement with owner).
Kelmscott House, 26 Upper Mall, Hammersmith (headquarters of William Morris Society).
Kelmscott Manor, near Lechlade, Oxfordshire (open in 1982 on 7 April, 5 May, 2 June, 7 July, 4 August and 1 September, or by application in writing to the Deputy Curator).

Houses with surviving decorative schemes that are open to the public:

Standen, East Grinstead, East Sussex
Wightwick Manor, near Wolverhampton, Staffordshire
Jesus, Queens' and Pembroke College, Cambridge all have a chapel or hall decorated by the Firm. The Morris rooms in St James's Palace can be seen by written arrangement. A list of churches that have stained-glass windows and other works by the Firm is published by the William Morris Society.

Notes on Contributors

Leonard Stoppani is the Principal of the West Surrey College of Art and Design.

A. R. Dufty is the past President of the Society of Antiquaries. His contributions to Morris studies include his edition of *Cupid and Psyche* and his pamphlets on the restoration and the contents of Kelmscott Manor.

Asa Briggs is Provost of Worcester College, Oxford. His many publications include *Selected Works of William Morris*.

Joseph Acheson is Senior Lecturer in Art History at the West Surrey College of Art and Design. He also teaches at the Open University and the Universities of London and Surrey.

Martin Shuttleworth is Senior Tutor Librarian of the West Surrey College of Art and Design.

Gillian Naylor is Senior Lecturer in Design History at the Royal College of Art. Her *The Arts and Crafts Movement, a study of its sources, ideals and influence on design theory* is the standard work on the subject.

Stuart Durant is Senior Lecturer in History of Design at Kingston Polytechnic. He contributes regularly to *Architectural Design* magazine. He has just completed a detailed study of Christopher Dresser which is due for publication in four parts in 1982.

Patricia L. Baker teaches at the School of Oriental and African Studies and at the West Surrey College of Art and Design.

Helen Snowdon teaches at Corsham and at the West Surrey College of Art and Design. She is currently reading for a Ph.D. in nineteenth-century design at the Royal College of Art.

Dorothy D. Bosomworth is Research Fellow in Design History at the West Surrey College of Art and Design. She is reading for a Ph.D. on Byzantine influence on Victorian design.

John Brandon-Jones is a leading authority on the Arts and Crafts Movement. His *C. F. A. Voysey, Architect and Designer* was published in 1978.

Larry Baker is Principal Lecturer in Complementary Studies at the West Surrey College of Art and Design. He is currently working on a book on nineteenth-century British historical painting.

Ray Watkinson was Deputy Warden of Goldsmith's College of London University. His massive contributions to Morris studies over the years include *Pre-Raphaelite Art and Design* and *William Morris as Designer*.

Jacqueline Herald teaches the History of Textiles at the West Surrey College of Art and Design, and at Goldsmiths' College, University of London.

Deryn O'Connor is Principal Lecturer in Textiles at the West Surrey College of Art and Design. Her principal field is printed textiles, but she is also engaged in research on natural dyes.

Picture Credits

Unless otherwise stated, copyright for the illustrations in this book is held by West Surrey College of Art and Design

Page	Copyright holder
13	Victoria and Albert Museum
16	National Portrait Gallery
22	Dr de Haas
24	Radio Times, Hulton Picture Library, London
27	Tate Gallery
34, 35	Victoria and Albert Museum
36	(Left) Birmingham City Museum and Art Gallery
45, 59	William Morris Gallery, Walthamstow
86	Victoria and Albert Museum
88	National Portrait Gallery
89	Victoria and Albert Museum
91	Birmingham City Museum and Art Gallery
92	John Brandon-Jones
112	Victoria and Albert Museum

WHEN ADAM DELVED
AND EVE SPAN
WHO WAS THEN THE
GENTLEMAN